Value
and
Price

An Extract

Value
and Price

An Extract

Eugen von Böhm-Bawerk

Two Supplements by the Publisher

Libertarian Press
South Holland, Illinois 60473, U.S.A.

Copyright © 1973 by Libertarian Press

Revised Second Edition

First Edition 1960

Library of Congress Catalog Card Number: 73-81132

International Standard Book Number: 0-910884-01-3

Printed in the United States of America

Publisher's Preface

Böhm-Bawerk's major work carried the title, *CAPITAL AND INTEREST*, in three volumes:

I	HISTORY AND CRITIQUE OF INTEREST THEORIES	512 pages
II	POSITIVE THEORY OF CAPITAL	480
III	FURTHER ESSAYS ON CAPITAL AND INTEREST	256
	Total	1,248 pages

Volume I analyzes all previous *unearned-income* theories and shows them to be untenable; Volume II outlines his new theory of the essential nature of unearned income; Volume III constitutes a rebuttal of critiques by other economists of the new theory which appeared in Volume II. *Value and Price* is a 164-page Extract from the middle of Volume II.

This Publisher's Preface will help a reader understand new and fundamental ideas presented in the middle of 1,248 pages of closely printed material.

Böhm-Bawerk and Carl Menger made the biggest contribution to the "revolution" that occurred in economics in the last half of the nineteenth century; their contribution, and that of others in the same movement, was in economics what Sir Isaac Newton's *Principia* was in physics. The following comments may be helpful:

1. What follows first is Böhm-Bawerk's classic text on (a) what is the essence of *value*, and (b) how *prices* are determined in free markets. The text was translated by George D. Huncke, with Dr. Hans Sennholz the Consulting Economist; however, all sideheadings are insertions by this publisher and are not by Böhm-Bawerk.

2. Next there is a photograph of Böhm-Bawerk and a brief Biographical Sketch by Dr. Sennholz, reprinted by permission from the 1959 edition of *CAPITAL AND INTEREST*; then there is a Preface written specially to introduce this Extract by the same Economist.

3. Pages xix through xxv present a Table of Contents for this book.

4. The next 102 pages pertain to *Value*; then another 62 pages pertain to *Price*. There is an index of new terms used by Böhm-Bawerk on page 165, "Location of Definitions of New Terms by Böhm-Bawerk"; for meanings of those terms, see pages on which they are first used; the terms of the Austrian economists, pertaining as they did to new (corrected) concepts, required an improved nomenclature.

5. A complete Table of Contents of Böhm-Bawerk's opus, *CAPITAL AND INTEREST*, is presented on pages 167 through 184 so that readers can see what portion *Value and Price* is of the whole of Böhm-Bawerk's thought. See marked pages 178 and 179.

6. Next, there are two Supplements which are applications or extensions of Böhm-Bawerk's thought, but for which Böhm-Bawerk can have no responsibility whatever:

Supplement I — Experiments with Matching Buy and Sell Orders in Different Ways
With Preliminary Reflections on the Problem of "Just Prices"

Readers who may wish to "check" Böhm-Bawerk's ideas on price should find Supplement I helpful to analyze variations from Böhm-Bawerk's presentation; all of these variations turn out to be unfruitful. Supplement I in effect demonstrates how right Böhm-Bawerk is. (To avoid cumbersome paging back and forth, some of this material is a re-quotation (in small print) from the original.)

Supplement II — ABC Optimum Price Computator
For Attainment of Pefect Competition in Auction Markets of Stocks, Bonds, Foreign Exchange, Fungible Goods, Etc.

An attainment for which economists yearn is "perfect competition." Supplement II describes a manner to accomplish what was formerly unaccomplishable. In a sense, Supplement II is based on conclusions reached from Supplement I. As a byproduct, readers will be able to understand how antiquated — unchanged from horse-and-buggy days—activities of famous markets still are (in this instance, the New York Stock Exchange). Appropriate devices can yet save millions of costly man-hours in new ways, thereby further raising the general standard of living.

6. Finally, beginning on the back cover there is a book review by the most famous of Böhm-Bawerk's students, Ludwig von Mises, with the title, "Böhm-Bawerk and the Discriminating Reader." In it the practical point is made that the "great issues" of the late twentieth century are basically *economic* in character, and that whoever wishes to participate in understanding the hottest issues of the age should certainly read this material by Böhm-Bawerk. Dr. von Mises wrote:

> The general reader should start with the second volume in which Böhm-Bawerk analyzes the essence of saving and capital accumulation and the role capital goods play in the process of production. Especially important is the third book of this second volume; it deals with the determination of value and prices.

This publication, *Value and Price,* is what Dr. von Mises refers to in the foregoing quotation.

THE PUBLISHER

April 9, 1973

HIS EXCELLENCY EUGEN VON BÖHM-BAWERK
(1851-1914)
Professor of Political Economy, University of Vienna, Austria
Austrian Finance Minister: 1895, 1897, 1900-1904

Biographical Sketch
of Eugen von Böhm-Bawerk

EUGEN VON BÖHM-BAWERK (February 12, 1851, Brünn, Austria-August 27, 1914, Vienna, Austria) was one of Austria's foremost economists and statesmen. His enduring fame rests on his lifelong defense of the science of economics and his stout resistance against the rising flood of interventionism and socialism. He was one of the first to see clearly the imminent destruction of our civilization through Marxism and all its related schemes of socialism. Böhm-Bawerk was a brilliant critic who also had the rare gifts of an originator.

He studied law at the University of Vienna and political science in Heidelberg, Leipzig, and Jena. In 1881 he was appointed professor of economics at the University of Innsbruck where he developed and defended the economic principles that Carl Menger and the classical economists had outlined.

His name as a statesman is associated with the best period of Austrian financial history. In 1889 he entered the Austrian Finance Department, where his abilities as an economist were needed for a projected currency reform. He was vice-chairman of the commission which led to the adoption of the gold standard with the krone as the unit. He was minister of finance in 1895, then again in 1897 and for the third time from 1900 to 1904. His tenure of office was characterized by far-sighted management, balanced budgets, stable currency and a successful conversion of the public debt. He also succeeded in abolishing the age-old special privilege of government subsidies to exporters of sugar. All this was achieved in spite of rising economic nationalism which was working continuously toward the disintegration of the Austro-Hungarian union. It was achieved in spite of the fact that Böhm-Bawerk was not associated with any political party. In 1904 he resigned from his position in protest against army irregularities in budgetary estimates and thereafter devoted his life to writing and teaching economics at the University of Vienna.

As an economist he won great fame by an unusual combination of qualities—extraordinary learning, independence of thought and judgment, dialectical skill, power of penetrating criticism, and mastery of exposition and illustration. An indefatigable scholar, he was marked by the ability always to go to the core of the subject. He showed lively interest in the problems of the Western democracies and in the controversies carried on in English and American journals to which he frequently contributed.

His labors were prodigious. In his famous treatise, *Capital and Interest,* he not only expounded a complete theory of distribution but also a theory of social cooperation which exerted a profound influence on the thought of other economists. His most important works are the following:

1. KAPITAL UND KAPITALZINS comprising three volumes:
     I *Geschichte und Kritik der Kapitalzins-Theorien*
       (first edition, 1884; second edition, 1900; third edition, 1914; fourth edition, 1921)
     II *Positive Theorie des Kapitales*
       (first edition, 1889; second edition, 1902; third edition, 1909-1912; fourth edition, 1921)
     III *Exkurse zur "Positiven Theorie des Kapitales"*
       (Printed as appendices to the third edition of *Positive Theorie des Kapitales* in 1909-1912; printed as separate volume in 1921)
2. *Rechte und Verhältnisse vom Standpunkte der volkswirtschaftlichen Güterlehre,* Innsbruck, 1881
3. "Grundzüge der Theorie des wirtschaftlichen Güterwerts," in Conrad's *Jahrbücher für Nationalökonomie und Statistik,* new series, volume 13, 1886, pp. 1-88 and 477-541; reprinted in the "School of Economics Series of Scarce Tracts in Economic and Political Science," number 11, London, 1932
4. "The Austrian Economists," in the *Annals of the American Academy of Political and Social Science,* volume 1, 1891, pp. 361-384
5. "The Historical vs. the Deductive Method in Political Economy," in the *Annals of the American Academy of Political and Social Science,* volume 1, 1891, pp. 244-271
6. "Wert, Kosten und Grenznutzen," in Conrad's *Jahrbücher für Nationalökonomie und Statistik,* series III, 1892, pp. 321-367
7. "Der letzte Masstab des Güterwertes," in *Zeitschrift für Volkswirtschaft, Sozialpolitik und Verwaltung,* volume III, 1894, pp. 185-230; English translation under the title "The Ultimate Standard of Value," in the *Annals of the American Academy of Political and Social Science,* volume V, number 2
8. "The Positive Theory of Capital and Its Critics," published as a series of essays in the *Quarterly Journal of Economics* in 1895 and 1896 under the titles:
     "Professor Clark's Views on the Genesis of Capital," volume IX, pp. 113-131
     "General Walker Against *Capital and Interest,*" volume IX, pp. 235-256

"The Views of Mr. White, Mr. Bilgram, Professor Mac-Vane and Mr. Hawley," volume x, pp. 121-155

9. "Zum Abschluss des Marxschen Systems," in *Staatswirtschaftliche Arbeiten, Festgaben für Karl Knies,* Berlin, 1896, published in English under the title "Karl Marx and the Close of His System" by T. Fisher Unwin, London, 1898, and by Augustus M. Kelley, New York, 1949

10. "Einige strittige Fragen der Kapitalstheorie," Vienna, 1899, in *Zeitschrift für Volkswirtschaft, Sozialpolitik und Verwaltung,* volume VIII

11. "Macht oder ökonomisches Gesetz?" in *Zeitschrift für Volkswirtschaft, Sozialpolitik und Verwaltung,* volume XXIII, 1914, pp. 205-271, published in English under the title "Control or Economic Law?" by Consumers-Producers Economic Service, South Holland, Illinois, 1951

12. "Unsere passive Handelsbilanz," in *Neue Freie Presse,* issues of January 6, 8 and 9, 1914

F. X. Weiss has collected the more important minor works of Böhm-Bawerk in *Gesammelte Schriften,* two volumes, Vienna 1924-1926.

HANS F. SENNHOLZ

PUBLISHER'S NOTE: The "specialty" of Libertarian Press is publishing English translations of Böhm-Bawerk's works. Those already published are listed on pages 235-242, which see.

Preface to
the First Edition

FOR ALMOST two thousand years the investigation of economic problems was handicapped by some utterances of Aristotle. In his writings *Politics* and *Nicomachean Ethics,* which greatly influenced the development of subsequent economic thought, Aristotle expressed the opinion that exchange is fair and just as long as each party gets exactly as much as he gives the other. Things that are exchanged are compared through a standard of value that lies in man's wants and then bartered on the basis of equality. This idea of equality in exchange together with many others on ethics, logic, and politics were adopted without further questioning by the Scholastics, especially by Thomas Aquinas. It permeated even the theories of the classical economists who, however, differed from Aristotle inasmuch as they considered the quantity of labor as the absolute standard of value. According to Adam Smith, "labor is the real measure of the exchangeable value of all commodities."

Beginning with the 1870's the Englishman Jevons, the Swiss Walras, and the Austrians Menger, Wieser, and Böhm-Bawerk irrefutably exploded this praxeological foundation. The Austrian School built a new foundation on the cognition that interpersonal exchange results from a disparity of individual valuation rather than equality of labor costs. According to Menger, the founder of the School, "the principle that leads men to exchange is the same principle that guides them in their economic activity as a whole; it is the endeavor to ensure the greatest possible satisfaction of their wants." Exchange comes to an end as soon as one party to the exchange should judge both goods of equal value. And we ascribe value to economic goods not because their manufacture has cost labor, but because of their "importance that we first attribute to the satisfaction of our wants, that is, to our lives and well-being, and in consequence carry over to economic goods as the exclusive causes of the satisfaction of our wants."

Professor von Böhm-Bawerk's enduring title to fame lies in his elaboration and popularization of the subjective value theory as applicable to direct exchange. His analysis of value and price, which this volume extracts from his *Positive Theory of Capital,* is one of the most lucid and cogent expositions of the causal relationship between individual valuation and price determination that has yet appeared. On its basis Böhm-Bawerk elaborated his famous time-preference theory of interest which was later perfected by Wicksell, Fetter, and Fisher. However, it was left to another representative of this prominent School, Ludwig von Mises,[1] to extend the subjective value theory also to the problems of money and indirect exchange, which in fact completed the general theory of interpersonal exchange.

Value and price constitute the very foundation of the economics of the market society, for it is through value and price that the people who are the sovereigns of the market economy give purpose and aim to the production process. No matter what their ultimate motivation may be, whether material or ideal, noble or base, the people judge goods and services according to their suitability for the attainment of their desired objectives. They ascribe value to consumers' goods and determine their prices. And according to Böhm-Bawerk's irrefutable "imputation theory," they even determine indirectly the prices of all factors of production and the income of every member of the market economy. The entrepreneurs and capitalists are merely their agents who must cater to their wishes and preferences. Through the operation of value and price the consumers in fact decide what is to be produced and in what quantity and quality, where it is to be produced and by whom, what method of production is to be employed, what material is to be used, and make numerous other decisions. Indeed, the baton of value and price makes every member of the market economy a conductor of the production process.

Unfortunately the teaching of these basic principles of economics has virtually disappeared from the curricula of our universities and colleges. Instruction in value and price has been replaced by courses on "national product and income," "labor economics," "agricultural economics," "the political setting of contemporary business," etc. Some instructors even deny the very existence of market laws that determine prices, wage rates, and interest rates. To them the system of unhampered enterprise is ruled by the law of the jungle which permits speculators and capitalists to prey on the sweat and blood of the workers. Only the fittest are said to survive. These critics obviously prefer all-round government control over the economic actions of individuals, i.e. socialism, to the system of individual enterprise. Others do not deny that there is a causal interrelationship of market phenomena, but they believe that the market laws harm the vital interests of the vast majority of the people. They denounce capitalism as an immoral system because it permits acquisitiveness, causes inequalities of wealth and income, and otherwise negates decency and justice. These critics who comprise the large majority of economic instructors recommend various degrees of government intervention in order to remove the undesired features from the free economy.

However, economic theory reveals irrefutably that government intervention causes effects that tend to be undesirable even from the point of view of those who design it. To interfere with prices, wages, and the rates of interest through government orders and prohibitions is to deprive the people of their central position as sovereigns of the market process. It

---

1. *Theorie des Geldes und der Umlaufsmittel,* 1912. English editions: *The Theory of Money and Credit,* 1934 and 1953.

compels entrepreneurs to obey government orders rather than the value judgments and price signals of consumers. In short, government intervention curtails the economic freedom of the people and enhances the powers of politicians and government officials.

The theory of value and price also demonstrates that government interference with the people's economic decisions hampers and mutilates the individual enterprise economy. Interference with prices, for instance, creates either shortages or surpluses. To raise artificially the price of grain is to create a surplus of grain. To increase the minimum wages above those determined by the market in order to benefit the low-income groups is to cause their unemployment. Similarly, the union methods that forcibly raise wages above those established by the market merely succeed in creating unemployment. Our union strongholds are the centers of unemployment and our unionized industries are plagued by maladjustment and depression.

Interference by taxation may aim either at suppressing or restricting the production of certain commodities demanded by consumers, or at expropriating certain income or wealth. But it causes capital consumption, or at least retards its accumulation, and thus reduces labor productivity and wage rates. It prevents production adjustments to the wishes and preferences of consumers. And, above all, it creates a class society in which changes in the individual's economic and social position are virtually prevented. Finally, government interference with the people's currency and capital market may aim at a more plentiful provision of money and credit or at a reduction of interest rates. But it inevitably results in currency debasement and destruction of the capital market. The ultimate outcome of a policy of continuous inflation must be the total destruction of the medium of exchange and the return to barter. It is obvious that the market economy with its extensive division of labor cannot for long survive the effects of such policies.

When the interventionist economy finally evidences defects that are deplorable from everyone's point of view as, for example, chronic mass unemployment or disastrous inflation, the interventionists and socialists then clamor for acceleration and radicalization of government measures. Socialism is ushered in. But socialism merely breeds more chaos and turns the people into wards and serfs of an omnipotent state. For it is the substance of socialism that all economic powers are centralized with one person or committee of persons. All orders and instructions proceed from a central authority whose value judgments and objectives are binding for the rest of the people. One central will controls the employment of all factors of production through orders, instructions, prohibitions, and penalties. One central employer manages and remunerates the labor exertions of the whole population.

The price theory also discloses the most crucial problem of socialism which is the impossibility of economic calculation. How is the economic director to calculate the results of production? Without the common denominator of market prices expressed in terms of money, he cannot compare the vast number of different materials, kinds of labor, capital goods, land, and methods of production with the yields of production. Without the price yardstick, he cannot ascertain whether or not certain production actually increases the productivity and output of his system. It is true, he may calculate in kind. But such a calculation permits no numerical comparison between the costs of production and its yields. Other socialist substitutes for the price denominator as, for instance, calculation of labor time, are equally spurious.

Economic activity without economic calculation is irrational and chaotic. This is why socialism impoverishes the people and enslaves them to the absolute will of economic dictators. At its best a socialist economy depends on a crude imitation of the market order in order to avert the always threatening collapse and disaster. It is in vain that the dictators of socialism and communism decry and disparage the capitalist economies and ridicule economic thought as an ideological disguise of capitalist class interests. The economic laws work silently and implacably even under communism.

HANS F. SENNHOLZ

Grove City College
Grove City, Pa.
January 1960

Contents

Part A — VALUE

Part B — PRICE

Part A

VALUE

Part A—VALUE [1]

Chapter I

The Two Concepts of Value

1. Economics Concerns Itself With Wirkungswert

THE concept of value does not belong solely to the science of economics. That particular sort of recognition which we call valuation is something we accord in the most varied fields of human activity. We speak of the value of virtue, of life, of health, or we prize the artistic or literary value of some product of the mind. The word is as frequently used in such connections as in speaking of the value of a commodity or a piece of real estate. It is the province of psychology to pursue to its ultimate conclusion the question of the common element which lies at the root of all these manifestations of that recognition. For our present purpose it will suffice to pursue our inquiry into just one type of valuation.

All things which are the object of our valuation fall on one side or the other of a single thoroughgoing line of differentiation. Certain objects are considered valuable for their own sake; they possess intrinsic value or what modern German psychologists call *Eigenwert*.[2] Other ob-

Cross references by Böhm-Bawerk himself are based on original pagination of CAPITAL AND INTEREST, *which are shown by these figures in the margin.*

1. My views on value were first published in my "Grundzüge der Theorie des wirtschaftlichen Güterwerts" which appeared in Conrad's *Jahrbücher für Nationalökonomik und Statistik,* new series, Vol. XIII, pp. 1-82 and 477-541. In the first two editions I included a very much abbreviated excerpt from that earlier treatment, adapting it to the special requirements of the theory of capital. In the third edition I enlarged the excerpt materially. This was partly out of deference to direct requests from friendly colleagues abroad who were anxious to have certain subject matter which had appeared in the *Grundzüge* more conveniently to hand in my chief work. But it was also because it was my unfortunate experience that my omission of some things was responsible for the assumption that I withdrew everything I did not expressly repeat, the further consequence of which was a multitude of troublesome misunderstandings. While I was able to adhere to the fundamental ideas of my first articles without any

change at all, and to a large extent to the original wording as well, it goes without saying that I took pains to make revisions, wherever it seemed necessary, as dictated by the lapse of years, and as seemed in order for the amplified and systematic development of my doctrine. The publications on the subject which had made their appearance in the interim also necessitated numerous additions of new material. To be sure, not all of it was incorporated in the text of the *Positive Theory of Capital* but was assigned a place in the various *Further Essays On Capital and Interest.* Even so I will have to refer any readers who may be interested in some of the material, especially that dealing with the history of theory, to my original treatment of the topic in Conrad's *Jahrbücher.*

2. The first of these was Ehrenfels whose "Werttheorie und Ethik" appeared in Avenarius's *Vierteljahrsschrift für wissenschaftliche Psychologie* for the year 1893, p. 76 ff.

jects are, on the contrary, considered valuable only as means to an end lying outside themselves; they possess extrinsic value or what the German psychologists call *Wirkungswert*. Economic value belongs exclusively in this second category. We do not prize and cherish goods for their own sake, but only because we expect them to promote our ends. The miser's unreasoning acquisitive impulse constitutes the only exception to this generalization. Every valuation of a good is nothing but a reflection of a more basic valuation which we accord to the life and welfare purposes which goods serve to attain.

2. Value in the Subjective Sense

In the last analysis, the value of all goods is bound up with man and his purposes. Now the position which man takes toward a given purpose determines whether or not in ordinary parlance he ascribes value to a particular good. And that position may be either of two kinds and on its kind is based the familiar distinction between value in its subjective sense and value in the objective sense. In its subjective sense value denotes the significance which a good or a quantity of goods possesses for the well-being of a certain subject. The word "well-being" is here to be understood in a very broad sense. It is in such a sense that I should say that a good has value for me, if I recognize that my well-being is bound up with it. By this I mean that possession of the good satisfies some want, provides some gratification, affords some pleasure or spares me some pain, which I should be forced to forgo (or suffer, in the case of pain) if I did not possess the good. In that case the presence of the good means a gain for my well-being, the loss of the good means a corresponding loss. The good has importance to me, it has value for me.

122

3. Value in the Objective Sense

The other kind of value is objective. It signifies our estimate of the capacity of a good to bring about some definite extrinsic objective result. When we accord value in this sense to a good, we are limiting ourselves to an appraisal of the relationship that exists between the good and the accomplishment of some single objective purpose or result. There is no admixture in our appraisal of what importance that particular single purpose itself may have for the well-being of any particular person. We refrain from projecting, as it were, the technical result achieved by the good, to the point where it has bearing upon the weal or woe of a particular person. In this sense of the word we speak of the relative fuel value of wood and coal. We mean by that the varying effectiveness in bringing about warmth through the use of a unit of these two goods. We do the same in ascribing relative objective nutritive value to different foodstuffs, fertilizing value to different manures, "combat value" to the different battleships of a navy, and so on. In all these uses of the word, value, there is excluded from the concept "value" any relation to the weal or woe of any person. If we make the statement that beechwood has more fuel value than pine, we are speaking only of the objective, "mechanical" fact, as it were, that a definite quantity (by weight, let us say) of beechwood will release a larger number of thermal units than an equal quantity of pine.

4. Difference Between Subjective Value and Objective Value

The profound difference in the nature of these two judgments as to value, and the difference in the factual situations on which they are based becomes manifest in several ways. One of these is the circumstance that the objective and subjective goods values do not necessarily coincide. That is to say that they need not be of the same order, and do not necessarily even coincide to the extent of each being present or absent in the presence or absence of the other. Two cords of beechwood, for instance, possess equal objective fuel value. And yet one of them may be the only fuel supply of a poor family in a hard winter and absolutely irreplaceable because of their lack of money. It will possess a far greater subjective value for the satisfaction of that family's wants than will the other cord which is owned by a millionaire. And again, where wood is to be had in such abundance that it constitutes a "free good," it may very well have no subjective value for anyone's well-being at all, despite the fact that its "objective fuel value" remains entirely unchanged.

5. Special Importance of One Kind of Objective Value, viz., Objective Exchange Value

There are as many kinds of objective value as there are concrete purposes and extrinsic results which we may wish to take into account. Economic science will have little or no interest in most of them. The "combat value" which I mentioned by way of example has, I should say, nothing at all to do with economic problems, and the "nutritive value" and "fuel value" I spoke of can have very little and certainly only indirect connection with the science of economics. It is not the task of economics to offer an explanation of, let us say, the fuel value of wood. Nor is there any reason why it should use it as a basis for the explanation of other economic phenomena, in a manner different from, or to a degree greater than applies in the case of any random physical or technical fact in some other field. I mentioned it and those other values purely by way of illustration. The purpose was to shed a more revealing light upon one particular kind of objective value of not dissimilar nature, but of exceedingly great importance in economic science. The value I have in mind is the *objective exchange value* of goods. By that term we designate the objective significance of goods in exchange. Expressed in other words, exchange value means the capacity of goods, because of the nature of the facts in any given instance, to command a certain quantity of other goods as an equivalent in an exchange. In this sense we say that a house "is worth" or "has a value of" $30,000, that a horse "is worth" $1,500, if in an exchange it is possible to secure $30,000 for the house or $1,500 for the horse. Just as in the similar judgments concerning fuel value, etc., so in these instances we are saying nothing about the influence those goods exert on the well-being of any individual. Instead we are limiting ourselves to stating the purely objective fact that it is possible for a good to procure in an exchange a certain amount of other goods.

123

6. More Remarks on Subjective Value

Each of the two concepts to which accepted speech usage attaches the name of "value" is called upon to play an extraordinarily important part in economic theory. Objective exchange value is one of the important results which it behooves economics to explain; subjective value belongs to the means or tools by which economics is to achieve some of its explanations. Subjective value is the significance for our well-being possessed under given conditions by the goods we deal with in our economy. That value must therefore inevitably constitute to a very large degree the criterion which determines our practical behavior with respect to other goods. It is pre-eminently what Neumann has in mind when he says that value is the "real quintessence and the turning point of all the activity embraced by our economizing." In much the same sense I myself once spoke of subjective value as the "compass and the universal intermediary motive of all our economic actions." And as befits the great contribution it makes to the orientation and the direction of all our economizing, it also has an egregiously important role to play in the theoretical explanation of our actions. When qualified by the term "subjective," value is one of the most important and most fruitful fundamental concepts in economics.

7. More Remarks on Objective Exchange Value

As for objective exchange value it must be said that economic theory has always conceded to it "all the rights and perquisites appertaining thereunto." To delve into the laws which govern the exchange relations of goods has at all times been considered one of the prime missions of economic science. There have even been economists who so grossly exaggerated this feature as to make it appear the one principal task of the science, and I can even remember a proposal to abolish the name "economics" and supplant it with "catallactics"—the science of exchange. Subjective value, by contrast, came into its own only much later. There had, to be sure, always been awareness of the fact that the word "value" is used in a double sense. But it was supposed that complete justice was being done to that double sense by drawing a distinction between use value and exchange value. But that basis of differentiation was completely different and far less profound. So-called use value was in truth only an inadequate representative of the concept which we designate today by the name of subjective value. Furthermore, it was subjected to some inappropriate elucidations which set it even further apart from subjective value. It is no wonder that it was quite unable to render to economic theory the service of which the other concept was capable. Economists did not quite know what to do with use value and so almost ignored it entirely. They neither took the trouble to make any profound investigation into its nature, nor availed themselves of its help in meeting the demands imposed by research tasks dealing with other topics. They placed its name on the roster of concepts, as it were, and then let it stand idly in the wings of the theater where economic doctrines are inculcated. It became an idle supernumerary. It was reserved for later research to discover that the neglected supernumerary was really one of the principals in the cast who was promulgating economic concepts of supreme importance, and at the same time the object of a series of most remarkable economic laws. Indeed, those laws have a significance that far transcends the scope of the theory of value, for they supply a fundamental basis and a point of departure for almost every theoretical explanation in the whole domain of economics.

8. Double Function of Economic Theory, Genuinely to Explain Subjective Value and Objective Exchange Value

The economic theory of value thus finds it must assume a double task. On the one hand it must develop the laws of subjective value; on the other hand it must also trace out the laws governing objective exchange value which, from the standpoint of economics, is by far the most important aspect of the matter of objective values generally. It is my purpose to meet the first half of this dual assignment in the ten chapters of Part A of VALUE AND PRICE. The second half of my obligations I hope to perform in Part B which follows and which deals with the theory of price. That does not by any means imply that the concept of price and exchange value are identical. Exchange value is the *capacity* of a good to obtain in an exchange a certain quantity of other goods; price is *that quantity of goods*. But the laws governing both are identical. For the law of price explains how a good really commands a certain price and why it does so. In the very act of giving that explanation it automatically furnishes the reason why the good in question has the capacity of obtaining a certain price. The law of price contains within itself the law of exchange value.

9. Dual Nature of Phenomena of Value

It is the duty of economics to do full justice to this dual nature of "phenomena of value," and to the explicatory burdens arising out of it. But the names it employs in fulfilling its duty constitute, after all, a question of only minor and terminological importance, provided the distinction itself is clearly and appropriately made. The names subjective and objective value apply to an adaptation of a pair of concepts originally set up by Neumann. Sometime ago I proposed using them for the present differentiation, and they have since been widely adopted. The only fault to be found with them, in my estimation, is that they have a slightly "academic" ring and can hardly hope for general acceptance by the lay public. However, I have been quite unable to discover any pair of names which has a "vernacular ring" and at the same time covers the distinction precisely. The terms "use value" and "exchange value" are still believed by isolated writers to be adequate, but they are based on a different distinction and are not at all appropriate as an expression of the dissimilarity with which we are dealing. That can readily be seen from the fact that there is such a thing as "subjective exchange value," a topic treated in Chapter v, Part A. Quite recently Wieser launched a tempting proposition by suggesting that we use the term *personal* for subjective, and *economic* for objective exchange value.[3] In and of itself I consider the first

125

3. *Der Geldwert und seine Veränderungen,* *Referat für die Generalversammlung des* *Vereins für Sozialpolitik,* 1909, in the 132nd   volume of the association's collected publications, p. 498 ff.

member of the proposed pair of terms entirely unobjectionable, and to the second I cannot raise any objection that I can call conclusive. The one trouble is that Wieser's terminology fails to designate a genuine *division,* because what it designates does not exhaust the field to be divided. Objective exchange value for which Wieser proposes the alternative expression "economic value" (*op. cit., p. 500*), is admittedly the most important value of interest to economic science, but not the only one. It is but one link in a whole chain of objective values including, for instance, "objective value of proceeds" and "productional value." All of these are of interest to economic science and thus constitute equally estimable kinds of economic value. And so Wieser's terminology would not make unnecessary the further and exhaustive classification of all values into subjective and objective. The best that could be said for it would be that it furnishes, within such classification, good synonymous terms for the two most important groups of phenomena that are embraced by the completely inclusive appellatives.

10. Danger From Ambiguity of Terms

But there seems to me to be, in addition, a certain amount of danger involved. Using for objective exchange value a term indicating the economic value of a good runs the risk, I think, of setting up an association with a misleading supposition. I mean the supposition that the only feature which distinguishes personal value from economic value is the enlarged circle concerning which and on behalf of which a judgment of value is arrived at—a judgment otherwise identical in kind. That would be tantamount to saying that economic value reflects a significance of a good for the total society which comprises an economy, in exactly the same way that subjective or personal value reflects the significance of a good for the well-being of an individual. That would be quite erroneous. That is why, in my *Grundzüge,** p. 478, I expressed my very decided opposition to the term "economic value." At that time this erroneous understanding of the term was the prevailing one and I felt it had to be combated. Subsequently to be sure, more accurate comprehension of the nature of the phenomena of value has gained the upper hand, and now the danger of being misled by a tempting bit of nomenclature into an erroneous supposition is materially reduced. Nevertheless, not all danger of that has yet been completely removed. And although I do not consider my objections as compelling as they were 25 years ago, I should still prefer to see nomenclature develop along lines that avoided renewed temblors which shake the foundations of the well-accustomed and completely unambiguous terms, "subjective value" and "objective value."

I should like to say in conclusion that one further question has been raised anent the concepts of subjective and objective value as I have defined them in the foregoing paragraphs. That question is as follows. Are they to be regarded as concepts that are completely independent of each other and entirely disparate as to content, or in a word, related

126

*Libertarian Press has prepared a translation of *Grundzüge,* but it has not been published yet.

only in the manner of any pair of "namesakes"? Or are they rather to be looked upon as subspecies of a unified and more general class to be imagined as constituting an immediately superior species? While I do not feel that the question is of great objective import, my answer would lie rather on the side of the latter alternative, and I should favor calling them a lower category of a unified concept of value.[4] I look on the matter this way. There are admittedly certain common features present in both concepts, though they are not particularly essential, and are more limited to externals. Still there seems to me to be nothing to prevent, even on the basis of such meager commonly possessed characteristics, the drawing up of a common definition. But of course it must be anticipated that this definition will turn out correspondingly meager, and it will have to be based on rather loose and elastic conceptual features. When it comes to framing a formal definition, recourse will necessarily be taken to such terms as Wieser's "significance of goods in economic life" or "measure of things in economic terms." As soon as the first attempt is made to elucidate these vague characteristics of the concept, it will become obvious that we are dealing, in the case of the two kinds of value, with "significances" of very dissimilar kinds which arise from very dissimilar arrays of facts. In short, it is clear we are here concerned with two sharply differentiated groups of phenomena. It happens also to be true that the facts pertaining to the one group of phenomena exert a causal influence on the facts belonging in the other group. That is to say, subjective valuations, as we shall see later, have a decisive influence on the determination of objective exchange value. But all that is utterly irrelevant and has nothing to do with the question whether the two groups of phenomena can be classified under a single unified rubric—no more, certainly, than the fact that rain has a causative influence on the life and development of plants is any justification for creating a superior classification which will include the two subspecies "rain" and "plants."[5]

4. In the "Grundzüge" of my early days (p. 6) I had come to a different conclusion which supported Neumann's.

5. The foundations of the modern theory of value, as everyone knows, were laid in the works of Carl Menger, Jevons and Walras who were all in agreement on the subject. The leading place among the three must be accorded to Menger because of the clarity and the completeness of his presentation. Some of the most important basic ideas had already been expressed 20 years earlier by Gossen in his remarkable volume on the "development of the laws of human commerce and of the rules to be derived from it for human behavior," which was published in Brunswick, Germany, in 1854. However, those ideas were consigned to the same complete and undeserved limbo as became the fate of the book itself, and they had to become the subject of a fresh and original discovery on the part of the three research scholars mentioned above. It is a highly remarkable coincidence that the discovery was made simultaneously by three different scholars living in three different countries, and working entirely independently of each other. It is at the same time no slight testimony to the correctness of their fundamental ideas, that all three were of one mind concerning them, though they differed in the degree of completeness with which they formulated them. Since that time they have undergone remarkable elaboration and have been very widely circulated.

Part A—VALUE

Chapter II

Nature and Origin of
Subjective Value

1. Mere Capability of Promoting Human Well-Being
Versus Being an Indispensible Condition of It

BY THEIR very definition all goods possess a certain relation to human well-being. But there is a greater and a lesser degree in that relation. The lesser is present when a good possesses the *capacity* to promote human well-being at all. But for the higher degree to be achieved it is necessary that a good be not only a competent cause of an enhancement in well-being, but also an indispensable *condition* of it. The gaining or the losing of the good must be the condition on which a gratification stands or falls.[6] The richness and responsiveness so characteristic of man's language have caused the development of a special designation of each of these two degrees. We call the lesser *usefulness,* the greater *value.*

It is a real distinction. Let us attempt to make it as clear as befits its fundamental importance for the whole theory of value.

One man is sitting beside a copiously flowing spring of fine drinking water. He has filled his cup, and sits watching the water flow past him in a stream that would suffice to fill 100 cups every minute. And now let us look at another man traveling across the desert. A long day's journey over the burning sands still separates him from the next oasis. He has one last single cup of water left. What is the relation, in these two cases, between the cup of water and the well-being of its possessor?

It is obvious at the first glance that the relation in the two cases is utterly dissimilar. But wherein does the dissimilarity consist? Simply in the fact that the first situation exemplifies the lesser degree of relationship to human well-being—it exemplifies the mere usefulness. The second case exemplifies in addition the higher degree as well. The cup of water is just as truly useful in the first case as in the second, since it is capable

---

6. The terms "well-being," "welfare," "enjoyment," "pleasure" and "pain," etc., are frequently used in this and succeeding sections. Although their use in connection with this topic represents a tradition of long standing, there have been numerous evidences of a recent tendency to interpret them as an avowal of a purely hedonistic or utilitarian attitude and psychology. I wish to say at the very outset that such is not the case, and to reserve the right to explain later in adequate detail why and in what sense I consider the use of these expressions advisable even without affecting to offer any opinion either way as to the correctness of a purely hedonistic explanation of human behavior.

of satisfying a want. And it is useful in exactly the same degree. For it is quite obvious that the qualities which enable it to quench thirst—its coolness, its palatableness, etc.—are not impaired in the slightest by the coincidental circumstance that the other cups of water possess the same qualities. Nor is the thirst quenching capacity of the water in the second instance in the least increased because it so happens there is no other water on hand. But with respect to the presence of the second and qualified degree of the relation to well-being [i.e., the indispensable condition— **128** Trsl.], the two cases differ widely and fundamentally. We regard the first man and we know that the possession of the cup of water does not render the satisfaction of a want any more attainable, nor does the loss of it make such a satisfaction less attainable than would have been the case in any event. If he has that particular cupful of water he can slake his thirst; if he has not he will slake it with any one of the 100 other cupfuls of water that the copious spring makes available to him every minute. If he wishes, the cupful of water with which he just happens to be quenching his thirst can be the *cause* of his satisfaction. But under no circumstances can that cupful be an indispensable *condition* thereof. That cupful of water, so far as the man's well-being is concerned, is dispensable, unimportant, a matter of indifference.

The second case is utterly different. Now we must recognize that if our traveler in the desert did not have that last cupful of water, he simply could not relieve his thirst at all. He would have to endure the tortures of an unslaked thirst, might even succumb to them. This cupful of water is not merely a competent cause of the promotion of his well-being; it is an indispensable condition of it, a *conditio sine qua non*. This cupful is of consequence, it is important, it possesses significance for his well-being.

2. Economizing Man Is Careless of Goods Merely Useful

It is not too much to say that the differentiation just described is one of the most fundamental and fruitful in all economics. It did not need the lens of the scholar with a mania for dissection and analysis to summon it into being. It is a vital factor in "everyman's" judgments, all the world knows it, uses it, makes it a guide for every contact with the world of goods, for intellectual estimates of their value, and also for actual day to day behavior. The practical economizing man is careless and indifferent about goods which are *merely useful*. The academic recognition of the fact that a good can be of use is incapable of arousing any effective interest concerning it when further recognition is also present that the same use can be derived without that good. From a practical point of view such goods are ciphers with respect to our well-being and we treat them accordingly. The loss of them does not cause us concern, and we make no effort to acquire them. Who will grieve over the spilling of a cup of water at the brookside, or put forth any energy to prevent the escape of a cubic yard of atmospheric air? But familiarity born of practice so sharpens the economizing eye that it perceives clearly how on this or that good depends a certain satisfaction, a particular bit of well-being, or the gratification of this or that vital desire. Then the effective interest we take in our well-being is transferred to the good which we recognize to be a condition of that well-being. We are concerned about and we cherish our well-being as it is bound up in that good, we recognize its significance for us as *value,* and finally, we evince an anxiety, proportionate to the magnitude of that significance, to acquire the good and retain it.

3. Formal Definition of Value

We thus arrive at a formal definition of value. It is *the significance which a good or a complex of goods possesses for promoting the well-being of an individual.* Any addition to the definition concerning the kind of significance or the reason for that significance or importance is, strictly speaking, unnecessary. For real significance with respect to our well-being can be attained by goods in only one way. That way is for them to become an indispensable condition, a *conditio sine qua non* of some usefulness that contributes to our well-being. But I must reckon with the fact that other definitions also frequently declare value to be a "significance" or an "importance," but erroneously base it on the mere capacity for usefulness. Or they base it, in a manner which is essentially no less erroneous, on the necessity for the expenditure of costs or some such thing. And so I wish to frame my definition with indubitable exactitude by saying, *"Value is that significance which a good or a complex of goods acquires as the recognized condition of a usefulness which could not otherwise be contributed toward the well-being of an individual."*[7]

4. For There to Be Value, Usefulness Must be Paired With Scarcity

All goods have usefulness, but not all goods have value. In order that there be value, usefulness must be paired with *scarcity.* This does not mean absolute scarcity but only relative scarcity in comparison with demand for the goods of the kind in question. Let us put it more exactly. Goods acquire value when the total available supply of goods of that kind is so limited as to be insufficient to cover the demands which call for satisfaction by those goods, or so nearly insufficient that the withdrawal of the goods which it is a question of valuing, would render the supply insufficient. On the other hand, goods remain valueless when they are available in such superabundant quantity that not only are all wants covered for the satisfaction of which they are adapted, but that in addition there remains an excess of such goods and no wants for them to satisfy; furthermore, the excess must be sufficiently large so that the withdrawal of the goods which it is a question of valuing would not imperil the satisfaction of any want.

After what has been said concerning the nature of value this proposition should not be difficult to prove. The supply of available goods may be inadequate, so that some of the wants dependent on them for satisfaction must remain unsatisfied. In that case the loss of even a single

---

7. Even the expression "usefulness," despite its being, apparently, a universally understood term, is to be the subject of subsequent explicit clarification.

specimen of that good entails the further loss of a satisfaction which would otherwise have been possible; conversely, the addition of a single specimen entails the undertaking of a satisfaction which would otherwise have had to be forgone. In a word, a certain degree of gratification or of well-being depends upon the existence of that good. The reverse is just as apparent. When there is an unqualified superfluity of any category of good, the loss of a single specimen can immediately be replaced out of the excess and no harm is done. Nor, on the other hand, does the addition of a single specimen of such good to the available supply add any usefulness, since the excess cannot, by the terms of our hypothesis find useful employment.

Let us assume for instance, that for all the purposes for which he can use water at all a farmer consumes a daily supply of 1,000 gallons. This will furnish drinking water for himself, his family and the hired help, will water his stock, and take care of washing, sluicing down, etc. The flow from the only source of water at his disposal is no more than 800 gallons a day. Obviously, the loss of even 100 gallons would mean a serious curtailment of the needs and activities of the farm. On that farm every 100 gallons constitutes a condition on which a certain group of uses depends. The same would be true if the flow from the spring were just 1,000 gallons a day. But if the spring flowed at the rate of 2,000 gallons a day there would patently be not the slightest damage to our farmer's interests if 100 gallons were lost. Since he can find useful employment for only 1,000 gallons, he must allow the other 1,000 to run off unused. If there is a loss of 100 gallons, it is replaced out of the excess, and the only effect is that the unusable excess is reduced from 1,000 to 900 gallons.

5. Economic Goods Versus Free Goods

Now goods which are available only in inadequate or barely adequate supply are also the very goods which men are prompted to make it their economic purpose to acquire and retain, whereas goods that are available in superabundant supply are at the free disposition of everyone. Therefore we amend our previous propositions to read as follows. "All economic goods have value, and all free goods are valueless." It must however always be borne in mind that it is only *quantitative* considerations which determine whether a good is merely capable of usefulness, or whether it is in addition a "condition precedent" of usefulness to us.[8]

8. There are numerous writers like Scharling (in Conrad's *Jahrbücher*, Vol. XVI, pp. 417 ff., 513 ff., and particularly p. 424, pp. 430 ff., 551 ff.) who cite as the decisive criterion of the "economic" or "valuable" character of goods, the *difficulty of acquisition*, the necessity for an *expenditure of labor* and the like. But that is a secondary manifestation rather than the genuinely determinative and primary distinguishing feature. There are times when we suffer or apprehend a deficiency in the satisfaction of our wants because of an inadequate supply of goods. It is only when that occurs, and because it occurs, that we make up our minds at all to submit to the difficulties of acquisition, to the expenditure of labor, etc. These latter characteristics would never suffice by themselves to establish the economic character of goods; one really distinguishing circumstance must always be present in conjunction with them, and that is the fact that those kinds of good which are difficult or onerous to acquire are also regularly *scarce*. However, it is not the "difficulty" but the *scarcity* that is the determining quality. Very striking proof of that is furnished by those cases—they are admittedly not numerous—in which the

I just said all free goods are valueless. Atmospheric air and drinking water are such free goods. And yet it is obvious that we cannot live five minutes without air to breathe, nor preserve life a week without potable water. Our well-being therefore is utterly dependent on those free goods. How can those two statements be reconciled?

6. Enigmatic Solution of Many Problems Depends on Exact Ratio Between Need and Supply

But what here seems inconsistent is only apparently so. To reconcile the statements, it is necessary to consider a circumstance which will repeatedly engage our attention during the course of our discussion of value, and which will furnish the key to many a riddle. I refer to the fact that our valuation may result quite differently with respect to one and the same species of good, even at one time and under identical circumstances. This variation goes hand in hand with a change between exercising a judgment of value with respect to single specimens and doing so with respect to larger quantities as a unified whole. As we shall see in the next chapter, our judgments in this respect may not merely vary, but may be directly opposed, and they may pertain not only to the degree of value but even to the presence or absence of any value at all. Strange as this may seem at first glance, it is readily explainable on the basis of what has just been said concerning the conditions surrounding the origination of value. For value presupposes scarcity, valuelessness presupposes superabundance. Indeed, we just found it necessary to amplify the latter statement above and to say that the superabundance must be sufficiently large to permit the loss of the very goods which are being subjected to a valuation, without converting the superfluity into an insufficiency. This supplementary statement indicates how a change in the magnitude of the unit being submitted to appraisal may bring about a variation in the judgment of value. Whether or not that variation takes place depends on the answer to just this one question. With goods of a given kind available in superabundant quantity, is the magnitude of the unit to be judged greater or smaller than the magnitude of the excess which constitutes the unusable superabundance? If it is smaller, then all of it can be replaced out of the excess and the loss of it has no disadvantageous bearing on well-being; hence it is adjudged valueless. But if it is greater, the situation oscillates, as it were, between superabundance and insufficiency. If the greater amount, the amount to be judged, is on

131

technical conditions are such that a good can be acquired only by overcoming difficulties, but then in complete superabundance. An instance would be the acquisition of a supply of drinking water by a farmer by means of a piping system which brings water right into his house. His water system may cause a constant expenditure of labor and other costs, as represented by the construction of the system, its maintenance and its operation. But if by means of it the farmer gets good water in superabundant quantity, it would never occur to him to "economize" with the water, despite those costs. In his most recent utterances on the subject (*Grenznutzentheorie und Grenzwertlehre, ibid.,* 3rd series, Vol. XXVII) Scharling presents his theory in a materially modified version in contrast to my own.—Stolzmann comments on my concept of "scarcity in comparison with need" which is presented with such care in this text and even illustrated with figures and computations, and says that it fails to exhibit the characteristic of definitiveness (*Zweck in der Volkswirtschaft,* p. 766 ff.). How he can advance that contention is utterly incomprehensible to me.

hand, the superabundance exists. If that amount is lost, then not only does the superabundance cease to exist, but there is even a resulting deficiency which causes some of the demand which had previously been met, now to go unsatisfied. Its existence is therefore in this case admittedly the condition of certain contributions to well-being, and it must accordingly be adjudged to have value. The principle is easily illustrated by our example. For our farmer who needs 1,000 gallons of water daily and has 2,000 available, any unit of 100 gallons has no value at all. But a unit of 1,500 does have value. For it not only embraces the 1,000 gallons which the farmer may regard with indifference, but also 500 of those other 1,000 gallons which constitute an absolute necessity for the running of his farm. The 1,500 gallons cannot be forgone without causing an impairment of the satisfaction of wants. It is a condition of the latter.

It may seem as if this results in a very dubious situation whereby man's judgments of value are deprived of any firm foundation and become entirely a matter of caprice. It may seem as if a good might arbitrarily be judged at a high or a low value, depending on the choice of a small or a large quantity of it as the unit on which to base the judgment. Doubts of such a nature are not sound. For man cannot arbitrarily choose the unit to be valued. Certain external circumstances determine in any event whether or not there is any necessity for a valuation at all. As a rule, there is inherent in those same circumstances a compelling mandate which prescribes what quantity shall constitute the unit to be valued. If I need to buy a horse, I have no intention whatever of forming a judgment on the value of 100 horses, or of all the horses in the world, and to make that the criterion of how much I am willing to offer. I shall of course form a judgment as to the value of just one horse. In every instance there is some inherent compulsion by virtue of which we make just such an estimation of value as the concrete economic situation demands. The fact that in different situations we are able to render different judgments need not be regarded as disturbing, but rather as inevitable. Let us imagine a miller who simultaneously receives two requests from neighbors. One asks for permission to draw a pitcher of water from the millstream; the other applies to the miller for his consent to a plan for diverting the entire course of the millstream. If with respect to the category "water" only one judgment of value were open to the miller, he would in any event have to follow a mistaken course in one case or the other. If his estimate of water is "valuable," pure and simple, he would be forced into an utterly unnecessary refusal of the perfectly harmless drawing of one pitcherful of water. If his verdict is "valueless" without any and's, if's or but's, he would not forbid the diverting of the whole stream and would suffer greatly thereby. In real life our miller will quite rightly render two different judgments of value. He calls the one pitcherful valueless and grants permission without ado for drawing it from the stream; he calls the whole stream valuable and summarily forbids its being diverted.

A simple application of the principles just laid down leads to a resolution of the apparent inconsistency in the valuation of free goods, of which we spoke a few paragraphs back. Free goods are available in utter superabundance. All smaller and partial quantities which do not exhaust the superabundance must, according to what has been said, be without value. And they are. The empirical evidence of everyday life proves that. On the other hand, if the total taken into consideration as a unit is so great a quantity of free goods that it embraces more than the super-abundance, or indeed, constitutes the total of all the free goods of a given category, then it is just as natural and just as much in keeping with what has been said, that value must be ascribed to this greater total. That is exactly what happens when the judgment is rendered that man cannot live without air and water. The thing that people then have in mind is the totality of all the air there is to breathe and all the water there is to drink. And thinking of it as a unit which is present, or a unit which is absent makes it entirely logical to ascribe value to that unit.

7. Insignificance of the Idea
Of "Abstract Categorical Value"

For quite obvious reasons we almost always deal in practical life only with limited and partial quantities of free goods, and for that reason the latter are almost always adjudged to be valueless. Virtually the only opportunities for an opposite decision arise by way of academic discussions such as this one. In rare and exceptional cases, there is nevertheless practical reason for rendering a unified judgment of value concerning great totalities of free goods. Those cases are then frequently decided in favor of positive valuation. A colony in the primeval forest, for instance, can very well regard an individual tree as a valueless free good. But if it were confronted with a proposal to cede or to clear away the entire forest on which the colony depends for fuel, the colony would then assuredly place great value and a high price upon it. Or let us cite an example that occurs fairly frequently in the practical life of modern Europe. There are cases which involve control over an entire watercourse or a considerable portion of it. Total quantities of such a nature are regularly treated by both parties as an object of value that is worth its price. Despite the continuing utter worthlessness of an individual gallon or an individual 1,000 gallons, large sums are demanded and paid for the rights to drinking water or to water power of a whole region. Instances of that kind furnish proof that the foregoing discussion of value and absence of value in the case of varying quantities of free goods is not based on a bandying about of subtleties, but rather on a genuine foundation that has real existence in economic life.

Earlier theories of value failed to propound any happy solution of the problem put by the facts just presented. They made the adequate accurate observation that judgment of value led to quite different results when applied to a whole category, and when exercised with respect to individual specimens. But they failed to recognize that they were dealing with a selective and specialized application of one single principle. Instead, they posited two different kinds of value. One was an abstract categorical value which was possessed by the category as such; the other was a con-

133

crete value that was possessed by concrete specimens and partial quantities in concrete economic situations.[9]

I consider the "abstract categorical value" a completely misbegotten creation. There simply is no such thing, insofar as value is understood to mean real significance for man on the part of goods. For any value that exists at all is concrete value.[10] Mere membership in a category or species bestows upon goods nothing more than the possession of the objective qualities characteristic of that species, and hence possession of the *capacity for usefulness* that is peculiar to that species. But that is not enough to serve as the basis of any significance for human well-being even *in abstracto* and with respect to some "abstract average human being." Genuine significance always presupposes that human well-being depends upon the goods in question, and that such dependence presupposes in turn, as we now know, a certain scarcity of these goods. But this last characteristic is never peculiar to a species as such; it only develops out of a situation in which the species is "scarce." In speaking of "drinking water," for instance, I cannot be certain of the correctness of any unqualified statement beyond the one that it has the capacity to quench man's thirst. But whether or not any quenching of thirst *depends on it,* is a question that is determined, even for the "abstract average human being," by the answer to another question. That question is, "Does he have a superabundance of drinking water or not?"

8. Significance of the Difference Between the Whole Quantity Combined And Every Fractional Part of It

In accordance with the situation prevailing in each particular instance, some drinking water has significance for man and other drinking water has not. Under those circumstances it is an impermissible generalization to maintain that all drinking water as such must have significance and possess value. It can be maintained only *in one sense* that "the category drinking water" has value, and that is if we understand by the category the totality of all drinking water in existence, or at least the totality of all the available drinking water. But it must be noted that "all the existing water" or "all the available water" is also a concrete quantity of water which owes its value not only to the qualities of the species water, but also to the circumstance that because of its great magnitude that quantity of it cannot be forgone with impunity. From all this we can draw two conclusions. The first is that the value of a species as a totality is a normal concrete value: the second is that there is no warrant for imputing to every isolated specimen of a species the value that properly may be ascribed to the species as the aggregate of all its specimens. That is the error committed by the theorists who propounded the "abstract categorical value." They were obviously misled into the error by the ambiguity which, in the use of the term "the whole category," is always a possibility and often an actuality. If I say "the whole category has value," it is equally possible that I mean *all water combined* or that I mean *every bit of water.*

---

9. Rau, *Volkswirtschaftslehre*, 8th ed., Vol. I, Sec. 62; he was followed by numerous others.

10. Already correctly stated by Schäffle—*Das gesellschaftliche System*, 3rd ed., Vol. I, p. 171.

134 Since it was perceived that the conclusion in the former sense was entirely correct, but that in the latter sense it proved untenable, the erroneous practice was adopted of ascribing an "abstract categorical value" to all water and to every bit of water.

9. More on Abstract Categorical Valuations. Erroneous Identification of Value With Usefulness.

A few incidental statements by several adherents of the theory contain ingenuous admissions that this abstract categorical value is not a genuine value. Consider, for example, Wagner's statement that the estimation which ascribes abstract value to a good "does not necessarily excite any impulse to acquire or retain the good."[11] Here certainly is an indirect admission that the value of the category is not based upon any actual importance for human well-being, since men would then feel under compulsion to modify their actions in deference to it. In actual fact, the only dowry that goods bring with them by reason of their membership in a particular species is the capacity for usefulness which is peculiar to that species. The categorical value that stems solely from membership in the category is therefore nothing but a second name for usefulness. Whether or not such a second name should be incorporated into the vocabulary of economic science is a question of terminological expediency. I think there are many extremely compelling reasons for answering that question in the negative. As a mere synonym for usefulness the term "abstract categorical value" is superfluous; as its competitor the term, being ambiguous to begin with, would lead to confusion and error. Since we do not need it for the purposes of economic science, let us rather give it up completely. That should be all the easier to do since it has never found popular support, and has been grafted, like an artificial scion, upon the stock of scholarly language by dint of scholarly abstraction.

11. *Grundlegung*, 2nd ed., p. 52. To make the quoted statement completely accurate, this excellent research scholar ought, if I may be permitted so to remark, to have gone a little further. For in my opinion the factual situation on which the concept of abstract categorical value is based not only does *not necessarily* stimulate us to action, but in and of itself does *not do so at all*.

Part A—VALUE

Chapter III

The Magnitude of Value.
The General Principle.
The Law of Marginal Utility.

1. Simple Principle Governing the Value of Goods

WHEN we seek to establish the principle that governs the value   135
of goods, we enter upon the field where the chief task of the theory lies,
but also where we find its greatest difficulties. The latter are the result
of a peculiar concentration of circumstances. On the other hand, the
correct principle seems to suggest itself almost automatically. If value
is the significance of goods for human well-being, and if this significance
is based on the fact that some gain in well-being is dependent upon the
disposition of those goods, then it is clear that the magnitude of value
must be determined by the gain in well-being that depends on the good in
question. A good will have a high value when an important advantage for
our well-being depends on it; it will have a low value when only some
trifling gain in well-being depends on it.

2. Apparent Paradoxes in Value Determinations

On the other hand, certain facts are found in the world of economics
that seem to give the lie to this most obvious and natural explanation.
Everyone knows that in practical economic life jewels enjoy a high valuation, goods like iron and bread have a modest value, air and water
have no value at all. But everyone also knows that without air and drinking water existence would be a sheer impossibility, that bread and iron
perform services that are extremely important for our well-being, whereas
jewels serve primarily to meet our desire for ornamentation which, so far
as human well-being is concerned, certainly has only minor significance
indeed. Suppose then, that a person adhered to the principle that the
magnitude of value is determined by the importance of the contributions
to well-being that depend on the goods. Such a person would necessarily,
it would seem, expect that jewels would have small value, bread and
iron great value, water and air the highest of all. Yet the actual facts
show exactly the opposite.

3. Recourse to False Solutions

This unquestionably astonishing phenomenon became a troublesome bone of contention for the theory of value. Supreme utility and minimal value—what a strange paradox! Admittedly, one reason why the situation was neither perceived nor portrayed quite correctly lay in the prevailing confusion between usefulness and "use value." By assigning (erroneously) a high "use value" to iron and a low one to diamonds, the causes for bewilderment were reduced to the mere circumstance that the "exchange value," in the case of these goods, seemed to follow a principle so radically different. But that of course merely shifted the name by which the contrast was known, without altering the sharpness of the contrast itself. There was no lack of devious expedients to reconcile the awkward contradiction. They all failed. It is therefore not difficult to understand that from the days of Adam Smith down to our own, numberless theorists have despaired completely of finding the essence and the measure of value in a relation to human welfare. They therefore seized upon other and singular lines of explanation, such as labor or labor-time, production costs, "difficulty of acquisition," "resistivity of nature toward man" and others of the sort. But since they could not entirely rid themselves of the feeling that there must be some connection between the value of the goods and their contribution to well-being, they recorded this disharmony between utility and value as a strange enigmatic paradox, a *contradiction économique.*

4. Common Man's Solution is Simple; And, All Paradoxical Solutions Are False

In the chapter which is to follow I shall submit proof that the early theory of value unnecessarily abandoned the most natural explanation. As a general rule,[12] *the measure of the benefit depending on the good is really also the measure of the value of that good.* In order to be convinced of the truth of this statement, all we need to do is employ sober and selective activity in our investigation of the question as to just which advantage to our well-being depends upon a good in a given situation. I say advisedly "selective activity." For actually the whole theory of subjective value is nothing but an extended selection as to how much depends upon a good in terms of promotion of our well-being, and when and under what circumstances that dependence manifests itself. It is a remarkable thing that the ordinary man is unerring in the selective decisions of this sort which he is called upon to make in practical life. He very rarely makes a mistake, and even then never in principle. He may be in actual error in taking a diamond to be a glass bead and in therefore assigning to it a very low value. But he will never allow himself to be misled into a selective error of judgment on the principle, say, of the value of drinking

---

12. At this point in the first edition I used the word "everywhere." The word is correct if the word *benefit* [or "use"] is employed in the broad sense of "contribution to well-being." Still, in one very narrow sense the word is not quite accurate with respect to the existence of one concededly insignificant group of exceptional cases. I made explicit mention of those cases even in my earliest treatment of this topic. Since I do not wish to have to rely on qualifiedly valid statements, I give preference to this quite unexceptionable wording and reserve the right to discuss the nature and significance of these exceptional cases explicitly at a later point in this work, as well as their relation to the rule. See following page 177 ff.

water. That is to say, the circumstance that man cannot live without water is, from the standpoint of principle, irrelevant; the common man would not be misled into the erroneous selective judgment that every quart of water he draws from the kitchen tap is therefore a treasure of immense value, and cheaply purchased at $1,000. It will now be our task to hold the mirror, as it were, up to the practice of making selective decisions in everyday life, and to discover the rules that the common man instinctively applies with such utter assurance. We shall then perceive them with equal assurance, but with far greater conscious recognition.

5. Specific Well-Being Depends On Satisfaction of Specific Wants

As a general rule, whenever the promotion of our well-being depends on a good, such promotion consists in the satisfaction of a *want*.[13] There are certain exceptions of minor importance, but we shall defer treatment of them until a later time. The correct selective decision as to how much depends on a good for the promotion of the well-being of a person really resolves itself into the answers to two complementary questions.

   1]   *Which among several or numerous wants depends on a good?*
   2]   *How important is the dependent want, or rather its satisfaction?*

For reasons of expediency let us consider the second question first.

6. Ranking of Wants, According to Importance

It is a matter of common knowledge that our wants vary widely in importance. We are in the habit of determining the degree of that importance by the gravity of the adverse consequences which ensue for our well-being when the wants are not satisfied. We therefore attach supreme importance to wants of such a nature that the failure to satisfy them would result in death. We attach the next smaller degree of importance to wants of such a nature that failure to satisfy them would entail a serious and long lasting impairment of our health, our honor, our happiness. Further down the scale are such wants as involve more transitory sorrows, pains or deprivations. At the very bottom we place wants of such kind

13. It is no part of the plan of this book to treat the highly important theory of wants *ex professo*. I think certain generally understood concepts and designations will suffice to enable me to elucidate those things which it devolves upon me to make clear. Nor do I intend to comment on them more extensively than my purposes make absolutely necessary. The elaboration of the theory of wants is a task of independent importance and one which is in crying need of the monographic treatment that it has failed to receive for far too long. There was recently, to be sure, an attempt by Čuhel (*Zur Lehre von den Bedürfnissen*, Innsbruck, 1907) marked by great devotion and industriousness as well as a number of objectively worthwhile results. But it is regrettable that this author has impaired the literary effectiveness of his meritorious work by certain inconsequential superficialities. Under this heading I should list his exaggerated zeal for hairsplitting analysis and schematic arrangements, as well as the heavyhandedness of his formulation arising from his striving for complete accuracy, but most of all a prodigal use of new turns of phrase which are by no means always felicitously or tastefully coined. There is a still more recent monograph by Lujo Brentano (*Versuch einer Theorie der Bedürfnisse, Sitzungsberichte der königlich bayrischen Akademie der Wissenschaften, Philos.-philolog. Klasse*, 1908, 10th Essay) which rather disappointed me, and I can hardly have been the only one. Brentano gathers together a host of interesting and instructive details in rather superficial fashion, but seems to me to fail conspicuously to give us the very things we have a right to expect of a *theory* of wants. He is an excellent "realistic research scholar," and his strength seems to lie in fields other than that of profoundly penetrative theoretical analysis.

137

that failure to satisfy them costs no more than some very slight discomfort or renunciation of some very lightly regarded pleasure. In accordance with these characteristics it is possible to construct a progression or graduated scale of wants in point of importance. That scale will of course vary from person to person because their varying physical and intellectual propensities, amount of education, and the like will result in widely varying wants. Even the same individual will vary widely in his wants at different times. And yet every practical economizing person, if he is to make a wise choice in the application of his limited means, will have to have his scale of wants more or less clearly in mind. There have even been several theorists who have taken occasion to set up such a graduated scale on the basis of "objective" unbiased scientific considerations.[14]

7. Difference Between Ranking Categories of Wants, and Individual Concrete Feelings of Wants

That would all be very simple and sure, if it were not for the ambiguity inherent in the expression "the ranking of wants." The expression may mean the rank and order of *categories of wants,* or may mean *concrete wants,* that is to say, the individual feelings of want. The two graduated scales differ materially from each other. If categories of wants, taken as units, are assigned to classes with respect to their importance for human well-being, there can be no doubt that the leading class would include the need of food; in a class very little lower would be found the need of shelter and of clothing. It would be only to classes much lower that we should assign such needs as the desire for tobacco, for alcoholic beverages or for the enjoyment of music. Finally the desire for ornament and the like would be assigned to a class far lower down the scale.

8. Different Results From Graduating Concrete Wants (Rather Than Categories of Wants)

Graduating concrete wants however, would lead to materially different results. For within each category of wants the individual wants are by no means equally intense and not all satisfactions are equally important. Consider, as an example, the case of a man who has not had a bite to eat for a week and who is close to starvation. The need for nourishment is inordinately more urgent than in the case of a man sitting at the dinner table, who has just completed the second course of his usual three course dinner and merely wants to eat the third as well. That modification puts an entirely different aspect on the question of ranking individual concrete

14. Very recently Lujo Brentano (*op. cit.,* p. 11 ff.) attempted to catalogue wants according to the degree of urgency which marks the influence they customarily exert upon human beings. Some of his results are a bit weird. For instance, in his empirical graduated scale of urgencies he assigns to the "Need for Provision for the Future" a place lower than that of the "Need for Cheerfulness" but higher than that of the "Need for Healing." The strangeness of his results is in part attributable to the infelicitous assembling of the groups of needs which he aligns for comparison, in part to the fact that his very groupings represent a departure from the principle underlying his classification in the first place, but for the most part to the very fact that he should attempt at all to establish a hierarchy of *kinds* of need. That attempt inevitably enmeshed him in all sorts of difficulties. The reasons for those difficulties are discussed in the immediately following pages of my text. Brentano seems to have taken too little account of those difficulties in the content of his exposition, and almost none at all in its form.

wants, and introduces far greater variability. On the graduated scale for categories, "need of nourishment," lumped together, was placed well ahead of need of tobacco, need of alcoholic beverages, need of ornament and so forth. But now the individual concrete wants from different categories cross each other's paths. Admittedly, the most important wants out of the most important categories will be ranked in the very forefront. But the less important wants of those categories will often be outranked by concrete wants from lower ranking categories. It will even happen that the last stragglers in the high categories will be of lower rank than the leaders among concrete wants of lower categories. It is analogous to comparing the European mountain ranges, Swiss Alps, Pyrenees, the Sudetic range, the Harz Mountains. It is one thing to rank these mountains as to altitude, taking each range as a whole; it is quite another thing to rank the individual peaks in the order of their altitude. Taken as whole ranges, the Swiss Alps outrank the Pyrenees which in turn are higher than the Sudetes, and the Harz Mountains have the lowest rank. But if the individual peaks are compared, there will be many Swiss mountain tops of a lesser altitude than some peaks in the Pyrenees, and some of them may even be outranked by one or two in the lowly Harz.

Now the question arises as to which scale to use, when we value goods, in order to determine the importance of the wants that depend on the goods. Shall we use the scale of categories, or the scale of concrete wants?

9. At First Fork in Road, the Old Economics Took Wrong Approach

Arriving at this crossroads—the first that offered an opportunity for error—the older theory chose the wrong turning. It seized upon the scale of categories of wants. Now on that scale the category called "need of nourishment" occupies a very high place, the category "need of ornament" a very low rank. For that reason the old theory of value rendered a verdict that, in general, bread has a high "use value," and jewels a very low "use value." And then, of course, there was great astonishment at finding that in real life the estimation in which the two are held is just the reverse.

The verdict is in error. The rationalization which determines the selection must run as follows. With the one piece of bread which is in my possession I can very well assuage one or the other concrete hunger pang as it manifests itself in me. But I can never in the world satisfy the aggregate of all real and possible stirrings of hunger, all the present and future appetites which constitute the category called need of nourishment. It is therefore patently ill advised, in gauging the importance of the contribution this bread can make to my well-being, to measure it by considering whether that universal aggregate of wants is of great or small importance. It would be comparable to the act of a man who, when asked about the height of the Kahlenberg hill (part of a tiny spur of the Swiss Alps), answered by stating the height of the entire Alpine range. As a matter of actual fact, no one in practical life would even dream of revering every slice of bread he owns as a life-giving treasure of supreme importance. Neither does anyone jump for joy because for two thin dimes he has preserved his life by buying a loaf of bread at the chain-store, any more than he would condemn his neighbor for wantonly risking his life by carelessly handing out a "slice of rye" to a hobo, by squandering it, or even **139** by feeding it to the dog! Yet those are the very things people would do, if they attached the same importance to every *specimen* as they do to the *category* "need of nourishment," the satisfaction of which actually is a matter of life and death.

Thus it becomes clear that the valuation of goods has nothing to do with the order in which categories of goods may be ranked, but only with the ranking of concrete wants. If full benefit is to be derived from that conclusion, a few points concerning the composition of that graduated scale of rank must be made clearer. It is especially necessary to supply a firmer foundation than the foregoing discussion has as yet furnished.

10. Where Crucial Significance of Marginal Utility Begins to Become Apparent

Most of our wants are fractionable in the sense that they are amenable to partial satisfaction. When I am hungry, I am not faced with the alternative of being fully sated or starving entirely. It is possible for me to assuage the worst of my hunger by partaking moderately of food, possibly to enjoy my fill later by means of a second and even a third ingestion of food, or possibly to content myself perforce by the first partial satisfaction. Such partial satisfaction of a concrete want has an importance for my well-being that is different from and smaller than that of a complete satisfaction of the same want. That circumstance alone would to a certain degree suffice for the existence of the phenomenon previously mentioned, namely that within a single category of wants individual concrete wants (including partial wants) manifest varying degrees of importance. But there is a further circumstance which allies itself to this one. It is a facet of human experience, as familiar as it is deep-seated in human nature, that the same act of enjoyment continually repeated, affords decreasing pleasure from a certain point on until it is finally transformed into its opposite and arouses disgust and revulsion. Everyone knows from his own experience that the fourth or fifth course of a banquet arouses far less appetite than did the first, and that as the courses continue to be served there finally comes a point where any further partaking of food is utterly repugnant. Similar sensations can arise in the course of a concert, a lecture, a walk or a game that continues for an unduly long period. This will apply, indeed, to virtually all physical and intellectual enjoyments as well.[15]

15. These views, as is well known, were recognized and accepted by economists under the name of "Gossen's Law of Diminishing Utility." Those interested in examining further into Gossen's predecessors, into parallel research efforts in other fields of knowledge, or into the validity of Gossen's law, its limitations and exceptions, its profounder psychological and physiological basis, may refer to a number of writers including Oskar Kraus (*Zur Theorie des Wertes, eine Bentham-Studie,* Halle, 1902, p. 41 ff.), Čuhel (*Lehre von den Bedürfnissen,* p. 232 ff.) and Brentano (*Versuch einer Theorie der Bedürfnisse,* p. 40 ff.). I do not need to go into exact details here, because the inferences I draw with respect to the theory of value are concerned only with the indubitably correct central thought of Gossen's law. For my purposes no importance attaches to the existence of certain exceptions, such as the initial phases of a satisfaction that is being experienced for the first time, the existence of "altruistic" wants, the collector's passion and the like. But I have considered these things to the extent of according to Gossen's law in my text only a widely applicable validity, but not a validity completely free of exceptions.

11. Important Phenomenon of Diminishing Utility

To express the essence of these familiar facts in the technical language of economics we can formulate the proposition as follows. The concrete fractional wants into which our sensations of want are divisible, or the successive partial satisfactions which can be obtained through equal quantities of goods are usually of *differing importance, and that importance tends to diminish progressively toward zero.* This principle explains a number of the foregoing statements which were there presented as bare assertions. In the first place we find here an explanation of the fact that within one and the same category of wants there can be concrete wants and partial wants possessing varying degrees of significance. Indeed, not only *can* such be the case but rather it *must* occur as an organically imperative phenomenon, as it were, simply for the reason that it is an obvious characteristic of fractionable wants, which is what our wants, for the most part, are. In the second place we find here an explanation for the fact that even in the most important categories gradations of wants are represented down to lower and lower intensities of importance. The only real difference between the more important and the less important categories is that the "peaks" in the former attain higher altitudes, so to speak. The base for all the categories is at the same level. And finally we find here an explanation for one fact which is not merely a *possibility,* as we said above, but rather a regular, usual and organically inevitable phenomenon. I refer to the circumstance that although a category may, on the whole, occupy a very high position in the scale of comparative importance, some individual concrete want within the category may be outranked by some individual concrete want in a category that, on the whole, occupies a lower position on that same scale. There will at all times be innumerable wants of nourishment that are less intense and less important than some concrete wants in quite unimportant categories such as the needs for ornament, for attendance at dances, for tobacco, for making pets of song birds and the like.

140

If we attempt to illustrate the classification of our wants by a typical schematic arrangement, we should on the basis of what has just been said arrive at something like the following.[16]

I	II	III	IV	V	VI	VII	VIII	IX	X
10	—	—	—	—	—	—	—	—	—
9	9	—	—	—	—	—	—	—	—
8	8	8	—	—	—	—	—	—	—
7	7	7	7	—	—	—	—	—	—
6	6	6	—	6	—	—	—	—	—
5	5	5	—	5	5	—	—	—	—
4	4	4	4	4	4	4	—	—	—
3	3	3	—	3	3	—	3	—	—
2	2	2	—	2	2	—	2	2	—
1	1	1	1	1	1	—	1	1	1
0	0	0	0	0	0	0	0	0	0

16. Cf. Menger, *Grundsätze der Volkswirtschaftslehre,* p. 93; *Principles of Economics,* The Free Press, Glencoe, Illinois, 1950, p. 127.

In the foregoing schematic arrangement the Roman numerals I to X denote the various categories of wants and their rank in descending order. Number I represents the most important category of wants—let us say, want of nourishment. Number V represents some category of medium importance—let us say, the desire for alcoholic beverages, while X represents the category of wants possessing the smallest conceivable importance. The Arabic figures 1 to 10 then represent the concrete wants and partial wants that occur in the various categories. The figure itself indicates the relative ranking of the concrete wants in question, the rank 10 designating a want of the greatest conceivable importance, the rank of 9 designating a want of the next greatest importance, and so on down to 1 which represents a want that has the least importance that will account for its existing at all. The table enables us to visualize the fact that the more important the category, the greater is the maximum importance that any concrete want within the category may attain. But it also illustrates that in addition all lesser degrees of importance are represented right down to the vanishing point. Categories IV and VII are exceptions to this rule in that certain gradations in the descending order are missing. These illustrate those infrequent categories in which for technical reasons successive satisfying of partial wants is either partly or entirely impracticable, that is to say, where the satisfaction of wants must take place completely or not at all. The need for a device for heating my dwelling, for instance, is so completely satisfied by *one* furnace that I should simply have no use at all for a second. There is a third and final point to be visualized by means of our table. In the most important category, Number I, concrete wants occur with the minimum ranking of 1, while at the same time in almost all categories of lesser importance than I, there are concrete wants with a rank in excess of 1.[17]

12. Perplexing Question: Which of Several Wants Depends on a Good?

Let us now turn to the other one (the first) of the two principal questions propounded on page 137 of this section. That question reads: *Which among several or numerous wants depends on a good?*

This question could not arise, if conditions in economic life were so simple that each single want corresponded to a single good. If a good is suitable for the satisfaction of just one single concrete want and if it is at the same time the only one of its kind, or at least the only one available, then it would be clear without any deliberation that on the power to dispose of that lone good depended the satisfaction of the only need which the good is capable of serving. But in actual practice the matter is almost never so simple as that. On the contrary, it is usually very complicated

17. To correct misunderstandings which have arisen despite my precautions, I should like to state explicitly that the descending scale represented by the arabic numerals 10 to 1 in this table do not symbolize anything beyond the fact that each concrete want designated by a given number has a lower intensity or importance than any want or wants designated by a higher number or numbers. The series of numbers is not meant to convey the *degree* to which the importance of a want with a higher index exceeds that of a want with a lower index. It is *not* by any means my intention to make the statement that a want with an index of 6 is exactly three times as important as one with an index of 2, nor that one with an index of 9 possesses an importance exactly equal to that of wants with indices of 6 and 3 combined.

in two directions. In the first place, one and the same good is ordinarily suitable for use in satisfying several concrete wants, which also exhibit varying degrees of importance. And in the second place there are often numerous specimens of the same kind of good available, and so it is the result of purely arbitrary choice that one specimen is used to satisfy an important want, and another to meet an unimportant need. Let us adduce as simple an example as possible. I am on a hunting expedition and the only food I have with me is two completely identical loaves of bread. I need one to satisfy my own hunger and the other to feed my dog. It is quite clear that my own nourishment is far more important to me than that of my dog. It is just as clear that I can make an arbitrary choice as to which of the two loaves I want to eat myself and which I will feed to my dog. And now the question arises, "Which of the two wants here depends on my bread?"

One could be easily tempted to answer by saying it is the want which the loaf in question was actually intended to satisfy. But it is easy to see immediately that such a decision would be erroneous. For it would mean that the two loaves, since they are destined for the satisfaction of wants of differing importance must also themselves differ in value. At the same time it is beyond question that two identical goods, available in identical situations must also be absolutely identical in value.

13. Answer to Question in Sideheading 12: The Least Important of All Wants Concerned

Here again some simple selective rationalizing leads to the desired goal. The simplest way to determine which one of several wants depends on a good is to observe which want would fail of satisfaction if the good which is to be valued were not present. That need is obviously the dependent one. And now it becomes easily demonstrable that the choice does not fall at all on the want which its owner's arbitrary option had selected. It will always fall on the least important among all the wants concerned, that is to say, among all the wants which would otherwise have been provided for through the total supply of goods of that kind, including the specimen to be valued.

142

14. Universal Principle Underlying Economics: Men Will Act (Surrender Satisfactions) According to the Ranking of Their Preferences

Regard for his own advantage, as obvious as it is compelling, will induce every reasonable economizing person to maintain a certain fixed order of precedence in satisfying his wants. No one will be so foolish as to expend all the means available to him on the satisfaction of trifling and easily dispensable wants, only to leave necessities unprovided for. Rather will it be every man's purpose to employ the means available to him for his most important wants to begin with. He will then go on to the next most important, proceed to wants of third rank and continue in such manner that the wants of a lower rank will not be selected for satisfaction until all wants in higher grades have been met, and as long as means of further satisfaction are available. These obviously reasonable rules are adhered to even when the previous supply suffers diminution by the loss of one specimen. This of course disturbs the plan of expenditure followed up to that point. Not all the wants which had previously been scheduled for satisfaction can now be covered, and a diminution in the number of satisfactions is inevitable. But the reasonable economizing subject will of course attempt to have the diminution strike at the least sensitive spot. That means that if the loss happens to involve a good that was intended for a more important disposition, he will not forgo satisfying the more important need and obstinately cling to the former plan of satisfying needs of minor importance. Instead he will in any event satisfy the more important need and leave uncovered the want which, among all the wants previously slated for satisfaction, he regards most lightly. Let us return to the example we were last discussing. If the hunter loses the loaf which he had intended for his own lunch, he will never expose himself to the risk of starvation and feed his one remaining loaf to the dog. He will on the contrary make a quick change in his plans for the disposition of his means, replace the lost loaf of bread by using the second loaf for the more important function and transferring the loss to the less sensitive spot, the feeding of the dog.

The case can be stated as follows. All wants which are more important than the often mentioned "last" remain unaffected by the loss of the one specimen, for satisfaction of them remains assured by requisitioning a replacement. Nor are those wants affected which are still less important than the "last," since they were not to be satisfied whether or not the one specimen was lost. Of all wants the only one affected is the last one of those previously covered. That want is satisfied when the good is present, it remains unsatisfied when the good is absent. It is the dependent want we have been looking for.

15. Summary of the Grand Principle Determining Value

That brings us to the goal of our present search. *The magnitude of the value of a good is determined by the importance of that concrete want or partial want which has the lowest degree of urgency among the wants that can be covered by the available supply of goods of the same kind.* Value is determined then, not by the greatest degree of utility which a good affords, nor by the average utility which goods of that kind afford, but by the smallest degree of utility for which, in whatever concrete economic situation obtains, it is rationally advisable to expend the good or its equivalent. That is rather a long-winded description of the situation, and to be entirely correct it really ought to be even somewhat more long-winded. But we must be spared such prolixity in the future when we wish to refer to this minimal usefulness which stands on the borderline of the economically admissible. So let us follow the example of Wieser[18] and

18. *Über den Ursprung und die Hauptgesetze des wirtschaftlichen Wertes*, p. 128. Jevons uses the terms "final degree of utility" and "terminal utility." Since that time the English term "marginal utility," which corresponds exactly to the German *Grenznutzen* has become the usual expression. Menger was the first to develop with complete clarity the law set forth in the text above, but he could not give it straightforward expression in brief technical phraseology. In his book (*op. cit.*, p. 98 f.) the law reads as follows: "Accordingly, in every concrete case, of all the satisfactions secured by means of the whole quantity of a good at the disposal of an economizing individual, only those that have the least importance to him are dependent on the availability of a given portion of the whole quantity. Hence the value to this person of any portion of the whole available quantity of the good is equal to the importance to him of the satisfactions of least importance among those assured by the whole quantity and achieved with an equal portion" (*Principles of Economics*, p. 132).

speak of it tersely as the economic marginal utility of the good. And now we can formulate the law of the magnitude of the value of goods as follows. *The value of a good is determined by the magnitude of its marginal utility.*

16. Universality of the Significance, and Applicability, of Principle of Marginal Utility

This proposition is the crux of our theory of value. But it is more than that. It constitutes, in my opinion, the key that opens the door to an understanding of the broadest fundamentals underlying the behavior of economizing men with respect to goods. It applies equally well to both the simplest cases and the exceedingly complicated situations which abound throughout the multiform manifestations of our modern economic life. Everywhere we see men making valuations of goods on the basis of their marginal utility and ruling their *actions* in accordance with the results of those estimations. And in view of that the doctrine of marginal utility may be regarded as the crux, not only of the theory of value, but of every explanation of man's economic behavior, and hence indeed of the entire field of economic theory.[19] I do not consider that pronouncement an exaggeration, and I am confident that anyone who understands the art of observing life accurately will be convinced of its correctness. To observe aright and to interpret observations aright is an art which is at times far from easy. To practice that art we will do well to avail ourselves of the theory of value insofar as such practice falls within the domain of that theory. I propose to follow my own advice in the pages to come, and I shall begin with an example of the greatest conceivable simplicity.

17. Principle of Marginal Utility Illustrated in a Case of Classic Simplicity

A pioneer farmer, whose solitary log cabin stands in the primeval forest far from the paths of commerce, has just harvested five sacks of grain. These he must "make do" until the next harvest. Being a methodical soul he lays careful plans for the use to which he will put them. One sack is absolutely essential as the food supply which is to keep him alive until the next harvest. A second sack will enable him to supplement his meals to the point where they will keep him at full strength and in complete health. He has no desire to eat more grain in the form of fancy breads and sweet puddings, but he would like very much to add some nutriment in the form of meat to his farinaceous diet. Therefore he determines to use a third sack for the raising of poultry. He devotes a fourth sack to the distilling of brandy. Now that his modest personal

19. Even when people act altruistically rather than selfishly they have good reason to take marginal utility into account. In this case it is the marginal utility which the goods to be given to other persons have for the recipients. Donations and alms are given when their significance in promoting well-being, as measured by their marginal utility, is far greater for the recipient than for the donor. The reverse is virtually never true.—It is a great pleasure to me to find myself, in respect to the thoughts expressed in the text at this point, in agreement with such an outstanding research scholar as Walras. In the preface to his *Théorie de la Monnaie*, (p. xi f.) he expressed himself on the significance of the idea of "marginal utility" for both economic theory and actual economic practice, and I can only say that I am in complete agreement with him.

wants are fully provided for by the arrangements just described, he can think of no better use for his last sack than to feed it to a number of parrots whose antics give him pleasure. It stands to reason that these uses do not rank equally as to their importance to him. In order to arrive at a brief numerical method of expressing our facts, let us set up a scale of 10 degrees of importance. In that event our pioneer farmer will naturally assign the maximum grade of 10 to the preservation of his life; he may call the preservation of his health worth a rating of 8; then descending the scale he might rate the improvement of his cuisine at 6, the enjoyment of his brandy at 4, and finally the keeping of parrots at the lowest conceivable mark of 1. And now let us put ourselves in the pioneer's position and ask ourselves what is the significance for his well-being of *one* sack of grain?

We are already aware that the simplest way to establish that is to determine what loss in utility would be represented by the loss of one sack of grain. Let us apply that yardstick. It is quite obvious that our man would have to be a bit addlepated to make good the loss of the sack out of the food that goes into his mouth and thus sacrifice his health or even his life, and yet continue to distill brandy and feed chickens and parrots as before. Upon sound reflection only one solution is conceivable. Our pioneer will use the four remaining sacks to cover the most urgent groups of needs and will renounce the enjoyment of only the least important, the final, the "marginal utility." In this case that is the keeping of parrots. Having or not having the fifth sack makes no greater difference to him than the ability, in one case, to indulge himself in the pleasure of keeping of parrots or in the other case, the inability to do so. And this unimportant utility will afford a rational basis for the estimation of the value of a single sack of his supply of grain. And that means *every* single sack. For if the five sacks are all exactly alike, it will be all one to the pioneer whether he loses sack A or sack B—just so long as its background harbors four other sacks with which to meet his more important wants.

Now let us modify the illustration. Let us assume our pioneer under the very same circumstances possesses only three sacks of grain. How high a value does he now place upon a sack of grain? The test is again quite easy. If our pioneer has three sacks he can cover the three most important groups of wants with them. And that is what he will do. If he has but two sacks he will restrict himself to satisfying the two most important groups, and have to forgo the third group of wants, the eating of meat. The possession of the third sack means for him nothing more and nothing less than the satisfying of the third most important group of wants, that is to say the final group that is provided for when his whole supply totals three sacks. When we say "third sack" we do not mean any certain individual sack, but rather any one of the three sacks, providing only there are still two more to "back it up." To value it on any other basis than that of its final or marginal utility would be contrary to the factual situation and therefore a fallacy.

Let us make a final supposition, namely, that our pioneer under the same conditions possesses only a single sack of grain. It is now crystal clear that every other disposition is out of the question, and this one sack must be devoted to and used for a bare subsistence, for which it is just adequate. It is just as clear that if the pioneer loses that single sack **145** he will no longer be able to maintain life. The possession of it therefore signifies life, its loss means death. The single sack of grain has the greatest conceivable significance for the well-being of the pioneer. And once more the valuation occurs in absolute adherence to the principle of marginal utility. For the supreme utility, the preservation of life, is now the only utility and as such is at the same time the last, the final, the *marginal* utility.

And all these valuations in accordance with the marginal utility are not merely "academic." Quite the contrary. Nobody will doubt that our pioneer's practical behavior will be governed thereby in whatever situation arises. Suppose someone made an offer to buy his grain. There is no doubt that any one of us in his position would be inclined to sell *one of the five sacks* relatively cheaply, and quite in keeping with its small marginal utility. We should be willing to sell *one of three sacks* only at a considerably higher price, while the irreplaceable *one and only sack* with its enormous marginal utility would not be for sale at any price, however high.

Let us shift the theater of action from the lonely primeval forest to the hurly-burly of a highly developed economy. Here the situation is under the veritable domination of the empirically familiar proposition that the value of goods is in inverse proportion to their quantity. The more goods of a given category are on hand, the smaller, other things being equal, will be the value of the individual specimen and vice versa. It is a matter of common knowledge that economic theory has utilized this elementary empirical proposition in the field of the doctrine of price, to set up the law of "supply and demand." But the proposition is also valid quite independently of exchange and price. How much more highly, for instance, does a collector prize the only specimen of a given category, than when that same category is represented by a dozen identical specimens! It can easily be shown that such facts as this, so well attested by experience, follow as a natural consequence from the operation of laws in full accord with the theory of marginal utility. For the more numerous the specimens of a given category of goods are, the more completely can the wants dependent on them be satisfied, the less important are the last wants which still achieve satisfaction and the satisfaction of which would be at stake if a single specimen were lost. In other words, the more numerous the specimens of a given category of goods, the lower the marginal utility which determines value. And to complete the picture, if there are so many specimens available that after complete satisfaction of all dependent wants there are still further specimens of that good available for which no useful employment can be found at all, then the marginal utility equals zero, and the goods are without value.

18. Solution of Paradoxes of Value
And Price That (So-Called)
Classical Economics Never Attained

And now we have the perfectly natural explanation of the phenomenon that at first seemed so startling—that things with little usefulness, such as pearls and diamonds, should possess such high value, while much more useful things like bread and iron should have a far lower value, and water and air no value at all. It is simply a case of pearls and diamonds being available in such small quantities that the need for them is satisfied to only a very small extent. As a result, the satisfying of the want "descends" only to a rank which denotes a final or marginal utility that is still relatively high. On the other hand—and fortunately—bread and iron, water and air are normally available in such great quantity especially for the rich who can buy pearls and diamonds, that satisfaction of all the more important needs dependent upon them is assured. And there are either very trifling needs or none at all that still depend upon the availability of a single example of the good or on a concrete partial quantity. Of course, under abnormal conditions such as the siege of a city or a voyage through the desert, water and bread can become scarce. In that case the very limited supplies no longer suffice to cover the most important concrete needs for food and drink. That causes the marginal utility to soar and the value of these otherwise so lightly regarded goods to rise rapidly, quite in accordance with our principle. The conclusion thus logically arrived at finds empirical corroboration in the proverbially exorbitant prices which the most modest foods and beverages customarily command in situations of that sort.[20] And so we can now once more consider those facts which at first glance seemed to deride our principle that the magnitude of value is determined by the magnitude of the utility dependent on it. And lo! instead of conflicting with the theory they furnish a brilliant corroboration of it!

19. To Determine Marginal Utility
Two Calculations Must Be Made

The cases we have considered so far were relatively easy to interpret. But practical life often offers economic complications which are more difficult for the research theorist to penetrate, even though the layman deals with them with consummate ease in actual practice.[21] The solution of the problems they present depends entirely on the accuracy of the selective decision that is arrived at concerning the rank which the marginal utility will under given conditions attain. To that end the following general precept may be applied, with confidence that it will furnish a universal rule for the solution of all the more difficult problems of value. The economic position of the person called upon to render the decision on the question of valuation must be taken into account from two points of view. In the first instance, the good that is to be valued must be imagined as included in the supply of goods possessed by the

20. The objection might be raised that the only conclusion that can be drawn with any assurance, is that these high prices indicate an increased "objective exchange value," while the subjective use value remains unchanged. But the demanding and the paying of high prices, as will be more fully expounded in a subsequent chapter, presupposes a high subjective valuation of a commodity. At the same time the readiness with which in normal times we give away such things as drinking water is a clear indication that, even from the subjective standpoint, we place no particular value upon the thing with which we part so openhandedly.

21. On the subject of the relation between theory and practice in the field of valuation the reader is referred to following p. 201 ff.

economic subject and an estimate must be made as to which concrete wants will represent the lowest grade that will be satisfied. In the second instance, the good must be imagined as excluded or lost, and a new estimate made as to how low a grade of want will now still find satisfaction. The two operations will reveal a certain layer of wants which is deprived of satisfaction. This is of course the lowest layer of the total wants covered by the good. *It is this lowest layer that indicates the marginal utility which determines valuation.*[22]

20. Simplicity of Marginal Utility Should Not Deceive Anyone Regarding Many Complexities

One immediate application of this formula is readily apparent and yet not without theoretical importance. It leads to a recognition of the fact that in some cases the valuation of a good sometimes involves the significance of only one concrete want, in others it involves the significance of many concrete wants which must be considered as an integral sum. In the very nature of things the depth of the layer of dependent wants may vary greatly according to the nature of the thing to be valued. When the latter is a single specimen of a perishable category of goods, such as food, the marginal utility will ordinarily embrace only a single concrete want, or even only a partial want. If on the other hand we are valuing a durable good capable of rendering repeated useful services, or a rather large quantity of goods considered as an integral whole, then the dependent layer of wants will naturally be so deep as to embrace a large number of wants. Under some conditions that number may be very, very large indeed. Hundreds of wants will, for instance, be dependent on the possession or nonpossession of a piano or of a ten-cask hoard of wine. In the first instance they will be musical enjoyments, in the second gustatory delights, but in both cases their significance must be summed up integrally to permit a valuation of the respective goods.

21. A Big Complication Which Is Not Finally Real

In cases of that kind it is possible under certain circumstances for a further phenomenon to be present which may at first blush appear incongruous, but which upon closer examination is susceptible of a per-

22. There are two principal types of occasion which cause a person to make a valuation. On occasions of the one type he is parting with a good, that is to say, he is giving it away, exchanging it, or using it up. On occasions of the other type he is acquiring a good. The line of thought which he follows in one case is, on the surface, different from the one he follows in the other case. A good which he already has, is valued according to the *deprivation* he suffers; that means it is determined by the last or lowest on the scale of his otherwise guaranteed satisfactions. Conversely, a good that he does not yet possess is valued according to the *addition* in the way of utility which its acquisition entails; that means it is determined by the most important of the satisfactions which the person in his previous situation, when not in possession of the good, would have been unable to procure. Of course, both methods of valuation lead to the same result, for the last or least of the satisfactions that is assured *with* the good is always identical with the first which is no longer covered when one is *without* the good. In the text above I have chosen a wording which is sufficiently general to embrace both methods.—Stolzmann condemned as unjustified the "master-key" which I recommended. The polemic which he launched, as verbose as it was mistaken, harks back in part to certain objections previously made by Wieser. I shall defer discussion of it until an opportunity arises to utilize that discussion for the simultaneous solution of another difficult problem. The reader will find it in my *Further Essays on Capital and Interest*, Essay No. VII.

fectly natural explanation. For it may be that the valuation of a rather large quantity will differ widely from that of a single unit of the same good, the large quantity being estimated at a far higher valuation.[23] "Five sacks of grain," for instance, will be rated as worth, not five times as much as *one* sack, but 10 times or 100 times as much. As a matter of fact this is regularly the case when the large quantity which is being valued as an integral sum constitutes such a considerable fraction of the total available quantity of the good in question that its removal will make deep inroads on the satisfaction of the wants of the individual making the value judgment, and leave some concrete wants still unsatisfied which are of a grade of importance materially higher than that of the final or marginal want. In that event, of course, the "lowest layer" which is dependent on the integrally valued quantity of goods embraces concrete wants that occupy several different steps on the graduated scale —that is to say, are of differing degrees of importance. It then becomes a matter of simple arithmetical calculation that the sum of a number of unequal factors is greater than the product derived by multiplying the final, the smallest factor (which is the one that determines the value of the single unit of the good) by the number of factors. It is inevitable that the sum of $5 + 4 + 3 + 2 + 1$ will be greater than the product 5×1.

22. Serious Problems Arising From Accidental Cases of Total Utility, But Especially From Purposeful Cases

The previous illustration of our pioneer permits us to envision the phenomenon quite clearly. As long as he had five sacks of grain, one of them had a value equivalent to the pleasure of keeping parrots as pets. But when it comes to a matter of three sacks, we find an aggregate of satisfactions dependent on them which is by no means merely the equivalent of three times as much pleasure as keeping parrots. What depends on the three sacks is the pleasure of keeping parrots plus the imbibing of brandy plus the eating of meat. And when all five sacks are considered as an integral unit, not only the last mentioned three wants of ascending importance are dependent on them but in addition the maintenance of health and the preservation of life itself. Surely that is a sum which is not merely five times, but infinitely greater than the pleasure of breeding parrots. Let us imagine that our pioneer is required to place a value on "three sacks" or on all "five sacks" as an integral quantity. Such a situation might arise if a second pioneer should wish to settle in the vicinity and offer to purchase one or the other quantity. It would occasion no surprise if our pioneer were quite ready to sell *one* of his five sacks at a moderate price, say $25. But we should not expect him to consider selling the larger quantity of "three sacks" unless he received far more than three times the price of one sack. And finally, he would assuredly not be willing to sell all five sacks together at any price, be it ever so high.[24]

23. Or also lower. See note 24 following.

24. The exact counterpart, that is to say, a disproportionately *lower* valuation of a larger aggregate, can be observed when, instead of being a case of disposing of a quantity of goods, it becomes one of an acquisition of them. If, for example, our pioneer had no grain at all, the purchase of a first and only sack would mean the preservation of life, the purchase of each

The subjective value of a rather large supply of goods is therefore not the equivalent of the marginal utility of a single unit of the good multiplied by the number of units comprising the supply. It is determined by the total value derived by adding together the marginal utilities of those units. And indeed, so long as the quantity to be valued does not completely exhaust the total available or existing supply, such value is determined in accordance with the principle of marginal utility by the smallest combined utility that is still economically feasible or admissible. The value of "three sacks of grain" in our illustration is not three times the marginal utility of one sack; nor on the other hand is it equivalent to the total utility which any "three sacks" would afford, and which could therefore be that derived from the three most important groups of needs, namely, preservation of life, maintenance of health, and ingestion of meat. Instead, it is determined by the marginal utility that can be derived from the "last three sacks," when expended for the last three purposes that are still economically justifiable. In our example this means the aggregate derived by totaling the keeping of parrots, the enjoyment of brandy and the eating of meat. Only when the supply to be integrally valued coincides with the total existing or available supply does the total utility of the supply coincide with its marginal utility. This is comparable to the valuation of goods which are available only in the amount of one single specimen of that kind of good. But this is of course no exception to the law of marginal utility. It simply means that because of the maximal limitation of numbers, there is no latitude for the characteristic development of the law to manifest itself. We can say with equal justice that it does not constitute a violation of the law of primogeniture when in any given instance an *only* son inherits the entire estate of his father.[25]

succeeding sack would mean correspondingly less, and consequently the purchase of five sacks would mean considerably less than five times the value of the first one. It is simply a matter of $5 + 4 + 3 + 2 + 1$ being less than 5×5. The attentive observer will be able to perceive numerous cases of this sort in practical life and will find that our theory furnishes a key to the ready solution of them.

25. It should occasion no astonishment to learn that writers who were strangers to the theory of marginal utility or even hostile to it should be bewildered by these complications, and derive from them material for objections arising out of misunderstanding. I refer the reader to p. 36 ff. of my "Grundzüge" and to my essay "Wert, Kosten und Grenznutzen" in Conrad's *Jahrbücher*, 3rd series, Vol. III, p. 347, note 1. In those two publications I discussed certain untenable objections made by Schäffle and Dietzel. Then there is Scharling's pedantic dissentient argument that the marginal utility theory always presupposes a *multiplicity* of available goods and is therefore not applicable to "single" goods, and for that reason cannot be a *generally* valid theory of value ("Grenznutzentheorie und Grenzwertlehre" in Conrad's *Jahrbücher*, 3rd Series, Vol. XXVII, p. 23 ff.). In view of

what I have said in the text above and also on an earlier occasion in reply to Dietzel, I think it is clear he is merely engaging in a mistaken quarrel about words. It is much more astonishing to find Wieser a prey to uncertainty at this juncture and guilty of being misleading, at least in his choice of expression. I call it astonishing in the case of Wieser because he is a research scholar who is exceedingly well versed in the theory of marginal utility and has to his credit such outstanding service in the development of that very theory. In his *Natürlicher Wert* (pp. 21-23) he points out quite correctly the difference between valuation of quantities of goods as integral aggregates and as individual specimens out of a quantity; and he correctly values a supply of goods taken "as an indivisible whole" on the basis of its "total utility." In all this he is substantially correct, but on p. 24 we find this misleading sentence: "A quantity of goods has in general a value equal to the product obtained by multiplying the pertinent marginal utility by the number of specimens involved." This sentence would certainly be an incorrect rule if interpreted in the usual sense of its words and applied to the *subjective* value of quantities of goods. The situation may be quite different with respect to the aggregate ob-

In practical everyday economic life there are innumerable estimations of subjective value. Probably the overwhelmingly greater portion of them will be concerned with single units of a good or a small, even a minute partial quantity thereof. For that reason valuation in accordance with the principle of the marginal utility of the single unit is by far the commonest. And yet there are cases—they constitute a small minority—in which we are impelled or even required to exercise our economic deliberation in connection with very large quantities of goods or even with the total supply of goods of a given kind. This minority of cases includes some that are particularly important and especially interesting. The duty therefore devolves upon me to develop the selective reasoning that deals with the subject of marginal utility to such a point as to offer a key to the understanding of these cases, too.[26]

I feel it is legitimate to ignore once and for all several other complications of selective rationalization, because they have no bearing on the specific purpose of this book.[27] Others I am ignoring for the time being because they have all too much bearing on our purposes and therefore require such detailed treatment that separate chapters must be devoted to them. At this point I am returning to the simple fundamental law of the value of goods because it needs a little amplification in a certain direction.

jective exchange value the goods represent. Now there is reason to believe that Wieser wanted to suggest a different meaning and one quite foreign to my reading. For he had previously (p. 23) drawn a subtle distinction between the value "of the sum of all the parts" and that "of the combined whole." Perhaps the sentence on p. 24 is intended to apply to the former rather than the latter. But the distinction itself is hardly clear enough nor sufficiently free of deceptive elements to prevent confusion and error. And indeed an ample sufficiency of the latter has been prevalent among the opponents of the theory of marginal utility who have evinced a special predilection for basing their attacks, significantly enough, on that very statement of Wieser's. And I have, moreover, some reason to believe that Wieser himself was confused by the dialecticism and equivocation that seems to have crept in at this point, and that he really allowed himself to become entangled in the meshes of a genuine factual error. We shall on a later occasion see that this same error played a part in his theory of complementary goods.—An entirely analogous point must be urged against the proposition which Wieser developed on p. 27 ff. It is to the effect that the value of a quantity of goods which is successively increased, must from a certain point onward become more decline. As a matter of fact, the subjective value of an increasing quantity of goods will be continuously augmented, so long as the marginal utility of the single unit does not sink to zero. And even then it merely ceases to increase, but does not diminish.—The English writers on economics developed completely accurate expositions of this relationship, employing the terms "total utility" and "final utility."

26. It may be of some interest to have it pointed out that the familiar power of strikes to exert pressure is founded in large part on the progressive increase of "total utility" in contrast to the "final utility" of the individual worker. The understanding of the theoretical aspect of such cases, and the correct incorporation of them into the general laws governing value becomes more important, the more strongly the tendency becomes manifest in modern economic life to unite persons and goods more and more into consolidated massive bodies by means of organized associations and unions of one kind or another.

27. For instance Menger, *Grundsätze*, p. 114 ff. He discusses in detail the selective reasoning concerning differences in the quality of goods. This may be compared with Clark's treatment of the topic in his *Distribution of Wealth*, p. 231 ff., and especially p. 238 ff. Clark is keen witted, but overly subtle and fond of expressing himself in bizarre turns of phrase. I have been unable to convince myself of two points. The first is that this bizarre imagery is indispensable for arriving at a correct theory of price. The other is Clark's contention (*op. cit.*, p. 213, p. 219) that if the theory of value and price as ordinarily and habitually formulated by the "Austrian economists" were valid, the prices for articles of high quality would necessarily attain heights from three to ten times as great as is actually the case in real life. It is probable that misunderstandings on Clark's part are at work here.

23. On What the Magnitude of Marginal Utility Depends

For we have been so far citing the magnitude of the marginal utility as the explanation of the magnitude of the value of a good. But we can go a step further in our research into the causes of the value of goods by asking this question: "On what, in turn, does the magnitude of the marginal utility itself depend?" The answer there is the *relation between wants and the wherewithal to satisfy them.* The manner in which these two factors influence the marginal utility has been so frequently and so thoroughly commented on in the foregoing explanations that I can dispense with any further elucidation and content myself with a brief formulation of the pertinent rule. It reads as follows. The more extensive and the more intensive the want is—in other words, the more wants there are, and the more urgently they demand satisfaction—and, *per contra,* the smaller the quantity of good that is available for that purpose, the higher will be the point in the graduated scale of wants where satisfaction will end, or in other words the greater will be the marginal utility. Conversely, the fewer wants there are to be satisfied, and the less urgently their satisfaction is demanded, the lower on that scale will be the point down to which wants are satisfied, and hence the smaller is the marginal utility and the value which must result. Approximately the same thing may be said, though somewhat less accurately, in a different form. One may say that *usefulness and scarcity* are the ultimate determinants of value. For insofar as the degree of usefulness of a good will indicate whether that good is by nature capable of contributions to well-being which are of major importance or only of minor significance, it simultaneously furnishes a basis for judging the maximum rank which the marginal utility can attain under the most favorable conditions. But scarcity determines the highest point which marginal utility can really attain in a particular concrete case.[28]

24. Difference in Marginal Utility For the Poor and the Rich

The proposition that the rank of the marginal utility is determined by the relation between want and coverage furnishes material for numerous applications. I shall rest satisfied with selecting two which we shall have occasion to make use of later on when we come to the theory of objective exchange value. The first is, that the relations of want and coverage vary so in individual cases that the same good may have quite a different subjective value for different persons. Indeed, if that were not so, the effecting of exchanges would not be conceivable at all. The second

---

28. I do not believe it is necessary to repeat the polemical remarks which I inserted at this point in earlier editions, directed against Scharling (*Werttheorie und Wertgesetze* appearing in Conrad's *Jahrbücher,* new series, Vol. XVI). My reason is that this excellent scholar very materially modified his views on this subject (*Grenznutzentheorie und Grenzwertlehre, ibid.,* 3rd series, Vol. XXVII). His opinions had seemed to be sharply opposed to my own, but his more recent exposition and formulation so closely approach my own point of view that there hardly seem to be any basic objective differences between us any more. At least Scharling regards the remaining points "in which we fail to agree, as being a matter of form rather than fact." He goes on to say that it is only a question of the selection of the best "expression" to describe a matter which is "in reality" correctly and clearly recognized, and that hence "the only thing that remains is a shade of difference in our common statement of the theory of subjective value." (*Op. cit.,* pp. 160, 163, 167 ff.)

150   is that under conditions that are otherwise identical, equal quantities of goods have quite unequal value for the rich and for the poor, that value being greater for the poor and smaller for the rich. For since the rich are more abundantly endowed with goods of all categories, their satisfactions in general extend downward to include even the more insignificant needs, and the addition or the loss of satisfaction which attaches to a single specimen of a good is therefore relatively unimportant. The poor, however, are able to cover only their most urgent wants anyway, and for them therefore there is an important use depending on *every* specimen of a good. And experience does in actual fact show that the poor man hails the gaining and bewails the losing of a sum of goods which the rich can gain or lose with complete indifference. Compare the emotional state of a poor clerk who on the first day of the month loses his whole monthly salary of $250 with that of a millionaire who drops the same amount at poker! For the former the loss means painful deprivation throughout an entire month, for the latter it can mean nothing more than the renunciation of some idle little luxury.

Part A—VALUE

The Magnitude of the Value Possessed by Goods Purchasable In Any Desired Quantity

1. First Reference to Final Utility (of All Goods) as Distinguished From Marginal Utility (Within Same Category of Goods)

THIS brings us to a complication that is of extremely great interest and has very far-reaching effects. As we know from our previous analysis, the marginal utility which determines the value of a good is not—barring accident—identical with the utility that is actually derived from the good itself.[29] It is as a rule a disparate utility, the utility of the last specimen of the good, or of the least partial quantity of uniform magnitude, which is available as an example of that good. In simple relationships this utility, though that of another good, is at least that of a good of the same category. In the illustration previously used, the value of each single sack of grain—let us say the first—was determined by that of another, namely, the last sack. But still it was at least a sack of grain. But the existence of a well-developed system of exchange can cause considerable complication in this respect. Since it makes it possible at any moment to exchange goods of one category for goods of another kind, it also makes it possible to transfer a loss from the category in which it occurs to a different category. Instead of making good the loss of a specimen by withdrawing one unit of the same category from a less important use and leaving the latter uncovered, it is possible to divert goods of utterly different categories from the purpose previously intended, and exchange them for the required substitute unit. What the loss of a good of one kind really causes us to be deprived of is the use which the substitute goods of a different kind would otherwise have rendered. However the latter, too, would be drawn not from the more important, but rather from the least significant uses in their own sphere of utility. Therefore what is lost is the marginal utility of the substitute disparate goods. Therefore the measure of the marginal utility and hence of the value of a good of one kind is the marginal utility of that quantity of goods of an unrelated kind which is required as a substitute.

---

29. Such equality or identity is present only in the case of specimens that are the only ones of their kind, or that just happen to be the ones selected for the least important service.

2. Illustration of Final Utility

Let us illustrate. My only winter overcoat is stolen. There can be no question of direct substitution of another specimen of the same category, because it was, as I said, my only one. Nor do I desire to endure the loss caused by the theft of the coat in the quarter where it was inflicted on me. For the need for warm winter clothing which is being deprived of satisfaction is a highly important want, and failure to provide for it may entail extremely deleterious consequences to my health or may even cost me my life. I shall therefore attempt to transfer the deprivation to other categories of goods. Translated into concrete acts, that means that I purchase a new winter overcoat with goods which would otherwise have been devoted to other uses. Naturally I draw the substitute goods from the uses which mean least to me, in other words, from their "marginal utility." If I am well-to-do, I shall probably simply draw a check for the $150 the new winter coat may cost me, and be able to draw on my reduced bank account for one or two luxury items fewer. If I am not well-to-do but not indigent either, the blow to my pocketbook will have to be made good through all sorts of economies that may affect my housekeeping budget for the next few months. If my means are so limited that I neither have the purchase price in cash nor can raise it in instalments out of my monthly income, I shall have to pawn or sell some furniture or other object that I can more easily get along without. And if, finally, I am so poor that I can meet only the supremely important concrete wants in all categories—well then I just cannot transfer the loss to any other category of wants, and I shall willy nilly have to "grin and bear it."

If we can succeed in vividly imagining ourselves in the very position of the owner of the winter coat, and then ask ourselves what contribution to well-being depends on the theft of the coat, we will find the following answers. In the first case it is an expenditure for a luxury or two; in the second place it is the practice of a few economies in housekeeping; in the third case it means the use of the articles that have to be pawned or sold; in the fourth case it is the effective safeguard of health. Only in the last case is the value of the winter overcoat determined by the direct marginal utility of its own category. That applies because here, where the category is represented by only one specimen, the marginal utility of the category coincides with that of the specimen itself. In all the other three cases the value of the coat is determined by the marginal utility of unrelated categories of goods and of wants.

3. Most Marginal Utility Considerations
Tend to Move Toward Final Utility Decisions

The modification in selective reasoning which I have described finds extraordinarily wide application in our economy, characterized as it is by a highly developed system of exchange. I should say that the majority of subjective estimations of value that are made at all, are of this kind.[30]

30. This sentence appeared word for word in my first edition and even before that in 1886 in my "Grundzüge." Nevertheless, it did not prevent Stolzmann from making the assertion (*Zweck in der Volkswirtschaft*, p. 722 ff.) that I "brand as exceptional the case which exemplifies the rule," namely, "the equal value of dissimilar

For reasons easily to be inferred from what has just been said, we almost never estimate the value of goods which are indispensable to us according to their direct utility, but in nearly all cases according to the "substitution utility" of unrelated categories of goods. Nevertheless I should like to point out explicitly and emphatically that even though we apply the latter method of estimation very frequently, we do so only under certain conditions. Those conditions do not by any means invariably prevail even amidst extremely highly organized conditions of exchange. We follow the method only when the marginal utility of the substituted unrelated goods is inferior to the direct marginal utility which obtains in the same category. It might be more accurate to say that the substitution method is employed when the prices of goods and at the same time the conditions under which needs are supplied are such that making good a loss occurring in any category by replacement from within that same category results in failure to satisfy wants that are relatively more important than those which must remain unsatisfied when a different category is drawn upon for the price of the substituted unit. No matter how involved the complications, it is always the *smallest* degree of utility directly or indirectly attaching to a good which indicates its genuine marginal utility and its value.

153

4. Important Case When Quick Replacement of Supplies Is Possible

Complications in the selective process similar to those attributable to facilities for exchange may also arise because of the possibility of quick replacement of requisite substitute units by means of production. Complications of this kind also possess very great significance for the theory of value, since they offer a key to the explanation of the influence of production costs on value. For that reason they demand particularly careful attention. I shall do more wisely to devote such attention to them and to other selective complications in a section of their own. First I should like to tarry briefly with the present topic on which I have a few supplementary remarks to make.

I am quite well aware that what has so far been said constitutes no completely conclusive explanation of the process of valuation in the case of goods purchasable in any desired quantity. For there is the matter of

goods." By this Stolzmann means valuation on the basis of the utility of the substituted good. From his whole context it becomes apparent that he has thoroughly misunderstood my contrast between the "simplest case" or the "elementary manifestation" on the one hand and the "more involved" developments or the "complications" of the situation on the other hand. He has interpreted my statement to mean that the first expression is tantamount to "the rule" and the second to "the exception" which is neither what I intended nor what I said. I regret to say that I do not feel able to suppress the remark that Stolzmann's polemics contain further and frequent instances of this tendency to make errors that result from the astonishing liberties he takes in interpreting what he attacks. It is the more extraordinary because Stolz-mann is indubitably inspired with the most ardent desire to be painfully correct in his polemics. Indeed, he tries to do justice to that desire by quoting at length—often for pages—from the authors he attacks, and certainly does too much rather than too little of that sort of thing. But he is also very fond of following up these long literal quotations with an interpretative summary, which is strongly colored by his subjective views. And then instead of attacking the author's original statement he attacks his own résumé. I think this and similar instances justify my formulating a general request, not directed against anyone in particular, and certainly not against Stolzmann alone, that any kind reader who professes to judge the merits of a polemical discussion, should not neglect to consult the original text.

the price at which substitute units can be acquired and which therefore constitutes a basis for subjective valuation, as for example the price of $150 for the winter overcoat. So far the price has been treated as if it were a fixed and determined magnitude. That was a legitimate thing to do for the time being, in order to avoid anticipating developments, but it would not be legitimate to continue to do so to the end. Quite on the contrary, the explanation of the price itself will be one of the most important tasks of a subsequent chapter. Now that explanation—if I may anticipate to this extent—will reveal the existence of causal influences of price upon subjective estimates of value as well as relations which exert their influence in the opposite direction. Since that is the case, it will devolve upon me as a special task, to expose the whole network of causal relations which exert their influence to and fro and to supply an exhaustive and satisfying solution.[31]

5. While the Concept of Marginal Utility Is Basically Simple, Its Universal Application To All Goods Necessarily Becomes Complex

Furthermore, I have pointed out that the characteristic and individual feature of this complication lies in the circumstance that the determinative marginal utility is transferred from goods of the same kind to goods of another kind. I should like to remark parenthetically that this was one of the reasons why I added to my description of "marginal utility" a further comment that the "longwinded" definition, to be entirely correct ought to be even more longwinded.[32] For the concluding words in italics "goods of the same kind" should be amplified to goods of another kind that are readily convertible into "goods of the same kind." Similarly the last words of the next sentence, "or its equivalent" should be expanded to read "all substitutes capable of prompt rendition of the same useful services." But there is still something more to be considered in that connection.

When we considered the elementary example we regarded the supply of goods which provides, as it were, "coverage" for the need of goods of a certain kind, as a given, definitely determined magnitude. The conditions of our illustrative hypothetical cases posited fixed and unalterable quantities. This was true of the loaves of bread in the first example and of the sacks of grain in the second. That presupposition must now be abandoned. We are now going to treat the supplies of a certain kind as what in practical economic life they are for the most part. There they are a magnitude which is, to a certain extent, elastic, a magnitude that within certain limits can be extended, supplemented or pieced out. We therefore now pose the problem of marginal utility with an inescapable added difficulty. That difficulty is the fact that with the magnitude of the variable supply its terminal point also becomes variable; that also shifts the situs of the "last unit" which concludes the supply of goods; and finally that makes a variable of the marginal utility which determines

154

---

31. I have been the subject of frequent strictures to the effect that my whole presentation argues in a circle in that I explain subjective value on the basis of price and then price on the basis of subjective value. I trust that the present occasion will furnish a thoroughgoing elucidation and refutation at the same time.

32. See foregoing, p. 142 f.

value. The thing which was a veritable Archimedean fulcrum when our supply of goods was fixed, now itself becomes an elusive x that has to be determined. But it is an x that is susceptible of determination. The elements required for its reliable determination are always inherent in the total situation. Even the "augmentable supply" is limited by conditions. It encounters its limitations as the result of a sort of "turn and turn about" which it enters into with the other classes or branches of wants and goods. It is capable of piecing out, but only at the expense of other categories of wants and of goods. From their "coverage" some additions can be pieced on, but only to the point where the substituting, the "turn and turn about" leads to an equalization, to a balance in the relationship of need and coverage among the different classes of need and of good, to a harmonizing of the marginal utility of the quantities of fungible goods in the various categories of goods. The situation may be compared to that which prevails when we consider the level of water in a number of vessels of varying size which stand beside one another and which are connected in such a way that valves, which can be opened at will or which open automatically permit free intercommunication between vessels. The water level in any *one* of these vessels is then not determined exclusively by the magnitude of the mass of water that happens to be in that one vessel at a given moment, nor by what happens in that one vessel. The drawing off of water to the extent of one-third of that vessel's capacity would not result in the dropping of the water level in that vessel by one-third. Instead, the opening of connecting valves to better filled communicating vessels would result in an influx of water until finally a uniform water level could be observed throughout the whole set of vessels. This water level would certainly not be anything arbitrary or fortuitous, but something which the conditions pertaining to the influx and efflux of water throughout the whole set of communicating vessels would determine and would render precisely de-   155
terminable.

6. Insufficiency of Goods to Supply Needs Are Universal, and Economic Problems Are Inescapable

In the same manner exchange opens up valves to partial supplies of goods in other categories. The same thing is also effected by production, as we shall later have occasion to convince ourselves, for production permits renewal or increase of whatever supply of goods is at the moment on hand in every category. In both cases we have an addition to the number of the facts and the data which exert a determining influence on the magnitude of the marginal utility, but there is no change in their nature. "Need and coverage" are no longer the isolated need of goods of an absolutely definite kind, nor the correspondingly isolated supply of those goods; the terms now apply to the data for needs and coverage throughout all communicating branches. But even in this extended field it is still true that a given magnitude of combined needs is faced by a similarly limited and fixed total magnitude of a combined supply. And the relation of the two magnitudes again supplies the basis for following our familiar rule and determining for each concrete partial quantity of goods the marginal utility applicable to the total supply of that good. But no matter how great the "augmentability" of supply may be, it is clear that we can never remove ourselves entirely from the influence of the element of limited supply—supply that is scarce in relation to wants. Nor can that be cause for astonishment to anyone who keeps in mind that the inadequacy of the means of satisfaction for coverage of the wants that demand satisfaction constitutes the basic relationship which stimulates and forces us into economic behavior at all. It must be remembered that the destruction of that relationship of insufficiency would mean the abolition of all our economic activity.[33]

33. The argument has occasionally been urged against the theory of marginal utility in general and my presentation of it in particular, that it deals too exclusively, or at least too long, with supplies of finished goods which are on hand "without production." I think I am entitled to deny this charge. My complete presentation is sufficiently extensive in scope to include all pertinent factors, one after the other. The fact that it begins with discussions of the simpler and more readily penetrable situations is a concession to didactic and methodological considerations. The "later" of my presentation certainly cannot be said to be "too late" for the content of the theory, since that is submitted as an integrated whole.

PUBLISHER'S NOTE: In this chapter, ideas under sideheadings 3, 4 and 5 must be mastered, remembered, and made usable for further reasoning, or else the reader will have difficulty in later chapters, as Chapter VII. Böhm-Bawerk himself warns the reader of this on page 153. If not thoroughly understood in its "complexity," readers can nevertheless proceed comfortably on "faith"; but they will not be able to follow either the challenging arguments of some professional economists or the rejoinders of Böhm-Bawerk in his several essays in Volume III, *Further Essays on Capital and Interest.*

Part A—VALUE

Chapter V

Specific Considerations Affecting Value Where Alternative Uses Are Possible—Use Value And Subjective Exchange Value

1. In Complex Situations, What Is The True Economic Marginal Utility?

FREQUENTLY a good permits of two completely different methods of utilization. Wood, for instance, can be used as fuel or as building material, grain can be used as a foodstuff, as seed, or for distilling whiskey, salt may be used to season foods or as an auxiliary in the manufacture of chemicals. In such case the good serves different needs in the various fields in which it is utilized and those needs are naturally unequal in importance; furthermore, the relation of need to coverage varies frequently from one field of wants to another; finally the good, though it may possess multiple capacity for utilization, does not possess that capacity to an equal degree in every field. For these three reasons, as may be readily perceived, the increment in utility which the good could yield by virtue of its utilization in various fields, and the marginal utility which it can afford in those fields, may vary greatly. It may, for instance, be quite possible that a pile of boards, used as building material, will afford its owner a marginal utility which could be designated by the figure 8, while the same boards used as fuel would afford a marginal utility of only 4. The question now arises, what is the true economic marginal utility that determines the value of the good?

2. Of Several Marginal Utilities The Highest Is the True One

The answer is easy. In such case the *highest* marginal utility is always the criterion. We worked out in detail in a previous chapter[34] that all true marginal utility of a good is identical with the smallest utility for the attainment of which it can, *from the economic point of view, be legitimately utilized*. Now if there is competition among several mutually exclusive uses for the services of an available good, it is obvious that under wise economic management the most important of them will gain the preference. It is the only one that is economically justifiable, all less important uses are ruled out and can therefore have no influence on the

34. See page 141 ff.

valuation of the good, since it cannot in any event serve them. To return to our woodpile! Suppose a farmer has met all his more important requirements in the way of building material and fuel and still has two desirable uses for wood, one of them with a utility value of 8, and the other with one of 4. But he has only *one* pile of boards left. It is clear that he will devote that pile to the more important use and leave the less important one unprovided for. As long as he can build with a utility of 8, he will not burn with a utility of 4. Hence for him the thing that depends on the possession or nonpossession of that pile of boards is the attainment or nonattainment of the greater utility of 8.

Let us put the rule in general terms. *Where goods permit of alternative methods of utilization and are capable of affording greater or lesser marginal utility in them, the use which has the highest marginal utility provides the measure of its economic value.* The rule can easily be corroborated by everyday experience. Nobody will value rosewood furniture on the basis of its "British Thermal Units," a fine saddle horse as so many pounds of horsemeat, nor a fine oil painting as antique canvas!

The wording used in the rule given above can readily lead to erroneous inferences which I should like to forestall before proceeding any further. For the impression might easily be gained that it contradicts what I said before. I am at this point stating that of several alternative dispositions of a given marginal utility the *most favorable* is the criterion. But previously[35] I developed the point that if the direct marginal utility of a good (or the utility of the last good in its own category) is greater than its indirect marginal utility (or that of goods of another category drawn on by way of substitution) then the *smaller* marginal utility serves as a criterion. That the contradiction is only apparent and not real becomes readily apparent from the fact that in the earlier statement we were dealing with a decision among several uses *still* covered by the available supply of goods, while in the latest statement we have to do with a decision concerning uses *otherwise unprovided for*. For it will be recalled that on a previous occasion[36] I pointed out that the least important of the uses that are *still covered by a good* always coincides exactly with the most important of the uses which *in the absence of the good are no longer covered*.

If, then, the formula I set down above speaks of *several* alternative uses affording a marginal utility, I was employing a phrase which, taken literally, cannot possibly be accurate. For of course only *one* of those competing uses can be the last economically permissible use and hence the use which affords a genuine marginal utility. All others must belong to the number of the economically excluded uses. Nevertheless they do engage our attention to a considerable degree because they are the leading and most prominent representatives of a whole class of uses. As soon as we consider the class at all, these occupy the forefront of our attention, and we make a sort of preliminary choice between whole classes of uses—"building and burning" in the case of the wood, between "riding and slaughtering" in that of the horse, and so on. That is the actual psychological process we go through, and that is what I felt the formula

158

35. See page 151 ff.   36. See Note 22 of this Part.

given above most aptly and most succinctly conveyed.

And yet it must be pointed out with some emphasis that such spurious marginal uses merely have a formally preferential position in the course of our deliberation, but do not receive the benefit of any materially favorable economic decision. *In any case the circumstance that the uses of a good can be classified in separate categories actually does not exert the slightest influence on the outcome of our valuations.* For just as we do not value goods according to categories of wants,[37] so also do we avoid classifying them in hard and fast branches of employment. Instead, each concrete use *as such* is taken into account in accordance with the rank it achieves by virtue of importance in competition with uses in all branches. And so we observe the principle of genuinely economic behavior and consistently follow a uniform procedure. We allocate the supply of goods on hand to concrete uses in the order of their importance, and the last one determines the marginal utility and the value of the good.

3. Exclusion of Spurious Marginal Utilities

Sometimes it happens that only uses of a single branch come up for consideration. That will quite regularly be the case of course, where only a single specimen of a good is at our disposal. But it can also occur when a whole series of concrete uses of one branch surpasses in importance those of another branch and when at the same time that series is long enough or the available supply of goods is so small that coverage is no longer afforded to uses of lesser importance. If, for instance, there are in one branch of uses 100 opportunities for employment with an importance rating of 8, while in another branch the only opportunities for use are limited to an importance rating of 6, and if, furthermore, the supply of goods totals only 50 specimens, then of course all 50 will be allocated exclusively to the first branch of uses. And then their value will be determined in accordance with the higher use rated at 8. But it also often happens that wants of various branches are met simultaneously. Then the numerical relation that happens to exist between goods and opportunities decides which branch of wants is drawn on for the "last" use, i.e., for the use which determines valuation. Let us suppose that in one branch there are four opportunities for use with importance ratings of 10, 8, 6 and 4, and that in a second branch there are also four opportunities with importance ratings of 9, 7, 5 and 3. If under these circumstances there are altogether five specimens of the good available, they will undoubtedly be assigned to the opportunities with ratings of 10, 9, 8, 7 and 6. The last of these happens to belong to the *first* branch of uses, and being a genuine marginal utility, it determines the value of the good. The next use in line, a member of the second branch, has a rating of 5 and thus is excluded, in accordance with our formula, as a "spurious marginal utility."

4. Significant Valuation of a Good
Based on Subjective Exchange Value

In connection with what has been said we must consider a concrete application that has as its basis an extremely widespread phenomenon.

37. See page 137 ff.

159   So far we have ascribed the capacity of a good for uses of many kinds to a technical versatility peculiar to that good. However, quite apart from such special assumed characteristics, practically every good has a second kind of usefulness, if it functions in the presence of a well-developed system of exchange. That second use lies in its exchangeability for other goods. It has become customary to pair off this kind of usefulness of each good against all its other kinds combined; and to correspond to these two uses which might be termed "individual use" and "exchange use," there has been set up a pair of values so that each good has both a "use value" and an "exchange value."

In a certain sense—and in this connection I should like to adhere to that sense—each of these values, even the exchange value, is a kind of subjective value. Use value is the importance that a good has for the well-being of a person, assuming that the person will make direct use of it to answer his own purposes. Similarly, exchange value is the importance that a good achieves for the well-being of a person by virtue of its capacity to procure other goods for the person by means of an exchange. According to rules we are already familiar with, use value is determined by the marginal utility which the good that is to be valued affords the person by way of utilization. The magnitude of the (subjective) exchange value, on the other hand, obviously coincides with the magnitude of the use value of those goods which are received in exchange. If I utilize a good for exchange purposes, I gain thereby, to further my well-being, just exactly the usefulness that is possessed by the goods I accept in exchange. The exchange value of a good is therefore to be measured *by the marginal utility of the goods for which it is exchanged*.

Now nothing is more common than that the use value and the exchange value which a good has for its owner are of unequal magnitude. The use value of a scholar's books, for instance, is usually far greater than their exchange value, while for the bookseller the opposite is ordinarily true. Now the question arises again, which of the two values in such cases is the true one.[38]

In dealing with this question we are dealing with a special case belonging to a group for which we have already devised a general rule. Employment in individual use and employment in exchange use are two different ways of using the same good. If the good has a different marginal utility in the two uses, then the higher marginal utility furnishes the determinant of its economic value. If then the use value and the exchange value of a good are unequal, then the *higher* of these two "values" is the true value. And that principal really does govern our behavior in practical life. We always devote our goods to that use which corresponds to the higher, the true value. The scholar keeps his books, the bookseller

---

38. It is readily seen that we may speak of two "values" only with the same inexactness we permitted ourselves in the foregoing, when we spoke of several "alternative dispositions of marginal utility." For a good can obviously always have only one value for any one person. Value is, by definition, the significance that a good has for the well-being of a human being, and that value cannot be at one and the same time large and small, cannot be both higher and lower. But that way of thinking and speaking of it, though not quite correct, is nevertheless the way we actually do think and speak in real life, and for that reason I have adapted my formula to it, both in preceding passages and at this point.

sells his. Or the scholar may sell them, if he feels the pinch of poverty; for in that case, although there has been no change in use value nor any change in objective exchange value of the books, their subjective exchange value has risen. Since there are wants in other categories of still higher importance which await satisfaction in vain, the possibility of satisfying 160 them by the sale of the books achieves an importance which easily surpasses that of the use value of the books.

5. Difference Between Subjective Exchange Value and Objective Exchange Value (see Chapter I, Sideheadings 3-8)

There is then such a thing as subjective exchange value, and it is something completely different from what economists prefer to call objective exchange value. The recognition of that fact is something of fundamental importance for our orientation in the matter of phenomena of value. For that reason I wish to devote a few words to the topic. The example of the scholar and his books is enough to show us that the subjective significance of a good based on the possibility of exchange may follow a course that is by no means parallel to that taken by objective power of exchange and price. For without the occurrence of any change in price the subjective exchange value of the books may rise. But it is possible for the two exchange values to move in opposite directions. Let us imagine a poor young chap whose last and only possession is an English banknote for five pounds, with the pound quoted at $2.80 in New York. There can be no doubt these $14.00 will have a high subjective importance for the satisfaction of his wants. Nor can there be any doubt that this importance is an *exchange value,* for a five pound note has no use value at all. Now our poor young chap comes quite unexpectedly into an inheritance of $100,000 and at the same time favorable political advices from London cause a rise in the rate of the pound sterling to $2.90. Now, how about the "exchange value" of his five pound note? The difference between the two concepts now becomes apparent. The *objective* exchange value, the market quotation for his five pounds has gone up from $14.00 to $14.50. But the importance that they possess for the satisfaction of their owner's wants, or in other words their *subjective* exchange value has undeniably dropped sharply because of the change in the ratio of need to coverage. If the young chap had lost his five pound note yesterday, he would have regretted it bitterly as the loss of his last resource, the only buffer to ward off starvation and misery. Today, in spite of its increased value, he might hand it out lightheartedly as a tip for some trifling service.

6. Basic Distinction, Between Objective Value And Subjective Value, With Further Subdivisions Of the Second According To Use and Exchange

This profound and intrinsic difference between the two concepts of exchange value is the principal reason why a differentiation into exchange value and use value can never serve as the supremely important basis for classification of the phenomena of value. The concept of subjective exchange value is much more closely akin to subjective use value than it is to objective power of exchange. Hence any move to make the chief distinction along the line "use value versus exchange value" would be a forcible sundering of related concepts and a commingling of heterogeneous elements for which it would be difficult to devise a common definition. If we are to orient ourselves clearly with respect to the phenomena which bear the label "value," then it will be necessary to do as we have just done and to set objective value all by itself on one side of the dividing line, and then all subjective value on the other side. Only after that has been done may we further subdivide the latter into subjective use value and subjective exchange value.

Part A—VALUE

Chapter VI

The Value of
Complementary Goods

1. Meaning of Term, Complementary Goods

IT OFTEN happens that some economic utility can be derived 161
only through the combining of several goods which cooperate in such
a way that if one of them drops out of the series the utility is not achieved,
or is achieved only imperfectly. The name we use for goods that combine
in this fashion to perform one complete operation is *complementary
goods,* a term originated by Carl Menger. Thus paper, pen and ink are
complementary goods, and so are needle and thread, horses and wagons,
bow and arrow, the two gloves and shoes that make a pair, and so on.
This characteristic of complementarism is a feature of a particularly
large number of production goods, if not, indeed, of almost all of them.

2. Effect Which the Fact That Goods Are
Complementary To Each Other Has on Their Value

It is easy to understand that the intimate reciprocal relationship in
which complementary goods afford their utility is also reflected in the
formation of their value. In respect to that value the interrelation of
complementary goods leads to a number of peculiar results which nevertheless are quite in accord with the general law of marginal utility. In
delineating those peculiarities we shall have to distinguish between the
value which we ascribe to the group as a whole, and that which we ascribe
to each of the members of the group.

*The value of the entire group is as a rule governed by the marginal
utility which it is capable of affording through its united functioning.*
If three goods, A, B and C, constitute a complementary group and if the
smallest economically permissible utility which can be achieved by the
combined utilization of the three goods registers 100, then the three
goods, A, B and C combined will have a value of 100.

The only exception to this rule occurs when, in accordance with the
general principle already familiar to us, the value of a good is not determined by its direct marginal utility within its own category, but by the
marginal utility of unrelated kinds of good which enter by way of substitution.*In our special case that will take place only if each individual

*PUBLISHER'S NOTE: See text under sideheading 2 in Chapter IV, where
an essential distinction is elaborated; see also the explanation under sideheadings
3, 4 and 5 in this chapter.

member of the complementary good is replaceable through purchase or production or through the withdrawal of a substitute specimen from some other isolated use. A further condition is that at the same time the resulting loss of "substitute utility" of all these members added together is less than the marginal utility which they afford when utilized as a combination. If the latter, let us say, can be expressed by the number 100, and if, by contrast, the "substitute utility" of the three members of the group amounts individually to 20, 30 and 40 respectively, a total of only 90, then what is dependent on all three together is not the combined utility of 100 (for that could have been procured in any event by bringing in substitute specimens) but only the achievement of the smaller utility amounting to 90, which is all that would fail of coverage if substitution were resorted to. But since in such cases complementarism exerts no real influence on the judgment of value, and the latter proceeds entirely in accordance with rules already familiar to us, it is therefore quite unnecessary to give any special consideration to it. In the succeeding pages I intend to devote attention only to the regular and principal sort of instance where the marginal utility to be attained by *utilization in common* is at the same time the true marginal utility—the utility which determines value.

3. Marginal Utility When It Is Attained by Utilization in Common

As we said before, marginal utility determines the integral value of the whole group. But the manner of distributing it over the individual members will vary widely from case to case depending on which principle emerges as pertinent in each instance.

4. Case 1, Infrequent

The *first* possibility may be as follows. If no member of the group can be adapted to use other than in combination, and if at the same time no member is replaceable in its collaboration toward the combined utility, then each single unit has the full aggregate value of the group while the other units are entirely worthless. For example, if I own a pair of gloves with an aggregate objective value of three dollars, and if one glove is lost, the entire utility of the good is lost, the entire value of the pair vanishes, and the remaining glove is entirely worthless. Of course either glove is capable of carrying either of the two values just mentioned, and the exigencies of any given situation alone will determine which glove is the one needed to complement the pair and is therefore worth "everything" and which glove is the useless "singleton" and therefore without any value whatsoever. Cases of this kind are relatively rare in actual practice.

5. Case 2, More Frequent

A *second* possibility is of more frequent occurrence and runs as follows. The individual members of the group are capable of affording utility outside of the combined activity, though a utility of lower rank. In such cases the value of the individual unit is no longer a matter of choice between the alternatives "all" and "nothing." That value will fall *within the range marked by the marginal utility it is capable of affording when isolated, as a minimum, and the combined marginal utility minus the isolated marginal utilities of the other members, as a maximum.* If three goods, A, B and C, can in combination afford a marginal utility of 100, and if individually they are capable of marginal utilities of 10, 20 and 30 respectively, then the value of A is established as follows: If it is possessed in isolation, it will make possible a marginal utility of only 10 and it is accordingly worth 10. But if the group is possessed in combination, and it is a question of selling A out of the combination, or **163** giving it away, or otherwise disposing of it, then the reasoning must be like this: With the good A, a combined utility of 100 is possible, without it only the smaller isolated utilities of 20 for the good B and 30 for the good C are attainable, making a total of 50; accordingly a difference in utility in the amount of 50 depends on the possession or nonpossession of the good A. When included as a member of the group it is therefore worth $100 - (20 + 30)$, and as an isolated unit only 10.[39] The distribution here falls between limits less extreme than those applicable in the first case, but still quite considerable.

6. Case 3, Most Frequent

A *third* possibility, which occurs still more frequently than the first or second can be described thus. Individual members of the group are not only adaptable for employment for other purposes but at the same time they are *replaceable* by other specimens of their own kind. If I am building a house, my plot, the bricks, beams and labor are complementary goods. If one or two thousand of brick, intended for construction of the house, should be destroyed or if some of the workmen hired for the job decide to quit, neither will under normal circumstances constitute the least obstacle to the attainment of the common utility, that is, the completion of the house. Instead, the missing workmen or the materials are simply replaced with others. This has bearing on the formation of the value of complementary goods in the following respects.

1] The replaceable members, if they are needed as complements, can never attain anything higher than their "substitution value," namely, the value derived from the loss in utility that arises in those branches of employment from which the replacements are drawn.

2] This considerably contracts the limits which encompass the possibilities for the value of the individual good which must be valued both as a complement and as an isolated unit. And the contraction is the more pronounced, the more the good in question has the character of an ordinary marketable commodity. For the greater the number of specimens on hand, and the more numerous the opportunities for employing them,

39. Naturally the peculiar nature of each case determines here, too, which member of the group is valued as a "last unit" and which ones merely as isolated units. Suppose, for instance, that the owner receives an offer to buy good *A*, then *A* will be his "last unit" and he will place on the goods *B* and *C*, which now remain isolated, the lower valuation appropriate to "isolated units." But if, contrariwise, he gets an offer to buy good *C*, then he will value *C* as a final unit, and estimate it at $100 - (10 + 20)$, in other words at 70. But the now isolated units *A* and *B* he will value only at 10 and 20 respectively.

the smaller will be the difference between maximum value as represented by the importance of that use from which it would be possible to withdraw a needed replacement, and minimum value as represented by the next highest use to which it would be possible to assign a superfluous isolated unit. Let us suppose, for instance, that the category A comprises the complementary good A_1 and two other specimens which we shall call A_2 and A_3. Let us further suppose that, in addition to employment in the complementary group, opportunities for employment exist with importance ratings, in descending order of 50, 20, 10, etc. In that case goods A_2 and A_3 will suffice only to cover the uses which have importance ratings of 50 and 20. If either A_2 or A_3 were withdrawn to form a replacement for A_1, a utility of 20 could not be covered and would be lost. Suppose on the other hand that the complementary group were broken up and the good A_1 itself has to seek isolated employment, its only opening would be the opportunity with an importance rating of 10. Under these circumstances its value would always fluctuate but only between 10 "in isolation," and 20 as a complementary good and by way of substitution. Now, if instead of only three, there were 1,000 specimens and opportunities for use, the difference involved would be that between the 1,000th and the 1,001st. The 1,000th use would be the one from which the necessary replacement unit would have to be withdrawn, the 1,001st would be the use to which it would be necessary for the "A_1" to be assigned, since it had been rendered idle by the breaking up of the combination. It is highly probable that the difference between number 1,000 and 1,001 would shrink to insignificance.

It is concededly unlikely that an individual will possess within the limits of his own economy 1,000 specimens of any one kind of good and 1,000 opportunities for utilization of them.[40] But the failure of our hypothetical situation to be realized in practice does not by any means militate against the effectiveness of the influences just described. It merely shifts the theater of operations in which they are exerted from an individual economy to a market economy. And this is how it does so. Individual economies buy what they need and sell their surplus on the market. Thus all the supplies and all the opportunities for their utilization that exist throughout that market region are brought together. And now, in a manner quite analogous to that which applied before, everything hinges on the question whether commodities and the chances for their disposition are scarce or not. If the commodity is very scarce, the determination of price will be materially affected by the answer to the question, "Is it a buyer or a seller who is attempting a transaction involving the one specimen?" Suppose, as in the previous example, there are just three specimens and three potential buyers who wish to cover uses that have importance ratings of 50, 20 and 10 respectively, and suppose further, that one specimen never reaches the market because it is required for utilization as a complementary good. Then the two remaining specimens will be acquired for the uses having intensities of 50 and 20; and in ac-

40. In a larger economy, with government ownership in the means of production, such as an economy organized along socialist lines of production, it would not be at all improbable that this would apply to such a degree that the conditions described in the preceding paragraph would become a literal actuality.

cordance with laws which are to be developed in the next chapter, the purchase price will inevitably be fixed at some point between 10 and 20, say at 15. But now suppose there is some change that abolishes the complementary uses and causes the third specimen to be offered for sale on the market. Now if a sale is to be effected, recourse must be had to the prospective buyer with the opportunity for utilization of an importance rating of only 10, and the result is that the market price will be depressed, and certainly *below* the order of 10. The two cases then exhibit a very considerable variation in price and in the subjective exchange value based on it. On the other hand, if it is a matter of a commodity of which 1,000 specimens are offered for sale and are sought by 1,000 buyers, it is probable that not the slightest perceptible influence will in actual practice be exerted upon the determination of the market price by the presence of a 1,001st buyer and/or seller. In this case the good commands a price and receives a value that are to all practical intents and purposes independent of the devotion or nondevotion of a single specimen to utilization as a complementary good.[41]

Under the presuppositions just presented, the value of the replaceable members is fixed at a point that is unrelated to their concrete use as complementary goods. That is also the value accorded them when the integral value of the group is distributed over its individual members. The method of making that distribution is as follows. *The integral value of the whole group is first determined according to the marginal utility of the combined utilization. Of that integral value the fixed or "substitution value" is assigned to each replaceable member and the remainder, which varies in accordance with the magnitude of the marginal utility of the whole, is assigned to the irreplaceable member or members as an individual value.* In terms of our own previous and repeatedly used example, if the members A and B have a fixed or "substitution value" of 10 and 20 respectively, and if the combined marginal utility is ranked at 100, then we can assign to the irreplaceable good C an individual value of 70; if the marginal utility amounted to 120, C's individual value would be 90.[42]

165

---

41. In this connection I wish to reply in explicit terms to a comment by Schumpeter (*Wesen und Hauptinhalt,* p. 252 ff.). These words were not intended to convey the impression that I deny "in principle" to the presence of a complementary use or to any other single opportunity for employment all influence on valuation in the case of "replaceable" goods. As a matter of principle it is undoubtedly true that every opportunity for employment (unless below marginal utility) contributes in some minute degree to the final result in the judgment of value. But under the conditions of fact assumed in the foregoing text that contribution will be so small that, as a matter of practice, it will be imperceptible. Where there is an infinite number of opportunities for use, each must make only an infinitesimal contribution. The general trend of my exposition might very well have enabled Schumpeter to infer that this is what I had in mind, rather than the absence of influence on the part of any group of uses, as a matter of principle. But there were

also specific evidences. In the preceding paragraph I discussed differences in estimations of value and spoke of a "shrinking into insignificance." The paragraph immediately following could then have been supposed not to advocate a contradictory thought, but quite on the contrary to assert that "the influences just described" were effective in a market economy in *identical* fashion, and that I was portraying only a change which "shifts the theater of operations in which they are exerted." In order to obviate any possible misunderstanding, I have now inserted the phrase "to all practical intents and purposes" which did not appear in earlier editions. See also Essay VII in *Further Essays on Capital and Interest.*

42. If *C* also were replaceable at a lower substitution value, the situation discussed on p. 161 f. would result, and the marginal utility of the combined utilization would be no criterion at all for the value possessed by the complementary group.

7. Clarifying Summary for Case 3

We have just considered three possible variants of situations involving complementary goods where selective reasoning must be applied. Of these the third type occurs by far the most frequently in common practice. Accordingly the method of valuation of complementary goods most frequently applicable is the one which follows the formula last presented. Its most important application is in connection with the assignment of the relative contributions to the product made by the productive powers which cooperate to produce it. For almost every product is the result of the cooperation of a group of complementary goods, of some form of uses of land, of labor and of fixed and circulating capital. The overwhelming majority of complementary goods will consist of marketable commodities and hence be replaceable at will. These are such things as labor performed by paid workers, raw materials, fuel, tools, etc. Only a small minority will be difficult or impossible to replace. Such would include the plot of ground which the farmer tills, the mine, the railway system, the activity of the entrepreneur himself marked by highly individual characteristics. As may be readily seen those very factors governing selection are here operative, which were to lend validity to that formula of distribution which was last presented. And in truth our formula does work out with extreme precision in actual practice. For in actual practice the first step is to deduct "costs" from the total product. These prove on closer inspection not to include all costs. The latter should include the uses of land that are involved as well as the activity of the entrepreneur, since both are goods having value. The costs that are deducted are the expenditures *for replaceable means of production which have a determinable substitution value,* such as wages, raw material, depreciation of equipment, etc. The balance is ascribed to the irreplaceable members as a "net return"; the farmer credits it to his land, the mine owner to his mine, the manufacturer to his factory, the merchant to his entrepreneurial activity.

If the combined return increases, no one dreams of crediting the increase to the replaceable members. We then simply say "the land" (or the mine) "has produced a greater yield." Similarly if the combined return decreases, it will occur to no one to enter the "costs" at a reduced figure in his computation. The reduction will simply be interpreted as the production of a smaller yield on the part of the land, the mine, etc. And as a matter of fact that is entirely logical and correct. For actually the only thing that depends on the elements of costs that are replaceable at all times is the fixed substitute utility; the entire balance of the total utility to be derived depends on the irreplaceable goods.

8. Value Determination When Several Combination Members Are Irreplaceable

Finally we have to consider the situation which obtains if several members are "irreplaceable" at the same time. As a practical matter that will prove to be a rather rare combination. But if it occurs they will occupy the position with respect to the remainder which the "replaceable goods" leave over, that was described above*in the paragraphs be-

*[on page 52, new pagination]

ginning "The first possibility," and a "second possibility." If C, with a fixed substitution value of 30, is replaceable and if A and B are irreplaceable and also not adaptable to any other use, then each of the two, depending on the situation that develops, will be worth 70 while the other is worth zero. Suppose, further, there is some other opportunity for the employment of A with a value of 10, and the same for B with the value of 20. Then A has two values, one of 50 as a complementary good, the other of 10 in isolation; and B likewise has two values, one of 60 as a complementary good, the other of 20 in isolation.

9. Correct Theory of Value of Complementary Goods Will Solve the Problem of the Contribution of Land, Capital and Labor, That Is, What Rent, Profit and Wages Should Be

The theory of the value of complementary goods offers a solution for one of the most important as well as one of the most difficult problems in economics. I refer to the problem of the distribution of goods as it takes place under the present organization of society, in which more or less free competition prevails and prices are determined by contractual agreement. All products arise from the cooperation of the three complementary "factors of production," labor, land and capital. Our theory tells us how much of the combined product is economically[43] attributable to each, and therefore how much of the integral value of the product is to be ascribed to each one. By doing so it reveals at the same time the most thoroughgoing basis for determining the amount of remuneration that each of the three factors obtains for itself. And even though the "production factor, capital," as is well known, does not exactly coincide with the "source of income, capital" the way is at least approximately indicated that leads to determination of the amount of income distributable over the branches called wages, rent and interest. But it does not as yet do so directly. That is to say, those portions which are received by the workers and by the owner of the collaborating land are without further discussion recognized as identical with wage and rent respectively. But the portion which is attributable to capital is very far from being interest, as has been assumed with an annoying prematurity countless times since the days of Say. No, it is only the *gross remuneration for capital's collaboration;* it is the nut which will yield the meat called interest only after the nutshell has been removed which consists in the value of the capital that is used up. Only if, and to the extent that there is then still

43. Not physically. The physical share would simply defy calculation. For how could one figure out what percentage represented the physical contribution of the marble, and what percentage the physical contribution of the sculptor toward the creation of a statue? However, this physical proportion is also a matter of complete indifference. On the other hand it is generally quite possible to determine what utility or value would have had to be forgone, if a certain single factor had not been possessed. And *this utility conditioned by the possession or the existence of a given factor* I call the economic share of that factor in the total product. For the problem of economic apportionment the physical conditions are just as irrelevant than the moral. It has nothing to do with the question of which portion of the joint product ought "rightly and justly" to be apportioned in the distributive process to one or the other of the collaborating factors. On the matter of what constitutes the problem, see the excellent observations by Wieser in *Natürlicher Wert*, 1889, p. 70 ff., and for further particulars Essay VII in *Further Essays on Capital and Interest.*

a remainder after the deduction, will there be net interest. And it constitutes an independent problem to determine why that happens.

10. Adumbration of the Acute Problem Of "Unearned Income," Also Called Originary Interest, But Designated "Net Interest" Here (See CAPITAL AND INTEREST, Volume II, Positive Theory of Capital)

167   Let us make it quite clear by means of an illustration. We shall assume that a product made with the collaboration of all three factors is worth $100. The law of complementary goods is helpful to the extent of enabling us to determine that the share of the labor directly engaged in production amounts to $20, that of the land is $10, and that of capital is $70. But the law of complementary goods does not tell us whether, after deduction for wear and tear of capital, there is any remainder in the form of net interest, nor how much that remainder amounts to. On the contrary, it would rather lead us to assume there is no remainder. For it is quite in accord with the spirit of that law to make the assumption that those components of capital to whose collaboration the $70 portion of the product is apportionable, and which are consumed in the attainment of the product, are themselves to be appraised at a full $70. If that assumption were valid, the yield from capital would completely counterbalance the wear and tear on capital. That such is not the case, is, so to speak, an "inside affair," something that goes on within the gross portion which belongs to capital and which is determined in accordance with the law of complementary goods. And it is, furthermore, the subject of an independent problem, the problem of interest. But before we can turn our attention to that question, we have many another little matter to clear up.[44]

---

44. Cf. my *History and Critique of Interest Theories,* particularly p. 96 ff. (concerning Lauderdale), p. 103 ff. (concerning Carey), p. 117 ff. (concerning Strasburger), p. 124 (concerning Say), etc. All these references concern the frequent confusion throughout economic literature between the undiminished share of capital for its collaboration, the so-called "gross interest" with net interest. It will hardly be expected of me that just "in passing" as it were, I should develop a complete theory of distribution. I advisedly refrain from going into the subject any more profoundly than is absolutely necessary for my special task, which is the development of the theory of interest. For that purpose it is sufficient for me to expound in their most general outlines the principles which underlie the distinction between the gross share of capital on the one hand, and the shares that can be ascribed to the collaborating forces, labor and uses of land, on the other. Our particular task is rather to show what happens to that gross share of capital.

Part A—VALUE

Chapter VII

Value of Production Goods
And of Goods of "Higher Orders"
Generally. Relation Between
Value and Costs.

1. Value of Goods Depends on Marginal Utility in Future Use, and Not on Value Of Goods Consumed in Origination of Goods

THE generally promulgated doctrine is that the value of goods is governed by the cost of their production. The principle of this doctrine was rarely attacked;[45] what happened more frequently was that by a listing of exceptions and the addition of all sorts of modifying and limiting clauses, the validity of the doctrine was restricted to a very much smaller field. At any rate within that field its authority remained almost unquestioned, right down to the present day.[46] And it is also beyond question that the experiences of every day practical life seem to lend it support of a sort. And it is also certainly true—and this is the most awkward circumstance of the three—that the theory of costs seems to contradict the theory that I advocate. For the "costs of production" are nothing in the world but the total of the production goods which had

45. Among older economists, Say opposed it in his *Traité*, Book II, Chap. IX, 7th ed., p. 404: ". . . ce qui nous ramène à ce principe déjà établi, que *les frais de production ne sont pas la cause du prix des choses*, mais que cette cause est dans les besoins que les produits peuvent satisfaire." A somewhat later era is marked by the noteworthy remarks of MacLeod (*Elements of Political Economy*, 1858, p. 111). The subject was however not grasped in all its implications until it was set down in the writings, epoch-making for the whole theory of value as they were, of Carl Menger, Jevons, and Walras. And of these the profoundest work was Menger's. Among Menger's successors Wieser is outstanding by reason of his closely knit and clearly thought out presentation of the subject.

46. Written in 1888. Since that time wide publicity has been given to the theory espoused in this book. It has been most effectively promoted through the particularly brilliant exposition of Wieser and his rebuttal of the older "theory of costs." In spite of that I have retained the present chapter in its early version, which was written with the point of view that the early theory of cost was something that needed to be opposed and overcome. I had two reasons for this. The first was that contrasting the two views allows the problems to be recognized most clearly. The other was that the older theory has by no means been exploded for so long nor so fully that an exposition pointedly refuting it can be considered superfluous. That is especially true because the obviousness of certain impressions to which it makes reference always makes it seem temptingly convincing for the layman's method of thinking.

to be used up in order to produce a good; they are the capital goods, labor, etc., that have been consumed in that process. In response to the questions why a good has value and how much value it has, my theory says: "It depends on the marginal utility the good is capable of delivering, in other words, *on its future use.*" The reply of the theory of costs is: "It depends on the value of the production goods used up in producing it, in other words *on the conditions of its origination.*

2. Making a Completely New Approach to Value Of Production Goods, and Hence, Concerning Costs

Let us forget this contradiction for a moment, and in fact, everything that we learned in school about costs, and let us investigate impartially what our theory of marginal utility, consistently followed through, must teach concerning the value of production goods, and hence, concerning "costs."

3. The Idea of Higher Orders of Goods

In order to conduct this investigation with entire clarity, we shall find it advisable to submit its object, production goods, to more exact definition. In contrast to consumption goods which serve to satisfy wants directly, all production goods have one characteristic in common, and that is the fact that they serve to satisfy wants only indirectly. But in that respect they differ from each other in the degree of their indirectness. Flour from which bread is made stands several degrees closer to the final satisfaction of want than does the field on which the grain is grown from which the flour is milled. These differences of degree are important as a matter both of theory and of practice. In order to express this difference in degree, let us follow the lead of Carl Menger[47] and divide goods into orders. The first order comprises those goods which serve to satisfy wants directly, or in other words consumption goods such as bread. The second order comprises those goods with the help of which goods of the first order are produced. Examples might be the flour, the oven and the labor of the baker, all things which collaborate in the production of bread. The third order comprises the goods that serve to produce goods of the second order. These might include the grain that is milled into flour, the mill in which it is ground, the building materials of which the oven is constructed, and so on. Goods of the fourth order would be the production goods from which goods of the third order are produced, such as the land on which the grain is grown, the plow with which the soil is tilled, the labor of the farmer, the building materials used to erect the mill, etc. This goes on into goods of the fifth, sixth, tenth order; in short, all those goods whose useful service consists in the production of goods of the succeeding lower orders.

4. Values in Higher Orders Depend on Their Utility Toward Producing Lower Orders

In the light of our understanding of the value of goods it is self-evident that a production good, like any other good, can acquire value

47. *Principles of Economics,* p. 56 f.

for us only when we recognize that the gaining or losing of some utility, of some satisfaction of want, depends on our possessing or not possessing that good. And it is just as self-evident for us that its value will be high when the dependent satisfaction of want is important and low when it is unimportant. There is only one difference between consumption and production goods. Consumption good and satisfaction of want stand in a causal relation directly beside each other; production good and the satisfaction of want dependent on it are separated from each other by a longer or shorter succession of intermediate members, the successive products of those same members. The remoteness and extensiveness of this connection results in an accretion of material and an increase in distance where relations are developed which are new in nature but which follow regular laws of development. These relationships develop, above all, between the value of the means of production and that of their products. But they neither violate nor disturb the chief law of value. It is merely that, in a manner analogous to what applied in the case of complementary goods, the law becomes overgrown, as it were, with additional provisions, the material for which is a natural outgrowth of the greater intricacy of the phenomena. It is these provisions that must become the object of our investigation.

For the purpose, let us imagine a typical production series. A consumption good which we shall call A, results from a group of production goods of a second order which we shall call G_2. These in turn proceed from a group of goods of third Order G_3—and these finally from a group 170 of means of production of fourth order, G_4. In order to make it easier to survey the entire scene, let us for the time being assume that each of these groups of means of production is exactly used up in the production of its products, with no remainder left over; and let us at the same time assume that the productive utilization designated is the only one of which the group is capable. Let us now determine what, in the way of the possessor's well-being, depends on each member of the foregoing series.

We already know what is dependent upon the final member of the series, the consumption good A. It is its marginal utility. Our investigation needs to begin only with the member G_2. If we did not have group G_2, we should not get its product A, and we should therefore have one specimen fewer of the category of the good A, than would otherwise be the case. But one specimen fewer, as we already know, means the loss of one satisfaction of want—to be specific, the least important one to which, economically speaking, a specimen out of the supply could legitimately have been devoted. All that is another way of saying it means the loss of the marginal utility of the product A. Therefore, what depends on group G_2 is exactly the same thing as depends on the consumption good A itself, namely, the marginal utility of that same A.

Let us continue our inquiry and proceed to the next member of the series. If we did not have the group G_3, then we should not get group G_2 which is derived from it, and as a further consequence we should have to forgo one specimen of the consumption good A, which is tantamount to losing its marginal utility. Hence the very same contribution to well-being is dependent on the group G_3 as on the members which follow it in the production series. The same thing is true of group G_4. If we lose it, we also lose one specimen of the group G_3 which otherwise would have been derived from it; that leads to the loss of one specimen of the group G_2, one specimen of good A and finally to the loss of its marginal utility. It is now possible to set up the following general proposition. *Where a group of means of production belonging to a higher order successively passes on into the next lower orders, the same gain in well-being is dependent on it throughout, namely the marginal utility of its end product.* This result will hardly cause astonishment. The conclusion is inescapable from the outset that a production series which is related to our well-being only through its end product, cannot be directed toward and cannot condition any utility, other than the utility which that end product itself conditions. In every successive link of the chain we hold in our hands the condition of the same final utility. It is merely a case of doing so, now at a further, and now at a nearer point on the road that must be traveled to reach that final utility.

5. General Principles for Valuing Means of Production

From the foregoing the following general principles may be deduced with respect to the value of the means of production.

1] Since the same utility depends on all groups of means of production which succeed each other in the production process, the value of them all must, as a matter of principle, be identical.

171   2] The magnitude of this value common to all of them is ultimately determined by the magnitude of the marginal utility afforded by the end product when ready for consumption. I emphasize the word "ultimately" because

3] The value of every means of production is also determined directly by the value of the product of the next lower order which is derived from it. Initially, the useful service rendered by any means of production consists in the production of its product, and that process exhausts its capacity for service: our valuation of the significance of the service and of its source will vary in proportion to the importance and value which that product has for us.

In essential content the second and third points coincide exactly, because in the goods of each succeeding lower order there is reflected the marginal utility of the ultimate product. I make the two points in order to convey the thought that while the value of all groups of means of production is derived from the end product, the derivation is a process that goes on in stages, as it were. As a first and direct step the magnitude of the marginal utility is expressed in the value of the end product. The latter constitutes the determinant of the value of the groups of goods from which it emanates; that value functions likewise to determine the value of the group of third order, and that, finally, does the same for the value of the last group of fourth order. The name of the determining element changes from stage to stage, but behind the different names, the identical thing is always active—the marginal utility of the end product.

In spite of the fact that the last two principles coincide in content, express formulation of the third is not superfluous. It affords the convenience of an abbreviated formula, which we use in practical life much more frequently than the full formula itself. When we estimate what contribution a means of production makes to our well-being, we naturally look first at the product which we derive from it, and then consider in what respect it promotes our well-being. If we cannot determine this at once, then we naturally must review the entire course through which utility was passed on from member to member of the series until we finally arrive at the marginal utility of the end product ready for consumption. But very frequently that is not necessary. On the basis of earlier consideration or experience, we find we have a judgment all ready to hand concerning the value of the products, and then without further ado we make that judgment the basis for a judgment as to the value of the means of production. A dealer in wood who wants to buy material from which to make barrel staves will not take long for deliberation concerning the value that the wood has for him. He estimates how many barrel staves he can make out of it and he knows how much staves are worth on that day's market. He does not need to bother about anything beyond that.

6. Familiar Identity of Costs and Value of Goods Produced Involves Use of an Interpretation Contradictory to What Is Presented Here

The foregoing statements about the value of means of production have so far been developed purely on their intrinsic merits, as postulates, so to speak, of economic logic. What does experience say to these logical postulates? It corroborates them. And indeed, we can turn for corroboration to that very "law of costs" which is apparently so hostile to our theory of marginal utility. Experience shows that the value of most goods 172 equals their "costs." But "costs" are nothing but the aggregate of the production goods having value—labor, capital objects, uses of wealth and the like—which had to be expended for the making of a product. The familiar identity of costs and value is therefore only another way of expressing the identity of value possessed by groups of goods of different orders which emanate successively each from the preceding one. Of course I am quite well aware that, so far as the cause of that identity is concerned, the law of costs is usually subjected to an interpretation exactly the opposite of our own. Instead of saying, as I do, that the value of the means of production, which is to say the goods that represent costs, is determined by the value of their products, the proponents of the law of costs ordinarily say that the value of the products is determined by the amount of the costs, which is to say by the value of the means of production from which they are made. We shall have occasion, a little later on, to go to the bottom of this matter of the reason for the identity. At this point I merely wish to register confirmation of the fact that the identity really exists, be the reason what it may. I am referring to the identity in value of the groups of means of production which successively pass from each stage to the next.

7. There Are Random Deviations In Value And Regular Deviations in Value Between Goods of Different Orders, Lower and Higher

To be sure, the equality in value is only approximate rather than absolute. One can really only speak of a *tendency toward equality in value*. The divergence from absolute identity is of two kinds: some of it is regular, some of it is random. Both kinds are attributable to the circumstance that production takes time. Often long periods of time will pass during which goods of sixth or eighth order pass through all the intermediate stages before being converted into the final form as mature consumption goods. And during that time people and things can change. Wants can alter, so can the relations between want and coverage, and above all, the insight into those relations can change. Naturally the estimates of the value of the goods in the various stages of their progress toward maturity will change correspondingly. It can be readily seen that the fluctuations which arise from that source may be extreme or slight, may be upwards or downwards. They are deviations that know no rule. At the same time we perceive a deviation from complete identity which is constant and regular. It may be observed that the value of a complete group of a remote order lags behind its product in value according to a regular pattern. And indeed, the difference in value varies directly as does the time which is required for conversion of the group of means of production into their product. If the value of the product is, say $100, then the aggregate value of the elements requisite for its production—labor, uses of land, fixed and circulating capital—will be shown by experience to be somewhat less than $100; it may in fact be $95 perhaps, if the production process requires a whole year, possibly $97 or $98 if the production process lasts only a half year. This difference in value is the fold, as it were, in which interest lies concealed. The explanation of it is a problem in itself, and one which will occupy us very fully in future chapters. But we must not lump together that problem and our present discussion which deals with the general relation of value to means of production and their products. For the moment, therefore, I shall ignore the existence of that difference in value entirely.

8. Egregious Heterogeneity of Production Goods Is According to the Higher Their Order

Up to this point in our discussion the law of the value of production goods was developed subject to the simplifying hypothesis that every group of means of production admits of utilization only to one very definite purpose. That hypothesis is in real life only very rarely in agreement with the facts. It is pre-eminently production goods, far more than consumption goods, which are characterized by egregious heterogeneity. The overwhelming majority of them will be capable of service in several productive fields, some are adaptable to thousands of such productive services. Examples are iron, coal, and, above all, human labor. Of course we have to take these factual circumstances into account in conducting our theoretical investigation. We must observe what modifications, if any, affect the law that the value of a group of goods occupying remote orders is governed by the value of their product.

9. How the Value of a Means Of Production Depends on Least Marginal Utility of the Produced Goods

Let us alter the order of the presuppositions of our typical example accordingly. Someone possesses a rather large supply of groups of means of production of second order (G_2). From each of these groups he can produce at will a consumption good of the category A, or one of category B or finally, of category C. He desires, of course, to take advance measures toward balanced provision for his various wants, and will therefore draw simultaneously on various parts of his supply of means of production to produce consumption goods of all three categories. And he will produce amounts in each in accordance with his needs. If there is genuinely balanced provision, the quantities produced will be so regulated that needs of approximately equal importance depend upon the last specimen in each category, and that thus the marginal utilities are approximately equal.[48] In spite of that it is not impossible that there will be differences —possibly even quite considerable differences—in the marginal utilities because, as we already know,[49] the gradation of concrete wants occurring in any one category is not always either uniform or continuous. The first stove in my room will afford me a very considerable utility, say one we might designate with an index of 200. A second stove will afford no utility at all. I shall most emphatically call a halt in providing stoves when I have a single specimen with its marginal utility of 200, even though in other areas provision for needs may see a dropping off of the average of marginal utility to as little as 120 or even 100. And so it is permissible and necessary, if our typical example is to be true to nature, to assume that the marginal utility of a specimen will be different in each of the categories A, B and C. Let us call it 100 for A, 120 for B and 200 for C.[50]

Now the question arises, "What is the value, under these circumstances, of a group of means of production, G_2?"

We have had so much practice with selective decisions of a similar nature that we can give the answer without hesitation. The value will be equal to 100. For if one of the available groups of means of production should be lost, the owner would naturally shift the loss to the least sensitive area. He would not curtail production in category B where he would be sacrificing a marginal utility of 120, and certainly not in category C where the sacrifice would go as high as 200. He would quite simply produce one specimen fewer of category A where the reduction in well-being is only 100. Let us express it in general terms. *The value of a unit of means of production is governed by the marginal utility and the value of that product which has the least marginal utility among all those prod-* 174

---

48. This is demanded by the principle of sound economic procedure. Cf. Wieser *Ursprung und Hauptgesetze des wirtschaftlichen Wertes*, p. 148 f.
49. See foregoing, p. 140 f.
50. Schumpeter (*Bemerkungen über das Zahlungsproblem*, in the *Zeitschrift für Volkswirtschaft*, Vol. 18, p. 129) registers an objection against this and similar examples. He contends that the occurrence of qualitative difference will necessarily lead to a completely continuous gradation of dependent wants and a complete levelling of marginal utilities in just the same manner as does the unlimited divisibility of goods. I shall meet this objection on another occasion when there will be a more particular reason for discussion of the point. See also my Essay VIII in *Further Essays on Capital and Interest.*

ucts for the making of which the unit means of production could have justifiably been used.

All the relations which we had declared to be plainly in force with regard to the value of means of production and their products under the simplifying assumption of only a single possible disposition, are therefore generally valid as between the value of means of production and value of its least valuable product.

And what is the situation with respect to the other categories of products, B and C? That question brings us to the origin of the "law of costs."

10. A Timesaving Method By Which Costs of Higher Order Goods Rather Than Marginal Utilities Are Used; But the Basic Explanation Is Still (as Always) the Same, viz., Marginal Utility

If under all circumstances the marginal utility attainable by a good within its own category were determinative, then the categories B and C would have to receive a value divergent not only from that of category A, but also from the value of its costs G_2. B would then have a value of 120, C a value of 200. But here we are confronted with one of the cases where, through substitution, a possible loss in one category is transferred to another, and as a result, the marginal utility of the latter becomes determinative for the other as well.[51] Thus, if a specimen of category C is lost, it is not necessary to forgo the marginal utility of 200 which the specimen would have delivered directly. Instead, it is possible to convert one unit of the means of production G_2 into a new specimen C, and in its place rather produce one specimen fewer in that category in which the marginal utility, and hence the loss in utility is least. And indeed, that possibility becomes a reality. The category in question in our example is the category A. Because of the opportunity which production offers for substitution, a specimen C is therefore not valued in accordance with its own marginal utility of 200, but in accordance with the marginal utility of the least valuable related product, the product A; its value is therefore 100. The same applies, naturally, to the value of category. B, and would apply generally to every category of good which is "productionally related"[52] to A, and of which the direct marginal utility is also greater than that of category A.

This leads to some important consequences. The first is that in this way the value of goods having a higher individual marginal utility occupies the same rank as the value of the "marginal product";[53] and *hence also the same rank as the means of production from which both emanate. The identity which exists in principle between "value" and "costs" therefore obtains in this instance as well.* But it is to be carefully noted that here the coinciding is brought about in quite a different way from that which was followed in the case of costs and marginal product. In the latter instance the two coincide because the value of the means of production accommodates itself to the value of the product. The value of

51. Cf. foregoing, p. 151 ff.
52. Wieser, *op. cit.*, p. 146.

53. Let us, for brevity's sake, use this name for the product with the smallest marginal utility.

the product is the determinant factor, the means of production is the   175
factor that is determined. In our present case it is the other way around,
and it is the value of the *product* that must do the accommodating. Ultimately it accommodates only to the value of another product. But initially
it accommodates also to the value of the means of production from which
it emanates and which brings about its substitutional connection with the
marginal product. The transmission of value proceeds, so to speak, along
a broken line. First it goes from the marginal product to the means of
production, fixes the value of the latter, and then ascends in the opposite
direction from the means of production to the other products which it is
possible to produce from them. In the end product, then, the products
of higher immediate marginal utility derive their value from their means
of production. Let us translate the abstract formula into terms of concrete practice. Good B or good C is, in general, a product of higher immediate marginal utility. If now we consider what good B or C is worth
to us our first response is, "Just exactly as much as the means of production are worth to us from which we can at any moment replace the
product." If we then inquire further and ask how much the means of
production themselves are worth, we arrive at the marginal utility of the
marginal product A. But on innumerable occasions we can spare ourselves this further inquiry. Time and again we already know the value
of the goods that comprise the cost, without any necessity for working
it out from its foundation and proceeding onward from case to case.
And on all these occasions we simply determine the value of products
by their costs, and in doing so we are taking advantage of an abbrevia-
tion which is as accurate as it is convenient.

11. The Idea Under Sideheading No. 10 Is Not a Different Law for Value, Nor an Exception, But Is a "Particular Law" Perfectly Subordinate to the General Law of Marginal Utility

And now the whole truth about the celebrated law of costs is re-
vealed. It is indeed quite correct to say that costs govern value. Only it
is imperative to remain aware of the limits within which this "law" is
valid, and of the source from which it derives its virtues. *In the first place*
it is only a *particular* law. It is valid only so long as the possibility is
present of furnishing, through production, substitute specimens in any
quantity and at any time they are desired. If there is no possibility of
substitution, then in the case of each product, value must be determined
by its immediate marginal utility in its own category. In that case its
value no longer coincides with that of the marginal product and of the
intermediate means of production. Therein lies the explanation of the
empirically established principle that the law of costs is valid only for
the goods that are "reproducible at will," and that it is a law of only
approximate validity. For it does not bind the goods over which it holds
sway to slavishly meticulous adherence to costs. On the contrary, it permits fluctuations above and below such costs, depending on whether
production at the moment lags behind demands or outstrips it.

A second and still more important consideration is that even where the law of costs is valid, those costs are not the final, but only an inter-mediate cause of the value of goods. In the last analysis they do not give value to their products, but *receive* it from them. That is clear as crystal in the case of production goods for which there is only one pro-ductive use. Surely no one will wish to deny that it would be erroneous to assert that Tokay wine is valuable because Tokay vineyards possess value; everyone will concede that the truth is the other way around, and that those vineyards have a high value because their product is highly valued. It is just as hopeless to deny that the value of a quicksilver mine depends on that of quicksilver, the value of a wheatfield on that of wheat, the value of a brickkiln on that of brick, and not vice versa. Only because of the manysidedness of most cost goods is it possible for the situation to present the opposite appearance, but somewhat closer inspection will surely reveal the fact that it is only an appearance. As the moon reflects the light of the sun upon the earth, so do the manysided cost goods reflect the value which they receive from their marginal product on their other products. The principle of value resides not within them, but outside of them and in the marginal utility of their products. We have here simply the great counterpart to the law of complementary goods. The latter dis-entangles the snarled relationships of value which arise from temporal and causal *juxtaposition,* from the simultaneous collaboration of several goods toward a common useful purpose. Just so does the law of costs perform the same service of enlightenment and clarification with respect to the relationships of value of those goods which operate in temporal and causal *succession,* which labor, one after the other and one through the other, toward the same ultimate goal. If we think of the relations of value among the intricately interacting goods as the meshes of a far-flung net, then we might say the law of complementary goods disentangles the meshes in breadth, the law of costs, in depth. But both operations take place within the all-inclusive frame of the law of marginal utility of which the other two laws are nothing more than special applications to special problems.

PUBLISHER'S NOTE: The reader should understand that the preceding chapters, in general simple and not complex, are not arrestingly warning enough adequately to alert the casual reader in regard to the revolutionary conclusions (applications) which Böhm-Bawerk will make with the foregoing as his base. This new foundation as formulated here by Böhm-Bawerk is radically and cogently and conclusively different from the confusion of the Classical economists including Smith and Ricardo on these subjects, and on the more extended fallacies in the economics of Karl Marx. Instead of "value" and "price" being based on *any* cost factor (particularly the labor cost factor of Marx) *all* value eventually derives from *utility* and not from cost or pain or sacrifice, etc. The foregoing exposition is brief; Böhm-Bawerk came back to this frequently; see especially his "Ultimate Standard of Value," Essay V in *Shorter Classics of Böhm-Bawerk;* also Chapters VIII and IX in *CAPITAL AND INTEREST,* Volume III, *Further Essays on Capital and Interest*; Libertarian Press, South Holland, Illinois 60473, U.S.A.

Part A—VALUE

Chapter VIII

Value and the Onerousness of Work (Disutility of Labor)

1. Exceptions, or Rather Pseudo-Exceptions, to The Basic Idea That Utility and Utility Alone (Not Costs at All) Is Determinative of Value

PREVIOUSLY I made the reservation that although, *as a general* 177 *rule,* the gain in well-being dependent on a good consists in the satisfaction of a want, that rule is subject to certain exceptions.[54] In order to avoid leaving a hiatus in my presentation, I now intend to take those exceptions under consideration, and to evaluate their importance for the theory of value.

The line of demarcation between the exception and the rule may be discerned from the following remarks. It is always the satisfaction of want which depends on goods when the amount of goods[55] in the possession of the person making the value judgment is of a definite magnitude. Then the elimination of the good to be valued causes a definite reduction in his means of satisfaction and hence in the satisfactions themselves. In such case one good more or one good fewer signifies one satisfaction more or one satisfaction fewer. However, certain combinations of circumstances can effect a modification. It is possible that the elimination of a good may bring about a very special kind of substitution by which the needed substitute specimen is acquired without any reduction in the amount of goods possessed, and solely for the price of some unpleasantness or some work or some exertion which would not have been assumed except through this special inducement. In such cases the elimination of the good by no means signifies the elimination of the satisfaction of a want, because the gap in the quantity of goods possessed is closed by means of the special substitution undertaken for that specific purpose. On the other hand, the elimination does signify a diminution of well-being through the imposition of an unpleasantness or a painful experience that would not otherwise have had to be suffered.

Let us consider an example. A coronation festival is being celebrated. Admission to this interesting event is by card, and the cards may be ob-

---

54. See foregoing p. 136 f. and closely related remark in Note 12 [on page 20, new pagination].

55. In this connection consideration must be given, not only to the amount of finished consumption goods, but also to the quantity of available means of production, including originary productive powers.

tained gratis but they are nontransferrable, and are issued only on application in person. I possess one of these cards. If I lost it, I should not have to forgo the pleasure of attending the festivity, but should have to put in another personal application for a card. What possession of the card therefore really means for me in that case is that I am relieved of the unpleasant burden of going to the proper office and making my request for a card.

For the situation to come to pass which makes for this sort of exceptional case, two conditions have to be fulfilled. (1) There must be an opportunity to purchase a substitute good at just the one price, namely, the suffering of something onerous that would otherwise have been avoided. (2) The detriment suffered must be smaller than the positive marginal utility of the good. If, for instance, I rated the inconvenience of a second application for a card of admission as greater than the positive enjoyment of the festival, then in case of the loss of the card I should simply forgo my substitution of the lost card, and the deprivation would once more fall into the category pertaining to positive satisfactions.

These two conditions obtain, I think, relatively seldom in practical economic life, and if they occur in unalloyed purity, they are particularly likely to involve only trifling and insignificant matters. There is, of course, in principle always the possibility of gaining increased concrete coverage of needs through voluntary assumption of a greater burden of labor.[56] This can be done in at least two ways. One way is to increase the number of daily working hours at gainful labor, and prolong that labor to the point where it entails a higher and a more painful degree of fatigue or weariness. The other way is to employ the regular working hours more intensively, to expend one's powers more energetically, more continuously, with fewer and shorter pauses for recuperation—all of which ordinarily has the same effect of heightening the feeling of onerousness connected with work. In either case coverage through concrete goods is subject to substitution or augmentation at the price of additional suffering of onerousness. It need not be any realization of a "least" or "last" positive satisfaction of want that depends on a definite good. It need be only the avoidance of some additional onerousness of labor undertaken to assume that satisfaction.

But the theoretical possibility of a combination of this kind probably becomes a concrete reality only very infrequently under the system of division of labor prevailing in our modern production process. Before an economic subject can perform voluntary additional labor for the sake of a definite satisfaction of want which would otherwise be eliminated, he must satisfy two conditions. First, he must have leisure time at his disposal, the use of which for purposes of recuperation he is able and

178

56. A much more infrequent means to such acquisition of goods would be the voluntary enduring of other burdensome or painful experiences. Yet a casuist would be able to cite or to imagine such cases. He might cite as an example a teacher or trainer whose purpose it is to harden a boy under his care into stoical disregard of pain. Such a person might promise the boy a much-longed-for toy as a reward for the courageous and voluntary enduring of pain. Unimportant as the occurrence of such cases may be, it is nevertheless important, as a matter of theory, to ascertain that labor and the burdensomeness of labor do not constitute the only circumstance which can form the basis for valuations that fall within the group of exceptions now under discussion.

willing to forgo. Second, he must have an opportunity to perform such labor in his free time. These two conditions are probably not very often met by the great majority of our population. Bound by the fetters of the wage contract or at least of long established vocational habits, we perform the serious economic tasks of our calling, for the most part at least, in a definitely fixed number of working hours per day. And we are seldom willing or, if willing, able to extend those hours for the sake of some special want. In a factory that has an eight-hour day, it is unlikely that the management will "keep open shop" for the sake of a single factory hand who would like to work a ninth hour so that he can replace a damaged piece of furniture at home. The work we do in the course of our regular vocation usually procures for us a definite measure of money and goods and so provides coverage for a definite measure of wants. Any impairment of that coverage does not result in any heightening of the vexatiousness of work, but in the elimination of satisfactions. And as we have already shown, the latter as a general rule furnish the measure for the value of goods.[57]

179

Conversely, little exertions of our leisure hours are not infrequently undertaken for the sake of acquiring goods which we should not be inclined to purchase from the earnings of our serious economic labors. On my pleasure strolls I gather flowers which add an ornamental touch to my rooms when dried and arranged in bouquets. If one of those bouquets is destroyed I do not lose the satisfaction of a single want. All it means is that I must again take the trouble to gather the flowers, dry them and so on, provided that I consider that trouble to be a lesser thing than the positive utility that I hope the bouquet will afford me.

In the light of what has been said, these exceptional cases seem, on the whole, to be of relatively minor significance. Do you ask me then, what is the criterion by which the magnitude of their goods value is determined? The importance of such goods for our well-being lies, after all, solely in the fact that possession of them enables us to avoid something

---

57. Such voluntary prolongation of a man's working hours will probably encounter external (as distinct from personal) obstacles more frequently than will his endeavors to acquire greater stores of goods through the intensification of his labors. When he works for a weekly or monthly wage there will of course be little opportunity for that, but it is quite possible when he does "piecework" or works under contract. But even then there is more likely to be a general disposition observable to assume heavier burdens for the sake of more copious providing of goods. It is quite possible, let us say, that a workman who has a particularly large family to provide for, or who is especially anxious to gain great advancement and rapid promotion, will impose more intensive exertion upon himself than his colleagues assume, in order to increase his earnings. But it is probable that only rarely and only in especially exceptional cases will such a concrete relation develop between a definite individual good and an increased exertion assumed for the sake of that good, as would be required in order that the good in question would be valued in accordance with the increase in exertion rather than with its marginal utility. I am inclined to believe that even pieceworkers and contractworkers will regularly value the economic goods with which their economy deals in accordance with their utility for the satisfaction of needs. When considering a purchase, for instance, and deliberating on the price up to which they will still be willing to buy, I think what they will take into account is the additional utility that will be theirs if they acquire the good, and the seriousness of the deprivation if they forgo it. In short, I think they will take the "marginal utility" of the good into account. And I think that they will count the "onerousness of work" only in those exceptional cases when they are determined and also clearly aware, that the means for acquiring a definite good are to be gained, not through the relegation of other wants, but through a special exertion exceeding the customary measure of intensity present in their ordinary labor. Cases of this kind are certainly conceivable, but I think I have every reason to consider them relatively rare and exceptional cases.

painful or burdensome. The more painful and burdensome it is, the more important it will naturally be to us to avoid it. We shall therefore attribute to those goods all the greater importance for our well-being, or in other words all the greater value, the more painful or the more burdensome is the experience which is averted.

2. Another Presumed Exception
(Pertaining to Varieties of Onerousness Of Labor) Is Not Truly an Exception

What is the relation of that dictum to the previously developed law of marginal utility? Upon cursory examination one might be tempted to conclude that we are violating the principle that has guided us hitherto, and even that we are relying on a principle that not only differs from the earlier one, but even contradicts it. It might seem that previously we were basing value on utility, and now were basing it on pain or labor. Any such view I should have to oppose emphatically. Our theory bases the explanation of the magnitude of every value on the same principle. In every case the basis is the gain in well-being that is connected with the possession of a good. But the situations presented by our economic life are complicated and heterogeneous, and consequently the opportunities for gain in well-being that are offered by that life are correspondingly varied. Now they take the form of gaining a positive benefit in the way of satisfying a want, at another time, though much less frequently to be sure, they assume the guise of the avoidance of some painfulness or troublesomeness, lesser in degree than is the positive benefit. By developing our principle in adaptation to the changing conditions of life, we still remain consistent; and far from abandoning that principle, we do but unfold its full significance.

3. The Advantage Inherent in the Use of
A Possible Substitute; Utility Still Determines How Much Onerousness Will Be Assumed

But it is possible to pursue this matter of the consistency of these two judgments still further. The distinctive feature of the doctrine of marginal utility lies in the fact that it declares the smallest economically admissible advantage to be the determinant of the magnitude of value. And the same characteristic feature asserts itself here again with full force. For, as we have just shown above, the exceptional cases we are discussing can occur only if the troublesomeness which the possession of a good enables us to avoid is of lesser degree than the positive satisfaction which is to be expected from the good. The avoidance of unpleasantness therefore does in actual fact represent the smallest, the truly marginal utility of the good. Anyway, it is of the very essence of marginal utility that it consists, not in the utility of the good itself, but in the advantage which is inherent in its possible substitute. We know that, according to the particular concatenation of circumstances, the substitute is sometimes found among goods of the same category and at other times, through the agency of exchange, is transferred from among goods of an entirely different kind. In exactly the same way, when the concatenation of circumstances is quite especially peculiar, the substitute is procured by the transfer of some painful or troublesome experience. To claim that in cases of this sort the value of the goods in question is to be explained by the painfulness that is avoided, is no deviation from the law of marginal utility, but—as witness the cases just described—simply an entirely correct instance of the application of that law.[58]

58. The cases we have been discussing will even fit without too much forcing into a class bearing the name of "marginal utility," provided we permit ourselves to use the word utility, not in the narrowest sense of the positive satisfaction of a want, but in the broader sense of an equivalent of "gain in well-being." In a general sense, the "utility" of a good must presumably be thought of as the effectiveness which the good displays in the furtherance of our purposes. Hence, insofar as those purposes concern our *well-being*—and that can be considered to be the case normally, to say the least—the utility manifests itself as an improvement in the state of our well-being effected by the good. (See Chapter x following.) This "improvement" may consist in the bringing about or the heightening of a state of pleasurableness, such as comes with the use of a piano to which I owe the pleasure of listening to a Beethoven sonata. Or it may consist in the avoidance or the alleviation of a painful state, such as is accomplished by the use of a dam for flood-control. Furthermore, it is possible to distinguish between the *direct* utility of a good and its *indirect* utility. We can apply the term "direct" to the utility which *the good itself delivers* directly through the functioning of the useful forces inherent in it. An example would be (returning to the illustration of our pioneer) the stilling of hunger that is effected by the sack of grain which he actually uses for his direct sustenance. We can apply the term "indirect" to the utility which a good is instrumental in delivering. It does so in the following manner. By being itself used for the attainment of a more important direct useful effect, it liberates some other good to be used for the attainment of a different, less important purpose, and by that liberation it makes the latter attainment possible. An example—again from the illustration of the pioneer—is the first sack of grain which helps to liberate the fifth sack for the raising of parrots, and thus *indirectly* delivers

the utility "raising parrots." The "dependent" utility which determines value is ordinarily, as we have sufficiently well proved in the course of our development of the theory of marginal utility, just such an indirect utility. And according to the nature of the want which it serves it can, in the light of what has just been said, consist in the effecting of a positive pleasure, or in the avoidance of a painful experience. We thus have worked out the thought that the marginal utility which depends on a good may be the avoidance of a painful experience, such avoidance being effected through the agency of a liberated substitute. There is but little difference—and that one of degree rather than kind—between that thought and the one which has engaged our attention in this section, namely, that on the possession of a good there depends, as its indirect utility, the avoidance of something onerous, such as the laboriousness of work, or other burden. Of course, when we are pursuing lines of thought which expressly contrast the "utility" of goods with the "sacrifices" that must be made to acquire them, then we must hold the concept of utility within correspondingly stricter limits. Otherwise we may incur the charge of playing with words. That is a circumstance which Dietzel failed to consider, with the result that the clarity of the controversies he carried on was greatly impaired. See my essay "Zur theoretischen Nationalökonomie der letzten Jahre" in the *Zeitschrift für Volkswissenschaft*, Vol. VII (1898), p. 405 ff. Many English and American theorists have shown a tendency to assign to onerousness of labor (they call it "disutility") a considerably more important position in the system of the theory of value than I had thought permissible. Because of its unavoidably extensive nature I am constrained to defer detailed consideration of this theoretically very interesting variant. See *Further Essays on Capital and Interest*, Essay IX.

PUBLISHER'S NOTE: American and British economists had difficulty grasping or reluctance in accepting the premises which Böhm-Bawerk, as the foremost expositor up to that date of Austrian NeoClassical economics, had elucidated. It is natural for (even) professional economists (let alone pseudo-economists who from an amateur ethical standpoint hold forth on the onerousness of work and that if a man worked hard, he ought to be rewarded *because* he worked hard and not because the product had high marginal utility) to find it difficult to shift appropriately and *entirely* from a theory that *cost* determines value and price, as distinguished from the *utility* of the product. That a man "worked hard" is finally irrelevant and irrational in regard to value and price; onerousness never *really* creates value.

Part A—VALUE

Chapter IX

Summary

1. The Sole and Unrivalled Primacy of Utility (in the Sense of Gain in Well-Being)

THE general and specific rules in the foregoing pages for valuation may be summarized as follows:

There is one very general principle which is, I believe, entirely without exception. That principle is that the value of goods is determined by that gain in an economizing subject's well-being which is dependent on his power of disposal over those goods. Such gain in well-being may be more exactly described as a difference in well-being, that is to say, the difference between the degree of well-being attainable with and the degree attainable without the goods to be valued.[59]

The dependent gain in well-being may be of either of two kinds:

A] In the very large majority of cases it consists in a positive advantage which emanates from the goods and which affords a *satisfaction of a want* which would not otherwise have been possible. Hence we esteem goods in cases of this kind according to the magnitude of the *utility* that depends upon them, of their "marginal utility," as has been elucidated in detail. When only a single specimen of a good is available, or when an aggregate of goods must be valued as a combined unit, marginal utility may coincide with "integral utility."*

B] A second kind of gain in well-being is characteristic of cases that constitute a minority which is in my opinion neither large nor important. This gain consists in the avoidance of some pain or unpleasantness which is of lesser magnitude than the positive marginal utility of the good which we could, if we desired, and would, if free to exercise a reasoned selection, procure by undergoing that pain. In this minority of cases we value the goods according to the magnitude of the pain which is avoided and which would have been required for acquisition of the good. This is termed its "cost" in the sense of the personal sacrifice required in the way of pain, troublesomeness and the like. In Chapter VIII I indicated the small extent of the field in which this limited rule

---

59. Concerning the meaning of the word "gain in well-being" see also following Section A of Chapter x on "Hedonism and the Theory of Value."

*PUBLISHER'S NOTE: See Chapter III, sideheading 22.

has validity, and pointed out that therefore cases to which it applies may be justly regarded as exceptions to the rule in paragraph A. Such cases may be briefly defined as those involving goods which are freely replaceable at the price of personal sacrifices.

2. Itemized Cases of the Primacy of Utility

We revert to the rule in paragraph A, applicable to valuation according to marginal utility, and find that we may record the following subdivisions.   182

1] When goods are available in definitely limited supply we value them in accordance with the immediate marginal utility of the category of goods involved. This criterion is applicable *in general and at all times* to those goods which cannot at will be increased in quantity—so-called monopoly goods or rare goods. In addition, this criterion is applicable *at certain times* to goods that can be increased in quantity at will. That is to say, it is applicable when and to the extent that the supply of replacement goods lags behind the demand of the moment, and therefore also behind "costs."

2] The quantity of most goods, however, can be increased at will and the goods themselves are replaceable. Assuming that there is no obstacle in the way of their prompt replacement, the estimation of their value is made on the basis of their "cost" in the sense that this cost is measured by the value of the goods that have to be diverted from other uses for such replacement. And this latter value itself goes back through one or more intermediate links to one or another marginal utility. In this case then, we no longer have a valuation according to the direct marginal utility of the category of goods in question. Instead, valuation proceeds indirectly and by way of "costs" in accordance with marginal utility; but it is now a question of the marginal utility (and value) of the replacement goods. *

This type includes primarily valuations that apply to goods that can be reproduced in any desired quantity in order to replace the supply on hand. Such value is then estimated at "cost of production" in the sense that it comprises an integral value, as represented by the goods needed for production, which is less than the immediate marginal utility of the good in question.

3] However, the general type just referred to also includes other cases. For it covers estimations of value in the case of goods which through purchase or exchange can be replaced by goods acquired at a price less than the immediate marginal utility. When a thing can be bought in any store for $10 it is completely reasonable to estimate its value at $10 in accordance with that "cost of acquisition," and we should still do so even if the thing possessed an immediate marginal utility, for our individual economy, far in excess of that amount. But in the last analysis

---

*PUBLISHER'S NOTE: See Essay V, "The Ultimate Standard of Value" in *Shorter Classics of Böhm-Bawerk*, Volume I, page 303; Libertarian Press, South Holland, Illinois 60473, U.S.A.

there always lies in the background behind such "cost of acquisition" *some* marginal utility, namely that marginal utility possessed by the purchase price that must be provided out of our limited means.

In our highly developed market economy, based on division of labor, type (3) forms the basis for an extraordinarily large proportion of the actual valuations which are exercised in everyday practical affairs. But in no sense does that fact impair the significance of type (1), since the influence of the latter is always effectively exerted in the background, even in cases that of themselves fall under types (2) and (3). In other words, it is the valuation as based on direct marginal utility which determines our decision whether or not, and to what maximal degree, we will consent to make the sacrifice requisite for replacement of the goods in question through purchase or production.[60] This is particularly true of the "cost of acquisition" which constitutes a factor in type (3). On the surface it may well appear as a magnitude objectively imposed upon the economizing individual by virtue of market conditions. Actually it is a product—and I intend to demonstrate this with due clarity at the proper time—of all those subjective valuations which interact upon the open market to determine the intensity of supply and demand, and which have their ultimate roots in an estimation of direct marginal utility. *

There is, finally, a special type comprised of cases which English and American economists specially emphasize, but which I have discussed only outside my text proper in my Essay IX in *Further Essays on Capital and Interest*. They are characterized by two conditions. The first is complete mobility and free divisibility not only of the labor-effort but also of the increase in quantity of goods to be obtained through such labor-effort. Moreover, the marginal utility which determines value in these cases tends to be equalized by the order of a marginal burdensomeness for which these economists have coined the English term "final disutility." However, these cases are, properly speaking, not to be classified under type B, but rather under type A. The reason for that is that in these cases too, the value of goods is determined by the magnitude of their marginal utility. But even within type A, they do not comprise a fourth type, coordinate with types (1), (2), and (3), for the simple reason that they do not fall outside the limits of these three types, but lie quite athwart the dividing lines between them. Their logically requisite conditions may be present either in the case of goods reproducible in any desired quantity, namely type (2), or in that of out-and-out monopoly

---

60. If in any particular instance there is any doubt as to the satisfactoriness of the substitution of one good for another, then to that extent there is an absence of the "free substitution" which is a condition prerequisite for the types (2) and (3). Any such case, therefore, belongs to type (1).

---

*PUBLISHER'S NOTE: Böhm-Bawerk indicates that his summary here presents conclusions which may still be argued by those not yet free from shackles to thought which consist of the idea that *costs* determine value and price. For the additional evidence, a reader should turn eventually to Böhm-Bawerk's comprehensive thesis in his three-volume opus, *CAPITAL AND INTEREST*.

The next chapter is a defensive chapter rejecting fallacious arguments against the positive theory presented in the first nine chapters.

goods, which is type (1) or even, finally, in the case of any sort of goods that are purchasable in any desired quantity, which is type (3). The last of these could be exemplified by advancing the case of a supposititious piece-worker or contract-worker who increases the daily effort he is willing to exert, or the daily fatigue he is willing to undergo to just such a point that the last additional increase just equalizes the marginal utility of the increase in wage or income which is gained thereby, and hence also of the purchase price which he thus enables himself to provide out of that limited income. *

*PUBLISHER'S NOTE: *Further Essays on Capital and Interest* is Volume III of *CAPITAL AND INTEREST*, which see; especially Essay IX, "On the Role of Disutility in the Value Theory," page 116.

Part A—VALUE

Chapter X

Some Psychological Considerations Supplementing Our Theory of Value[61]

A. Hedonism and the Theory of Value

184   THE theory of value I have just presented is frequently given a bad name on the grounds that it is in essence "hedonistic" or "utilitarian."[62] And since hedonism is in many quarters regarded as an antiquated philosophy,[63] this theory of value was deemed to be tainted with infirmity in that it derived support from a philosophy no longer considered capable of furnishing a solid foundation for it. At the same time the opinion was repeatedly expressed that it was quite unnecessary for the theory to expose itself to criticism on these grounds because all its tenets of any economic importance could be defended with equal success no matter whether its psychological aspects were formulated in terms of the utilitarian or the anti-utilitarian philosophy.

1. Dubious Repute of Hedonism Is Irrelevant to Marginal Utility Economics

I should like to declare my position with respect to this question in the following three statements.

1]   I concur entirely in the last-mentioned opinion. That is to say, the explanation of economic phenomena arrived at by the theory just

---

61. Chapter x comprises material which is in its entirety an addition of new matter which first appeared in the third edition. It contains only a discussion of rather subtle matters, the clarification of which supports and confirms the matter previously presented, without adding to it anything that is new. Any readers who feel that the course of the discussion up to this point constitutes a perfectly satisfactory theoretical investigation which merits unhesitating confidence in its correctness, may with a perfectly good conscience skip the entire section, in order to avoid being sub-

jected to delay in the progressive presentation and development of the theory.

62. Cf. Davenport, *Value and Distribution*, pp. 303-310; Marion Parris, *Total Utility and the Economic Judgement*, Philadelphia, 1909, *passim;* Gide and Rist, *Histoire des doctrines économiques*, Paris, 1909, p. 592 ff.; Oskar Kraus, *Zur Theorie des Wertes, eine Bentham-Studie*, Halle 1901, p. 59 ff.

63. "The preliminary step is to recognize that utilitarianism, or any form of hedonistic theory, is a thing of the past," Davenport, *op. cit.*, p. 304.

presented may prove correct or incorrect. But its correctness will be entirely unaffected by the interpretation of certain psychological premises.
The theory relies, and in view of their factual verity is quite well justified
in relying on those psychological premises. But the correctness or incorrectness of the economic theory remains the same no matter whether the
further conclusions drawn from the premises in the field of psychological
science are interpreted from the utilitarian or the anti-utilitarian viewpoint.[64]

2] I myself *abjure* any adherence to the tenets of hedonism, and in
the presentation of my theory of value I desire to avoid any statements
that could be interpreted as an expression of such adherence.

3] The terminology that I employ does include such frequently recurring terms as "well-being," "gain in, (or advancement of) well-being,"   185
"pleasure," "displeasure," "pain," "distress" and the like. It is true that
these are the very terms which have from the beginning been customarily
employed by economists who were avowedly utilitarian in their point of
view. To be sure, they are perhaps also terms employed by economists
generally, without distinction as to philosophical faith! Nevertheless, and
despite any false appearance they may create of a leaning toward hedonism on my part, I have sound reasons for refusing timorously to avoid
the use of those terms. On the contrary, I retain them deliberately because
they promote clarity in my explanation.

But we should not permit ourselves to discuss a name until we are
clear as to the thing to which it attaches. And what is really the deciding
criterion of a "hedonistic" viewpoint, such as the theory of value just
presented is accused of representing?

2. The Popular Definition of Hedonism

Ordinarily a viewpoint is described as "hedonistic" if it maintains
that there are no primary goods or primary values other than pleasure
and freedom from pain. From that the further doctrine is derived that
there can also be no other ultimate aims of human endeavor than maximum accretion of pleasure and avoidance of unpleasantness.[65]

Of late it has become customary to oppose this once widely dissemi-
nated doctrine, and to point to several groups of facts which cannot be
reconciled with the hedonists' contention that the motivation of all human
action is to be found *exclusively* in man's teleological striving for pleasure
and for the avoidance of pain. It is not denied—nor would it be possible
to deny—that an extraordinarily large proportion of human actions actually is determined by teleological motives of pleasure and pain. What
is denied, however, is the *exclusive* domination of such motives, and the

64. Cf. Davenport, *op. cit.,* pp. 307-310;
along the same lines see Schumpeter, *Wesen
und Hauptinhalt,* p. 542, and H. W. Stuart,
"The fortunes of the Austrian economics
are in no wise bound up with those of
the Benthamite psychology" (Journal of
Political Economy, Vol. IV (1895), p. 75).
65. Cf. Kraus, *op. cit.,* p. 4 ff. Similarly
Paulsen, *Enleitung in die Psychologie,* Berlin, 1892, p. 432: "To the question, what
is the ultimate purpose or the highest good

to the attainment of which all other effort
is directed, hedonism answers, 'Pleasure.
That is the goal to which every act of the
will is directed.'" The term "utilitarian" is
often used as a simple synonym for "hedonistic." But it is also frequently employed in
a narrower sense as a description of a very
special variant of the hedonistic philosophy.
But I do not believe I have any occasion
to go into detail on the subject in this place.

denial is supported by reference to some groups of cases in which other factors supply the motivation. In this connection reference is sometimes made to *altruistic actions,* at other times to *instinctive actions* and the like, which are performed "intuitively" or "habitually" but in either case "without deliberation," and without "hedonistic calculation" of pleasure and pain.[66] But principally and most emphatically, reference is made to cases in which something other than pleasure and pain constitutes "the primary value" which causes a thing to be loved or hated, to be sought or avoided. Some examples cited are knowledge, religious ideals, moral perfection, complete development of one's personality and the like.

I do not wish to enter into any argument as to the extent to which these groups of facts can be relied upon as a refutation of the hedonistic doctrine. But I do wish to make the following prefatory remarks concerning them, and to advance them from the standpoint of economic theory generally, and specifically from the standpoint of the theory of value which I propound.

3. Böhm-Bawerk's Rejoinder to Any Imputation That His Economics is Tainted With Hedonism

It was never my intention to limit the motives of economic acts, and hence the motives of economic judgments of value to *purely selfish* consideration of the economizing subject's *own individual* pleasure and pain. On the contrary, I pointed out from the very beginning that in my theory of value the words "purposes of well-being" or "our well-being" are to be taken in the sense that "they include not only the selfish interests of the economizing subject, but also everything that appears to him as worth striving for." Indeed, it was pointed out that such words refer specifically not only to the well-being of the particular person but also to that "of those other persons to whom we extend our economic care, either upon occasion or as a permanent consideration."[67] Hence my definitions do formally and in actual fact provide that the psychological basis of my theory of value embraces the altruistic motives as well. It may be remarked, incidentally, that this is also done by many genuinely hedonistic economists, such as Bentham himself. To be sure, they append to it that well-known interpolative bit of reasoning, the logicality of which has often been questioned, to the effect that the promotion of the well-being of others affords pleasure to the ethically disposed human being, and therefore becomes the goal of his action because of the pleasure he himself derives from it.

I have likewise no desire to deny the existence of the second group of factual phenomena consisting of instinctive and otherwise spontaneous actions. But insofar as we are dealing with actions that are genuinely devoid of all deliberation whatsoever, that group plays no part at all in connection with the theory of value. For where an act is really performed

186

66. Cf. Davenport, *op. cit.,* p. 306.
67. "Grundzüge der Theorie des wirtschaftlichen Güterwerts," 1886, in Conrad's *Jahrbücher,* New Series, Vol. XIII, p. 13, note 1, and p. 78. Similarly in the article "Wert" in Conrad and Lexis's *Manual* (2nd ed., p. 746): "We ascribe value, in a subjective sense, to a good if, and to the extent that we recognize that our well-being is dependent on it, or that it signifies the satisfaction of a need or of any vital interest, whether selfish *or altruistic.*"

in complete absence of teleological reflection or deliberation, it is impossible for a judgment as to economic value to be arrived at. For every such judgment considers the goods with which it deals as the means to a considered and valued end. It therefore inevitably and necessarily presupposes some sort of reflection upon the importance of that end. Wherever there is no judgment as to value, there is also nothing to be explained by my theory of value or by any theory of value. For that reason, it has never devolved upon me to establish any relationship between those spontaneous actions and my explanation of such valuations as do actually take place. It is therefore for my purposes a matter of complete indifference whether such actions do or do not occur. It is possible that their occurrence may constitute a point to be urged in rebuttal of psychological hedonism but such occurrence in no way impinges on the course it became my duty to pursue in an explanation of *de facto* judgments of value.

But it is just possible that those who cite that group of spontaneous actions may have something else in mind. For in a certain sense we do have genuine judgments of value which are pronounced in purely "mechanical" or "nondeliberative" fashion. As I already pointed out a long time ago,[68] and as I intend to expound once more at the proper place in this book, our economic judgments of value are by no means always constructed "from the ground up." That is to say, we do not, in every instance in which we need to direct our economic actions, reflect anew upon all the elementary factors involved in our judgment. Quite on the contrary, on innumerable occasions we revive our judgments entirely mechanically and on the basis of our memory which has stored up those judgments as the fruit of earlier reflections and experiences. It is even possible that these are not our own reflections and experiences but those of other persons. In all such cases our judgments are merely a matter **187** of habit and repetition. Now if that sort of judgments of value "made without reflection," is what the objectors to my theory of value have in mind,[69] my reply is that it should easily be seen that such an argument fails to penetrate beneath mere surface appearances. For the judgments of value stored up in the memory and then applied as a mere matter of habit must at some earlier time have been reasoned out as original judgments of value and must at that time have been based on genuine reflection. A calculation of that sort, having once been followed through, is then availed of not only for the first case for the sake of which it was undertaken, but also for numerous other cases which benefit by the results stored up in the memory or from the habitual character of the reaction. However, that does not mean there has been an elimination of the original calculation of well-being. It means, on the contrary, that the influence of that reflective process has been prolonged and multiplied.

In the case of instinctive actions we might be confronted with a variant involving a situation where a goal is striven for purely on the basis of instinct and without hedonistic weighing of the balance between pleasure and pain, and yet where a subsequent reflective process is inter-

---

68. "Grundzüge," p. 75 ff.
69. It would seem that Davenport (cf. *op. cit.,* p. 304 ff.) has some inclination in this direction.

polated which takes into account the means of achieving the goal and the importance of those means as derived from the importance of the goal. Let us cite an extreme example. A person considering the merits of suicide engages in a process of hedonistic deliberation, comes to the conclusion that life provides him with far more pain than pleasure, and so determines to commit suicide and jumps into deep water. At that moment the instinct for self-preservation comes into play; by chance a beam of wood floats nearby; that beam of wood, as a highly prized means to the preservation of life, becomes the object of extreme desire and a frenzied effort is made to obtain it. Now because cases of this kind lead to genuine judgments of value, they are, in some measure, the concern of an economic theory of value. Hence the latter is compelled to construct for itself a sufficiently broad psychological basis to accommodate cases of that kind. But this does not by any means signify that the economic theory must therefore set up a special category for nondeliberative instinctive judgments of value. It is true that some sort of deliberation does occur here, even though it may not be of a hedonistic nature. But cases of this sort simply call attention once more to that third group of facts which is, in its fundamental significance, by far the most important of all. They point up the question whether something else can be esteemed and striven for as a "primary good" in addition to pleasure and freedom from pain; whether, for instance, the instinctively pursued goal of self-preservation might not be such a "something else." Actually, even the first group of facts, the altruistic actions and motives, really belong here too. Let us assume that the factual existence of altruistic motives is conceded (and it would be difficult for anyone not to concede it), but that at the same time validity is denied to the previously mentioned intermediate explanation concerning the pleasure that is striven for by a given individual in the form of advancement of the well-being of other individuals. In that case the point that really requires to be settled is the question whether it is possible to consider as primary goods (or evils) both the individual's own pleasure and pain and also the pleasure and pain of other individuals. The third group then, becomes the one on which all the interest in the contention over the psychological principle becomes concentrated.

188

Now I have neither any reason nor any inclination to deny the existence and the potency for motivation of other primary goods in addition to individual pleasure. Twenty-five years ago I put myself on record to that effect[70] in a remark made without particular emphasis and therefore often unnoticed. I wish to repeat the statement here with all possible clarity. Whether the psychologists' dispute is settled in favor of the hedonists or against them is utterly without bearing upon the validity of the theory of value that I am advancing. For the economist, and for the theory of the economic value of goods, it is a matter of complete indifference *what* people love and hate, *what* they seek and *what* they avoid,

---

70. "I suppose it is hardly necessary for me to make particular mention of the fact that I am here using 'well-being' in the widest sense, and that it does not apply merely to the selfish interests of an individual, but *rather to everything that in his eyes appears worth striving for.*" ("Grundzüge," 1886, p. 13, note 1.)

and what, with greater or lesser intensity, they try to attain or attempt to escape from. It matters not whether it be only pleasure and pain, or whether it be in addition other things that are "desirable" and "worthy of being desired," "odious" or "worthy of odium." The only thing that is important is that people do love and hate *something,* that they seek with greater or lesser intensity to attain or to avoid ends for which their economy is to supply the means, and that their "golden opinions" of those more highly or less highly prized goals lend some of their color to the economic means of attaining them. Under these circumstances the economist's theory of value has one primary purpose. For all the varying instances that life has to offer it must explain with which goals, striven for with whatever degree of desire and esteem, a given good is so connected that the value attached to the goals is transferred to the goods as their "goods value." In the performance of that function the reasoning behind the theory of marginal utility loses no jot or tittle of its soundness because of the nature of the goal. The fulfillment of any kind of goal of human desire is subject to the limitation that the supply of goods is inadequate for the complete attainment of all goals. But a theory of value is not affected in its validity by the fact that some of these goals may not be of the nature of a pleasure. A marginal utility can just as well be a smallest rationally obtainable pleasure as any other smallest utility that may compete with desired pleasures and may be desired and sought after from other adequate motives.

4. The Matter of Nomenclature

My presentation of my theory of value could have met this aspect of the situation in either of two ways. One would have been to throw overboard entirely the whole terminology reminiscent of hedonism which employs the expressions pleasure, pain, gain in well-being and the like. I could then have substituted a different and colorless terminology which leaves room for goals of a somewhat different nature. Thus for instance, instead of gain in well-being I could have used in every instance the expression "gain in achievement of desired and avoidance of undesired effects," or "gain in wish fulfillment"; instead of "pleasure" I could have said "what is desirable," and in place of "pain" I could have used 189 "what is undesirable" or "what is contrary to desire"; I could have defined value as the importance "which a good possesses for the purposes that are highly regarded by an individual" and so on. The alternative procedure open to me was to adhere to the old traditional terminology of "well-being" and all the rest, and at the same time to provide for such extension in applicability of the terms as the situation calls for by appending a commentary to my terminology. That commentary would state that the terms were not to be understood in any narrow hedonistic sense, but rather were intended in a sense sufficiently broader to include as well other and desired and sought for goals in addition to the individual's selfish pleasure.

5. Böhm-Bawerk Declares Motivations Which
His Economics Implements Are, In Any Event,
Not Restricted to Hedonism, But Are Broader

I had ample and cogent reasons for choosing the latter alternative. Pre-eminent among them is the fact that striving after well-being, even if it be not the sole representative of all human striving, certainly does represent an exceedingly great and influential proportion of it. And that proportion is even greater when we consider those goals which are reflected in the specifically *economic* value of goods. Fervidly glowing enthusiasm for lofty ideals and elemental outbursts of the primal instincts are much more likely to manifest themselves in connection with non-economic or extra-economic activities than in connection with the cool and calculated considerations which ascribe economic value to a good on the basis of the best reasoned utilization that can rationally be devised for it. In the latter process it becomes, furthermore, particularly manifest that—to borrow a phrase from Wieser—"the *lower* limit of the line where utility ends is the point at which value begins." It is not in the lofty and exalted strata of human endeavor, but rather in its low-lying regions that marginal utility has its habitat and performs its function of determining the value of goods. And at these profounder depths man's banal and prosaic needs are certainly in the vast majority and signify more than a greater or lesser degree of pleasure and enjoyment. There are probably very few people indeed for whom the last minor tendrils of their needs would not descend into the region of banal "need of enjoyment." There must be few who do not use their most trifling, most dispensable means on things that imply no more than a choice of more abundant or more tasty dishes, of this or that cocktail, of one or another brand of tobacco, of more comfortable or more stylish clothes, or furniture, in short, a choice among all manner of the more agreeable and more pleasant details of living. There is a close interrelation between the values of goods of all kinds, by reason of the possibility of "substitutions," which include exchange and production. That interrelation creates a situation which renders the influence of the differing degrees of pleasure and pain on the determination of value universally and infallibly effective. The thought processes which characterize a theory of value and the necessity for illustrating it by concrete examples make it inevitable that such theory concern itself with the consideration of specific interests in well-being. This theory of interest in well-being always remains, as it were, the center of gravity of a sphere of thought that extends to wider limits. If, for the sake of complete formal accuracy, the theorist allows that wider sphere of thought to determine the form in which he presents his theory, he will find it impossible to avoid the necessity for a sort of duplicative or parallel presentation. Sterile generalizations will have to be repeated, revised and supplied with concrete illustrative references drawn from the domain of interest in well-being—a domain more limited, perhaps, and yet in its truly practical significance more limited to only a negligible degree. Under such circumstances I do not consider it either unjustified or inexpedient, when examining the psychological basis for economic phenomena of value, to place the terminology of the

190

interest in well-being in the foreground. Indeed, it may be more nearly correct to say that it should be allowed to *remain* in the foreground which it has traditionally occupied from the very beginning in economic science.

That minority of factors which the foregoing principle may fail to take care of is nevertheless accorded its day in court if an express reservation is registered in their favor, and if, in the explanation of the terminology that is accepted, provision is made to allow room for them within the system. And since that minority does concern itself with the general welfare of humanity, it appears not improper to preserve terminological contact between them and the striving after well-being, even though they do not coincide completely with hedonistic motivation. For there are, to my knowledge, psychologists who insist on the recognition of other primary values and "disvalues" and who still hold the opinion that the latter bring along in their train, as it were, accompanying "pleasures" and "displeasures," and that these likewise affect the well-being of the individual under discussion, even though the method of doing so does not follow the motivating channels envisioned by the hedonists. We should arrive at somewhat the same result if we accepted as completely valid a doctrine advanced today by many reputable psychologists completely independently of any connection with the outmoded hedonistic or utilitarian theory. I refer to the doctrine that all desires must necessarily emanate from the emotions. Under that doctrine, to be sure, the emotional qualities of pleasure and displeasure do not function *teleologically* as the hedonist believes, but they are at least active *causatively* in every human wish to accomplish a desired purpose.[71]

But terminology is, after all, an incidental matter, and if anyone wishes to modify it, I shall certainly not make an issue of it. The only point which I feel to be essential is establishing that the theory of value which I present is not firmly rooted in a specifically hedonistic psychology. It is no party to any ethical or psychological dispute over the boundary which determines whether, or how many, or which particular motivating factors so successfully defy classification as hedonistic motives that they require recognition as independent "primary values." For other primary values are just as capable as are primary pleasure-values, of playing the

71. Perhaps I may be permitted in this connection to point to one very significant sign which bears witness to the powerful and pervasive importance which is accorded to welfare interests throughout all the phases of endeavor and behavior that comprise man's economizing. The religious systems evolved by man most assuredly have reason to ascribe extreme importance to absolute and extra-egoistic ideals. It is certainly not merely fortuitous that man's religions have by no means forborne to invite the powerful assistance of motives of pleasure and pain in influencing human strivings. Indeed, they have on the contrary conducted a veritable courtship to gain their help, by devising such numerous conceptions, created with such originality, of the blessings of the hereafter, of paradise, of heaven and hell. And it is also significant that one author, who must be regarded as the head of the "ethical" school of economics and hence certainly invulnerable to the charge of blind hedonism, has yet felt called upon to say, "The longing for happiness, which in the last analysis arises from the absence of pain and the presence of pleasure, is the most indestructible element in human consciousness. It is identical with life itself" —(Schmoller, *Grundriss* Vol. I, p. 20). With specific reference to the value of goods, Schmoller says "Exchange or market value . . . has its ultimate basis in the consumer's feelings of pleasure and displeasure, and it is they whom the whole mechanism of production and exchange is meant to serve. . . . The origin of use value and enjoyment value lies in the world of human emotions; such value is under the domination of the myriad human feelings of pleasure and displeasure in all their infinite interaction, in all their baffling incomparability." (*Grundriss*, Vol. II, p. 106.)

part assigned to them by my theory of value. That part is to supply the basis for secondary goods' values, provided their relationship to particular goods meets certain specifications. Many details of the theory of value are admittedly derived from a consideration of motives that belong specifically to the category of pleasure and pain. Such, for example, are conclusions based on Gossen's law of diminishing enjoyment, or on the experience that the subjective onerousness of labor increases with prolongation of the labor itself. But in order to establish the validity of these details it is not necessary, as I have been careful to point out upon proper occasion,[72] for us to presuppose that they comply without deviation or exception with laws governing such influences, but only that the compliance be widespread. And thus they will still possess such validity, even if the principle that the purely hedonistic influences hold *exclusive* sway should be demonstrated to be without validity.

6. The Questions of Trespassing Freely, Cautiously, or Not at All, Over the Border Between Economics and Psychology

The controversial nature of certain basic psychological questions, and the further fact that the essential consequences of an economic theory of value are not dependent on a definite solution of those basic questions, has been recognized by several recent writers on economics. But it has led them to draw from those premises a conclusion to which I should not care to subscribe. They claim that the greater part of the psychological basis of the economic theory of value ought to be entirely excluded from economic science, on the ground that its content belongs to a different science, the science of psychology, and is unnecessary for that part of the explanation of value which it is the duty of economic science to examine. Thus it is the contention of Čuhel[73] that economic science should not go beyond the existence of the so-called "use demands," that is to say, the demand for the employment or utilization of goods and their capacities. He would have economics simply accept these and their intensities as "given quantities" and would oppose any steps to investigate the "well-being demands" from which the "use demands" are derived. He is most particularly averse to any treatment of the emotions of pleasure and pain which give rise to the "well-being demands." The investigation of these remoter causes of the use demands, Čuhel contends, economics should hand over to its sister sciences. In a manner similar to Čuhel's, Schumpeter[74] advocates setting more restricted boundaries for the territory to which economic science should restrict its explanatory activity.

Now I do not mean to deny that those more profound fundaments of the value of goods are intrinsically a part of psychological rather than of economic science, and would have to be treated there if strict technical adherence were observed in the division of labor among sciences. But

---

72. See foregoing Note 15 [on page 24, new pagination].

73. *Lehre von den Bedürfnissen*, Innsbruck 1907, Sec. 68 ff.

74. *Wesen und Hauptinhalt der theoretischen Nationalökonomie, passim,* e.g., pp. 29 ff., 63 ff., 76 ff.

even such division of labor as that between the sciences cannot be practiced without some community of labor too. It is impossible for the
explicatory processes to be sheared off with a smooth unbroken edge that
coincides exactly with the boundary of their respective sciences. There
must be some dovetailing and consequent overlapping of the borderline.
And indeed, it must be the more highly specialized science which extrudes
or projects itself, as it were, a greater or lesser distance into the realm of
the adjacent more general science. For it can hardly be expected that the
more general science would undertake to extend its labors into the fields
of all contiguous specialized sciences. That is the reason why economics
must deal with the processes that are pursued in evaluating goods. Those
processes are, to be sure, economic phenomena which have their roots in   192
psychological ground and it becomes the province of economic science
to trace those roots far enough into that ground to make the explanation
which it evolves understandable and convincing as a unified whole. And
such a duty cannot be performed without some trespassing beyond
boundary lines.

Trespassing of that nature would be less extensive in proportion to
the care and accuracy with which psychological science pushed out its
"feelers" into the adjacent economic field and cultivated them into readiness for grafting onto the explicatory plantings on the economic side of
the border. Unfortunately the science of psychology has at least until
quite recent times done very little to lighten the economist's task in this
particular. It is, on the contrary, a generally known fact and one admitted
by the psychologists, that the latter did nothing toward a systematic
tilling of their own arable field lying in juxtaposition to the economist's
field of the theory of value until aroused to action by the incursions,
undertaken under the spur of necessity, of the trespassing economists. It
is no mere coincidence that numerous treatments of *general* psychological
theory of value followed hard upon the heels of the propounding of a
"psychological theory of value" by the economists. And the content of
these very recent additions to the literature of psychology bear unmistakable evidence that they were inspired by certain contributions to the
literature of economics.[75]

75. I cite by way of example the writings
published in rapid succession between 1893
and 1902 which concerned theories of value
and which emanated from the pens of
Meinong, Ehrenfels, Kraus and Kreibig. Cf.
also the more extensive surveys of the literature on this subject found in M. Parris's
*Total Utility and the Economic Judgement
Compared with their Ethical Counterparts,*
Philadelphia, 1909, pp. 6, 12 and 13, and in
Wilbur Marshall Urban's *Valuation, its
Nature and Laws, being an Introduction to
the General Theory of Value,* London, 1909,
particularly Chap. vi, as well as his smaller
works, cited by M. Parris, *op. cit.,* p. 13.
Under these circumstances it must appear
strange indeed that some famous and some
not very famous representatives of economic
science reproached the economic scholars
specializing on the theory of value with a
failure to quote with sufficient frequency
from the writings of "psychologists pure and
simple!" Indeed, the case has been much
better put by one such "pure and simple"
psychologist himself who makes the statement that since research by the ethicists
has left certain questions unanswered "the
economists were well within their rights
in attempting to find the solution by their
own efforts" (Kraus, *Bentham-Studie,* p.
92). Cf. also the statement by the philos-
opher Ehrenfels in the preface to the first
volume of his *Systems der Werttheorie*
(1897), p. xii: "While the *economic theory
of value* . . . is perhaps on the point of
accomplishing its enormous quota of the
work, insofar as it can be isolated at all,
the *ethicist* and the *psychologist* have hardly
become aware of the problem that confronts
them. Indeed, an attempt to set up a comprehensive 'system of the theory of value'
bears the appearance of a completely new
departure in the field of philosophy."

The measure of such trespassing beyond the border must be controlled by considerations of expediency and tactfulness. To cease discussing the point in purely abstract terms, let it be clarified by means of a concrete example that I employed once before in a similar situation and that I shall simply repeat here in the same words. "We all have a very strong instinct for the preservation of life, or more specifically to avoid dying of hunger and thirst. Whence we get that instinct, whence it derives its power, why it is so much stronger than, say, the impulse to derive enjoyment from music—all these are questions which psychology may answer, if it can. Economics can at any rate reckon with the existence of that instinct in some degree of vigor as a given quantity constituting one of the factors of its problem. Why that given instinct concerns itself from time to time now with one good, now with another and invests it with much or with little importance—that is an entirely different question. Why is it that, though the strength of the instinct itself remains unchanged, it regards certain goods at certain times as being of supreme importance, and at other times as being of only the slightest significance? For we always have the instinct to defend ourselves against death from hunger and thirst, and it is always food and drink that serve to satisfy that instinct. And yet, how does it happen, that at certain times we struggle for bread and water with all the intensity of that tremendously powerful instinct, while at other times, and indeed ordinarily, we take only a very lukewarm interest in the possession of bread and water or even, as in the case of a particular quantity of drinking water for instance, evince absolutely no interest whatsoever? The explanation of that phenomenon does not devolve upon general psychology at all, for which it would constitute supererogatory rationalization. But it is the very kind of ratiocination in which the economist must become expert if he is to understand the behavior of mankind in relation to goods, and is to go forward from there to clarify the nature of the social laws governing exchange value."[76]

And I should like to add now that to that end he will inevitably be required to introduce into his presentation some psychological experiences and principles and these, incidentally, will have to amount to just about what the theory of marginal utility has, up to this time, been in the habit of introducing into its presentation.[77] He will certainly not be called on to furnish a genetic explanation of the instinct of self preservation or of the promotion of well-being, and he would be well advised to stay carefully aloof from any clearly superfluous participation in the controversy as to whether the instinct of self preservation is merely an offshoot of the instinct for individual well-being or an entirely independent and parallel instinct in its own right. On the other hand, he will hardly be capable of a lucid and convincing explanation of the absence of value attaching to concrete quantities of some of the most indispensable means of subsistence, unless he weaves into the fabric of his clarification, ex-

---

76. "Grundzüge," p. 79 ff.

77. And then it might very well happen that one of his critics would find nothing psychological in the theory or its presentation, while another critic would bar it from the field of economics altogether and insist on its classification under the rubric of psychology because, allegedly, of its predominantly psychological content!

periences and facts like Gossen's law of diminishing enjoyment. To follow the practice, as Čuhel and Schumpeter seem inclined, of omitting this "filling in" of the contour means reducing the whole presentation to a mere empty framework. The result may perhaps be logically correct, but it lacks objectivity and plasticity, and hence it remains unconvincing. Why did the use value theories of the eighteenth and the first part of the nineteenth centuries fail to convince as did the later marginal utility theory? The framework for both was the same. There were use aims of admittedly varying importance on the one hand, and goods in limited supply on the other. But there was a lack of illustrative presentation as to why within the same category of needs there was a downward gradation, in accordance with the law of diminishing enjoyment, in the importance attaching to more remote acts of gratification and correspondingly to more distant accretions of goods. Personally, I should dislike being asked to stand or fall on my ability to present a graphic and conclusive theory of economic value that was completely purified of any and all trespasses over the border of the domain of psychology. My experience might easily parallel the one jocularly but aptly illustrated by saying that even from behind you can recognize that a man is blind if you already know so beforehand. We of today have encountered and absorbed the modern theory of value as it is presented in contemporary literature, with its impugned gift of the theory's psychological nature "thrown in to boot." Knowing that, we can perhaps imagine away the additive and still find the theory intelligible and convincing. But whether that would be possible for a succeeding literary generation to whom the theory would be presented from the outset minus its "bonus" is quite a different question and one I am not at all prepared to answer in the affirmative. Nor has either Čuhel or Schumpeter subjected his methodological standpoint to a practical test. As to Čuhel, he did not in any event extend his literary task to the point where it included the development of the theory of value from the theory of needs. As to Schumpeter, while he did not present the fully worked out theory of marginal utility in his own name he took it for granted that his readers were acquainted or indeed familiar with it from beginning to end. And although he was merely borrowing, as it were, and though he hedged himself about with all sorts of methodological reservations, he did not scruple to avail himself of parts of its content to illustrate his own propositions which were otherwise presented in rather general outline only. I am inclined to believe that it would have been considerably more difficult to present his ideas of "the exchange relation" and the "function of value" to his readers as vivid concepts if he had been compelled to forgo all such borrowing, and had not permitted himself to presuppose his readers to be possessed of any of that concrete knowledge which the theory of marginal utility had imparted to them.[78]

194

---

78. Wieser expressed a very similar opinion concerning Schumpeter in the course of the exceedingly ample discussion of the latter's principal work which Wieser contributed to Schmoller's *Jahrbuch für Gesetzgebung*, Vol. 35 (1911) p. 909 ff. particularly pp. 924 ff., 929.

7. Examples of Economists Dabbling in Psychology, And Border-Raiding in Territory of Economists

And I have, finally, one more sound reason for not completely avoiding some careful trespassing upon the field of psychology. My reason is that there are, as a matter of fact, some few economists who do a bit of dabbling in psychology and conduct their own little psychological border raids into the territory of the economists. These raids have to be resisted. These men, in the name of an alleged psychological truth, contest well-grounded economic statements or they give distorted descriptions of the psychological facts which constitute the basis for some related economic phenomenon. In this category, for instance, must be placed any attempt by an economist to deny the entire theory of subjective value on such grounds as the following. Value (he will say) is something that is mathematically determinable, and hence something which must in turn have its roots in something mathematically determinable, something by which it can be measured. Now subjective wants, emotions and the like, he will say, can *not* be such a root because (and here is the psychological thesis that furnishes the ground from which to launch the attack against economic territory) such emotions and wants are not measurable nor commensurable. Just as untenable is the position occupied by a Jevons or a Sax in describing the status of the psychological factors wherever so-called "future needs" enter the picture. Nor is the empiricist Lujo Brentano on any firmer ground with the equally impractical assertions which constitute his intrusion into these same questions. All these and similar pseudo-psychological assertions and pronouncements are anomalous foreign bodies in the system of economic theory. But since, willy-nilly, the economist is confronted by their actual presence, what shall be his attitude toward them? Is he to exercise respectful restraint and ignore them on the ground that he, as an economist, is not competent to touch upon psychological matters? That would probably be interpreted by most readers as a confession of inability to refute those statements and the arguments based on them. Or at the very least it would leave the economist's readers open to the full force of an uncorrected misstatement. Or is the economist to wait until the "pure psychologist" himself confutes the incorrect assertions which arise in economic literature but impinge on the psychological field? Since it is these very border regions of psychology and economics which have so far been the object of very little attention or research on the part of the psychologist, the wait would be a long one indeed. Certainly, too great a delay for the economist to tolerate in cleaning his own house and throwing out misapprehensions and misstatements. It might, furthermore, very well be, that pure psychology takes no interest at all in such economic refinements of its own general problems. And it is also possible that, in the absence of any special incentive to investigate them, pure psychology has not even acquired sufficiently detailed knowledge concerning the special and determining facts necessary to adjudging these questions.

8. Along the Economics/Psychology Boundary, Böhm-Bawerk Favors Economists Carefully Trespassing Over the Line

What, then, is the economist to do? I think he should quietly but carefully step over the boundary line. Not that he should make sciolistic attempts to solve the ultimate and profoundest riddle of the human psyche. But he should do some industrious and painstaking collecting, sifting and combining of those facts from the neighboring domain which lie closest to his own boundary line. And they are facts concerning which the economist will, in any event, usually possess knowledge which is more exact and which extends to more characteristic details than that possessed by the scholar versed in general and pure psychology. And in most cases the economist will not have to go very far across the border nor penetrate deeply into the inner regions of pure psychology. For the fact of the matter is, fortunately, that the doubts and differences which are relevant for the economist do not really lie deep below the surface. For the most part they can be cleared up and corrected through a simple check on relatively superficial facts which are accessible to the layman. And that can be accomplished long before it is necessary to consider those deep and very profound problems the solution of which in any case is uncertain and likely to be attained only in the distant future. Our economic problems require us to plumb only the shallower depths, as it were, of the psychological waters. We deal for the most part only with facts which, as Wieser once so aptly and truly remarked, are present "in the general economic consciousness with its treasury of universal experience." They are therefore available to us all without any need for the adoption of special scientific methods to gather them.[79] And if only these facts are reliably and correctly observed *as* facts, then it can remain a matter of indifference to us economists, what the profounder explanation of the facts may be, and how much the psychologists in that profounder explanation may differ from one another or actually go astray. Aberrations at those profounder levels, the correction of which we must, in actual fact, leave to the pure psychologist, do not exert any influence on the confines within which our science moves. And divagations in the superficial strata of fact which are a disturbing factor solely within the limits of *our* explicatory activity we are able and are entitled to help correct. In that action we must rely on our scientific need and on a knowledge of the borderline facts, which it is at least likely that we are more intensively, more intimately and more minutely acquainted with than is even the pure psychologist himself.   196

It is in this sense that I have, in the course of this book, permitted myself a few careful trespasses across the border and then for the most part only in my *Further Essays on Capital and Interest*.[80] The care I exercised consisted mainly in taking pains not to go beyond the ascertainment of facts. But it also extended to calling a halt at the point where

79. "Das Wesen und der Hauptinhalt der theoretischen Nationalökonomie," a critical glossary by Wieser contributed to Schmoller's *Jahrbuch für Gesetzgebung*, Vol. 35 (1911), p. 914.

80. The most noteworthy of these are the investigations into the "measurability" of emotional magnitudes which are taken up in Essay X, and into the motivation of present economic actions through future wants which is treated in Essay XI.

the investigation ceased to be relevant to economics—the point beyond which only purely psychological considerations prevailed. It may not be impossible that the modest "leg work" performed in the collection and sifting of a special mass of factual material may promote or stimulate the cause of pure psychology. At least that has frequently been the case in the past in the matter of the relationship between the economic and the psychological theory of value.[81] Should that be the case, I could not consider that my activity were any disadvantage to the cause of psychology.

B. Degree of Value and Degree of Emotion

WE SET up the proposition before that the essential nature of value lies in the importance which goods have for our well-being. We laid down the rule that the magnitude of value is to be measured by the difference in well-being, the difference in pleasure or pain, which depends on the possession or nonpossession of a good. According to our theory then, what we must in the final analysis reckon with is magnitudes of feeling, of emotion.

But the objection we hear is that one cannot, one must not reckon with magnitudes of emotion. They are not of a rational nature, they are not commensurable, says one objector.[82] They cannot be measured says another. "It is impossible for me to say that one object is 1¼ times as pretty, or 1⅙ times as delicate or elegant as another, that this personality is 1⅕ times as charming or as cultured as that one. By the same token

---

81. There have been statements in recent years, as interesting as they are thorough, concerning the relation between economic theory and psychology. Pre-eminent among these are Max Weber's "Die Grenznutzlehre und das psychophysische Grundgesetz" in the *Archiv für Sozialwissenschaft*, Vol. 27 (1908), p. 546 ff., and the work by Wieser which has already been mentioned, the discussion of Schumpeter's work entitled "Wesen und der Hauptinhalt der theoretischen Nationalökonomie" which appeared in Schmoller's *Jahrbuch*, Vol. 35 (1911), p. 909 ff. I believe that *in the main* I am in agreement with both writers. I am completely so with respect to two points, namely, that most of the psychological facts which we have to take into account are familiar to us through our ordinary everyday experience, and that our economic explanations are by no means bound up with acceptance of any definite psychological doctrine. I believe, as Weber at one point so very aptly says (*op. cit.*, p. 552 ff.), "the results of the marginal utility theory do not in the slightest depend for their correctness on even the greatest conceivable revolution in the basic hypotheses of the biological and psychological sciences." However, I do believe that in their *manner of expressing themselves* both authors are more vehement than is either necessary or correct in deny-

ing the relationship which, after all, does exist in some measure between ourselves and the psychologists. Even Wieser, it seems to me, appears to go somewhat too far when he says, "You may say, if you wish, that we are and wish to remain psychological laymen" (*op. cit.*, p. 915). But certain statements of Weber's may definitely be said to overshoot the mark—statements the intention of which is to convert the divergence between psychology and economics into outright opposition. "The theory of marginal utility and any economic theory at all does this" (namely, an "overcoming" and a "sublimation" of "everyday experience") "not in the manner and by the methods employed by psychology, but rather along lines *diametrically* opposed to them . . ." (?) "All that" (what the economic theorists do) "is assuredly *the opposite* of any sort of psychology" (*op. cit.*, p. 554). In conclusion, I should like to refer anyone who wishes to be agreeably oriented on the general subject of the relation between economics and philosophy to the distinguished and soundly worked out book by Bonar which appeared in London in 1893 under the title *Philosophy and Political Economy in Some of Their Historical Relations*.

82. E.g., Schellwien, *Die Arbeit und ihr Recht*, Berlin, 1882, p. 198.

it is impossible for me to say this picture of my father or that book dedicated to me by a friend is worth to me 1¼ or 1⅓ times as much as the picture of my brother, or some other gift from an acquaintance, etc. The totality of the emotions, desires, interests, etc. that are in question in the one case as compared with those involved in the other case, is simply not divisible into units and is therefore not subject to measurement."[83]

The conclusions which our opponents draw from these premises vary, but in every case they are hostile to us. Some of our opponents admit that value (that is to say, subjective value) is founded on such incommensurable personal things as "interests, wishes, wants, purposes, aims, etc.," and yet declare that for that very reason such value is itself not measurable.[84] Others, again, accept it as a fact that value is measurable and indeed, that it is mathematically determinable, but consider that it is for that very reason impossible that the basis for measuring its magnitude can lie in incommensurable human needs, emotions and the like. A value that can be mathematically expressed, they say, must have its roots in and be measured by something that in turn can be mathematically expressed, such as, perhaps, labor or cost of production.[85] And quite frequently other and similar objections have been casually voiced or formally promulgated[86] and always specifically intended as a refutation of the theory of marginal utility and a denial of its fitness to furnish a competent foundation for the explanation of the phenomena of economic value.   197

9. Our Wants Are, in a Nonpedantic Way, Commensurable

If those opinions were followed out to their strictly logical conclusions, the resulting findings would be something that the originators of the opinions themselves probably never anticipated. For if our wants were really completely incommensurable, any sort of economic activity would become a sheer impossibility. For the generally recognized principle pervading all economizing consists in the attempt to derive the greatest benefit from the smallest sacrifice. But how is that to be accomplished, if we are not able to judge which benefit is the greater and which the lesser, whether a given benefit, because of its magnitude, outweighs the sacrifice that it requires? And how could we make that judgment if it were not possible at all to compare our needs, wishes, exertions from some single point of view, to reduce them all to a common denominator, and to form a judgment concerning their absolute and their relative intensity? In actual fact we do weigh and estimate our most subjective feelings and wishes every day of the week, every hour of the day. Even though every kind of satisfaction of a want provides us a different kind of pleasure, that does not by any means prevent us from forming a comparative judgment concerning the *degree* of that pleasure. It is quite true that the

83. Neumann in Schönberg's *Handbuch,* 2nd ed., Vol. I, p. 159 ff.
84. Neumann, *op. cit.*
85. E.g., Schellwein, *op. cit.*

86. By Lexis, among others, in his article "Grenznutzen" in the supplementary volume to the first two editions of the *Handwörterbuch der Staatswissenschaften.*

pleasure that I derive from a cold bath and the pleasure afforded by listening to a symphony concert are as far apart as the poles, and both of them widely different from the pleasure I take in appeasing my hunger. And still every one of us knows perfectly well which of the three enjoyments is for him the greatest at any given moment. In exactly the same way the pain that is caused by a pin prick is entirely different in nature from that of a toothache, but that prevents no one from deciding that a toothache causes greater pain than a pin prick. If our feelings of pleasure and pain were really indeterminable, we should forever be utterly perplexed. For since even the richest man does not have sufficient means to satisfy all his wishes, we should have absolutely no basis for determining which wishes and which needs should be accorded preference. And then we might one fine day have the experience, in all seriousness and not in jest, of dying of thirst amid a plentitude of water, simply because, being confronted by the necessity for choosing between using the available water to slake our thirst, and irrigating our fields with it, we unfortunately accorded too exclusive a preference to the latter alternative. The fact that we economize at all is the best proof of the fact that our feelings of pleasure and pain cannot be said to be inherently impossible to determine. The only point that can be in dispute is what kind of determination can be achieved.

198 We should be permitted to hope for unanimity on the question of man's ability to decide whether one pleasurable emotion is stronger or weaker than another. And it should even be reasonable to suppose that there can be no doubt that we can judge whether one feeling of pleasure is considerably or only negligibly stronger than another. But is it possible for us to determine the degree of difference more exactly, and express it in numerical terms? Can we judge whether pleasurable emotion A is, let us say, three times as great or strong as pleasurable emotion B?

10. Examples of Practical Commensuration in Everyday Life

I believe we can really do that or something very much like it. Or, to express myself more carefully, that we at least *undertake* to form numerically determined judgments on the magnitudes of pleasures. And as a matter of fact, we *are compelled* to undertake to do so as a practical necessity, because it is the only way for us, in cases without number, to arrive at a basis for a rationally practical decision. For we are on innumerable occasions in everyday life placed in the position of making a choice between several enjoyments which, because of the limitations of our means, it is impossible to attain all at the same time. Moreover, the situation is often such, that our alternatives consist of a rather greater pleasure on the one hand, and on the other of a multiplicity of smaller enjoyments of a single kind. No one will doubt that it is quite within our capacity to come to a rational decision in cases of that sort. But it is equally indubitable that for such a decision it is not enough to be able to judge merely that a pleasure of one kind is greater than a pleasure of another kind. Nor is it enough to judge that a pleasure of the first kind is considerably greater than one of the other kind. No, the decision has to be based strictly on how many smaller pleasures will counterbalance one pleasure of the first kind. And if we may assume that within the group of smaller pleasures, each is equal to each of the others, we are then actually making a decision as to how many times greater the one pleasure is than the other.[87]

Let us imagine a very simple example. A boy owns a dime, let us say, and wants to buy some fruit. His dime will buy either one apple or six plums. Naturally he will make a mental comparison of the gustatory pleasure to be derived from each kind of fruit. But in order for him to make his choice it will not be sufficient for him to decide whether apples taste better to him than plums. He must give his preferential judgment numerical definitiveness to the extent that he must make up his mind whether the enjoyment of one apple in comparison with the enjoyment of one plum (provided we can assume equal enjoyment of each of the six)[88] attains a ratio of more or less than six to one. Or we can modify the example so as to make the point stand out even more sharply. Let us imagine two boys, one of whom has an apple and the other of whom has some plums. The latter would like to make an exchange by which he can acquire the apple and he offers the first boy some of his plums. The latter, imagining the amount of enjoyment he will derive from the taste of the plums, refuses to accept four, and five and then six plums. When he hears the offer of seven plums he begins to hesitate, and finally gives up his apple in exchange for eight plums. How can we regard this transaction, if not as a clear-cut numerical judgment that the enjoyment of eating one apple is more than seven times but less than eight times as great as the enjoyment of eating one plum?[89]   199

What the boys in this example do with apples and plums we all do with more serious things in our economic life. Certainly everyone has been in the position of having something offered to him for sale, finding it too dear, then having the price reduced, say from $30 to $25, and buying at that price. A transaction like that, too is nothing but a judgment that the enjoyment one anticipates from the good to be bought is more than 25 times as great, but less than 30 times as great as the

---

87. Let us suppose the smaller pleasures are not equal each to each of the others but rather that they represent a diminishing series, which in practical life occurs quite frequently in accordance with Gossen's law of diminishing utility. In that case the judgment as to the number required for a counterbalance would no longer be describable as a straight-forward addition of equal units. But it would still represent a mathematical determination of the sum of a number of intensities which is something closely akin to the former, and most certainly presupposes the possibility that a decision can be arrived at by that former method. For a more detailed treatment of this interesting complication the reader is referred to Essay x in my *Further Essays on Capital and Interest.*

88. See Note 87 just preceding.

89. This general line of thought was presented by me in my "Grundzüge der Theorie des wirtschaftlichen Güterwerts" where I used essentially the same language though I phrased it with perhaps just a little less precaution. Čuhel (*op. cit.,* Sec. 264 ff.) recently presented a series of well thought out and interesting counterarguments. However, I do not believe that his arguments impair the soundness of the idea itself, but rather bring out the necessity for formulating it more carefully, which is what I have this time made an effort to do. See my Essay x in *Further Essays on Capital and Interest.*

enjoyment one could derive from spending one dollar some other way.[90] Anyone who is fond of making psychological observations will find it easy to multiply examples of this sort of thing from personal experience. Of course we perform innumerable economic actions purely through habit and mechanically, as it were. But in many situations that do not follow the well-worn rut of every day habit, we do have reason for economical deliberation. And in those situations numerical computation and determination of the degrees of enjoyments and sacrifices are not at all rare. I might even maintain that for decisions of that kind we frequently make use of what can justly be called a sort of unit of measure. That unit is the degree of the enjoyment that we can procure by means of a unit of money, a quarter, a dollar, a ten-dollar bill, a hundred-dollar bill, etc. I believe that each one of us has in his head a definite conception of the degree of the enjoyment he can procure for certain sums of money, and that in any doubtful case he uses it to determine whether a given enjoyment is worth the money it costs. Naturally the degree of enjoyment that attaches to the unit of money varies with each individual, and it is smaller for the rich man, for instance, than for the poor man. Also, the kinds of enjoyment which furnish the measure will be very different for different individuals, and the man, let us say who has a refined taste for intellectual pleasures will use entirely different measures from those employed by the man of little culture.[91] But no matter what the situation may be with respect to the employment of degrees of emotion as virtual units of measure, there is one proposition which I confidently believe the foregoing exposition has in any event proved. And that is that we are not satisfied merely to judge whether

---

90. I should like to interpolate at this point the remark that the example of the dollar has much wider practical application than the example of the plums. Indeed, it may be less accurate to call it an example than an actual rule of practical life. But it is also subject in far lesser degree to the limitation pointed out in Note 87 preceding. For it is a matter of common knowledge that the marginal utility of the unit of money diminishes at a far slower pace as the number of available units increases, than is the case with supplies of some specific type of goods. The very simple reason is that most types of goods can serve only one type of need, and an accumulation of examples of a good within this one type of need soon encounters concrete needs of only diminishing grades of importance. But the means of exchange known as money serves for the satisfaction of every kind of need. And so any given degree of importance, even if within each category of need it can be paired with only one single concrete need, still will encounter, through all categories of need taken together, an extremely high number of concrete needs with which to be paired. Consequently a very large number of units of money can find parallel employment at the same level of utility in the various categories of need, that is to say, at the "marginal" level of utility. And the further consequence is, that for a moderately well-to-do man the value of a supply of $50 has a value which differs very little or not at all from a value fifty times that of a single dollar. On the subject of the slow decline of the marginal utility of money, see also Weiss, "Die moderne Tendenz in der Lehre vom Geldwert" which appeared in the *Zeitschrift für Volkswirtschaft*, Vol. XIX, pp. 536 and 543.

91. The cultured man, for instance, will waver when considering whether or not to make an expenditure of $20 and will say to himself, "For the same money I could go to the theatre five times." But I once knew a bricklayer who under the same circumstances was fond of saying to himself, "For the same money I could drink 200 schooners of beer."

one feeling of pleasure is greater than another at all, but that we also undertake to determine the amount of the difference.[92]

11. Concessions on Commensuration, Which However Do Not Invalidate the Principle

I am perfectly willing to make numerous and, in fact, quite extensive concessions. I concede without ado that determinations of magnitude of the kind described may not deserve the name of "measure" (at least not in its strictest sense) and that the expression "estimate" may better suit the case. It is obviously impossible in our field of activity to furnish a mechanical and accurate measure, like a footrule or a surveyor's chain. But it does appear to me that we are in no worse case than someone who has left his footrule and his surveyor's chain at home, and who nevertheless likes to judge the height of the people he meets on the street or the height of the buildings and trees that he sees. Even without using a tape—in other words, without actually measuring—I can judge whether, in absolute terms, a house is high or low, and whether in relative terms, it is higher or lower than another house, and indeed, I can approximate whether it is twice as high or three times as high. And it is just as possible for me to call upon my memory and to determine with approximate accuracy whether the enjoyment provided by the satisfaction of a given want is, in absolute terms, great or small or whether, in relative terms, it is greater or smaller than the pleasures derived from another satisfaction. And finally—though admittedly with less precision—I can even determine how many times as great or as small it is. 200

12. Nor Do Erroneous Estimates Themselves Invalidate the Principle

And I gladly make the further concession that estimations of the kind just described are by no means infallible, and indeed that they often turn out to be quite badly in error. For one thing, we never experience

---

92. Anyone who wants to draw very fine distinctions may make the observation that the decision "I like an apple as well as I do eight plums" is not identical with "I like an apple eight times as well as I do one plum." The first judgment contains no estimation of the difference between the two pleasures, but is, on the contrary, a statement that no difference exists between the two pleasures which are compared. That person will admit our ability to render a judgment of that kind but will deny our capacity for any direct measurement of differences in intensity. I am glad to concede the justice of that claim! But it is also true that the former judgment leads to the second which is inherent, as a logical conclusion in the first. We may very well be incompetent to determine by direct comparison the difference in intensity between the enjoyment of an apple, let us say, and that of a pear. But if we are competent to judge that we like an apple exactly as much as we do eight plums, and a pear exactly as much as six plums, then we are competent by way of a conclusion based on these two

judgments, to decide that we like an apple exactly 1-1/3 times as much as we do a pear. For our theory it makes no difference whether we arrive at such judgments directly or indirectly, so long as we are competent to arrive at them at all. The point of view set forth in this footnote is in all probability the same as that expressed by Wieser in his interesting remarks in the chapter called "Rechenbarkeit des Wertes" in his *Ursprung und Hauptgesetze*, p. 180 ff. He there makes the statement, on the one hand, that value is completely measurable and computable, and on the other hand expresses the opinion that we never reckon in differing but only in equal degrees of intensity. Incidentally, Čuhel (*op. cit.*, Sec. 273) speaks of the "scaling" of the need of well-being and of intensities of feeling which is not quite the same thing as a "measuring" of them. And still it would seem to represent a kind of numerical determination of the difference between two intensities of feeling. Indeed Čuhel himself makes that assumption (Sec. 272). Cf. also my Essay x on this point in *Further Essays on Capital and Interest.*

simultaneously the emotions of pleasure which we compare as to degree, but base our comparison only on pictures drawn from our memory, or even from our imagination and these can very often be quite deceptive. Each one of us can prove from his own experience that a pleasure that seems highly tempting at the moment is badly overestimated, at the cost of forgoing some acquisition of lasting usefulness for the future. But I cannot emphasize too strongly that the correctness of our theory is entirely unaffected by the question whether or not those estimations are *correct*. All that matters is whether they are *in fact* made. The matter stands as follows. We maintain that the magnitude of value of a good is derived from the magnitude of some gain in well-being. We encounter the objection that gains in well-being are not subject to measurement because emotions are "incommensurable" and cannot be computed. We answer by proving that, whether they should or should not be, *as a matter of actual fact* they really are computed, and thereby we have proved the reality of the supposition upon which we relied to begin with. The fact that the computations which are actually performed turn out to be inaccurate or erroneous does not establish the inaccuracy or erroneousness of our theoretical *explanation* of the estimations of value, but only of the *estimations themselves*. The case is simple. A correct computation of a gain in well-being leads to a correct estimation of value, an inaccurate computation to an inaccurate estimation, a wrong computation to a wrong estimation. And those all occur in real economic life with untold frequency. But the erroneous computation serves just as well to explain correctly the erroneous estimation of value, as the correct computation serves for the correct explanation of the correct estimation of value.[93]

If we draw up a balance sheet, with our assertions as against our concessions, I think we can register as the unshakeable net balance the following propositions.

1] Our wants, desires, and emotions are actually commensurable and the common point which serves as the basis for comparison is the intensity of the pleasure and pain that we feel.[94]

2] We have the capability of estimating, both absolutely and rela-

---

93. Perhaps this is the proper place to add what might seem a rather obvious commentary of a related character which, nevertheless, not all economists who deal with the theory of value seem to have retained constantly in mind. Philosophers and ethicists have, from their own point of view, ample justification for placing the greatest emphasis on the point that only on *worthy* things and aims should value be placed, in other words that valuation should coincide with the "true value" of things that are *rightly* "loved" and valued. But for the explicatory purposes of the economic theorist the distinction between a true value and a value erroneously or fallaciously attributed deserves no consideration at all. An unjustified and fallacious valuation, provided only it is as a matter of fact actually made, serves just as reliably to explain economic phenomena as does a justified and correct valuation. Our economic behavior is affected, not by the *true* importance attaching to the aims and objects with which our economic activities deal, but by the *opinion* that we have formed of them whether right or wrong. And so wherever in my exegeses I ascribe to the value of a good an influence on our economic behavior, I never mean, whether I say so expressly or not, an ideal "true" value, but the estimated value which is reflected in our opinion of the good.

94. I wish to state, with respect to the *duration* of these emotions (as contrasted with this intensity) that sensations are "two dimensional," as Jevons, following in Bentham's footsteps, has said (*Theory of Political Economy*, 2nd ed., p. 31). I am restricting myself to this very aphoristic comment on the factor of the duration of emotions, since the rôle it plays has encountered no doubts or objections.

tively, the degree of pleasure and pain which goods afford us or avert for us, respectively. And we actually exercise that capability, entirely aside from the occurrence of errors in the estimation itself.

3]   It is just these determinations of the magnitude of pleasure and **201** pain which constitute the basis for our behavior with respect to goods. And that not only applies to the mental judgment concerning the magnitude of the importance which those goods have for our well-being, or in other words to our estimation of value, but it applies as well to our practical economic activities.

4]   Hence it follows that economic science is by no means in a position where it may permit itself to leave out of consideration the subjective needs, emotions, etc. and the subjective value based thereon. Quite on the contrary, economic science must seek in those very phenomena the roots of the explanation of things economic. A science of economics which fails to develop the theory of subjective value is building its house on a foundation of sand.

C. The Intellectual Demands of the Process of Valuation [95]

THE objection may be raised against the theory of subjective value that has been presented here that it gives credit to the common man for complicated deliberations which he does not actually perform. The computation of marginal utility—so the charge may read—requires us on each occasion to muster before our mind's eye all the concrete wants which can be satisfied by a good and then all the examples of the good that are at our disposal and finally to observe what is the last degree in the scale to which the satisfaction extends. But that—the charge would continue—represents highly involved labor to be performed by the imagination, and would attain astronomical proportions where goods of remotely higher order are concerned, since there it would have to be done not only for the good itself which is to be valued, but also for all its intermediate products. And the objection would follow that we do not in actuality make our valuations by any such laborious and time-consuming process.

That is quite correct. Our valuation is not a laborious process. Why?

The first reason is that through unremitting practice we have become astonishingly expert at it. The beginner in the act of reading finds it necessary to study the individual characters in every word in order to spell it out and combine them. The tyro at the piano, when he strikes a chord, must bear in mind the individual notes of which the chord is composed and give his attention to each of the intervals between them. In the same way the tyro at economizing would find it necessary to perform an assembling of the economic situation on which he is to base his valuation, comparable to the composing of a mental mosaic, stone by imaginary

95. The statements in this section are, for the most part, taken word for word   from my "Grundzüge der Theorie des wirtschaftlichen Güterwerts," Part I, Chapter VII.

stone. The experienced economizing subject creates and oversees the whole in one rapid sweep. There is one additional circumstance which places the economic expert in a position much more favorable than that of the piano virtuoso. It is the virtually universal rule that the former has absolutely no need for such minutely exact performance to arrive at his judgments of value. As long as his errors in valuation are not excessively wrong, as long as *he* strikes *his* keys with only a tolerable number of "sour notes," his performance will do well enough for the purposes of economic life. In fact, the underlying principle of economic behavior not only does not encourage overmeticulous care in ascribing values, it positively forbids it. To be sure, the most exact judgments of value do guarantee the most correct and therefore the most successful activity. But greater exactitude is to be purchased only at the price of a sacrifice in time and energy which increases as the exactitude increases, a sacrifice that is inevitably connected with careful consideration of all the circumstances. Up to a certain point the advantage to be gained for the conduct of our lives through more careful orientation may outweigh the sacrifice it entails in intellectual effort. And up to that point the expenditure of such effort is economically well advised. But beyond a certain point the reverse certainly becomes true. If anyone insisted on deliberating with maximum scrupulousness every one of the economic acts he undertakes every day, if he insisted on rendering a judgment of value thought out to the last detail concerning the most trifling good that he has to deal with by way of receipt or expenditure, by utilization or consumption, such a person would be too much occupied with reckoning and deliberating to call his life his own. The correct maxim and the one which would be observed in economic life is "Be no more accurate than it pays to be." In really important things, be really exact; in moderately important things be moderately exact; in the myriad trifles of everyday economic life, just make the roughest sort of valuation.[96]

Then there is a *second* reason why we very frequently find it quite unnecessary to strain our virtuosity to its full extent in the appraisal of economic situations. There are aids and auxiliaries to make the business of ascribing values considerably easier. One such aid is memory. It is not necessary, every time we decide on an economic act with reference to a good, to build up our judgment of its value from the very foundation. On some former occasion we already formed a judgment on its value, we remember it and make use of it again in the present case. We may safely use it so long as our economic situation has not changed essentially— and in the lives of most people economic cares describe such a regularly repetitious course that the old judgments of value remain usable for a long time. It would never occur to a housewife who goes marketing every day to propound questions and work out answers each day all over again

---

96. Does that mean, then that we do not, in the majority of cases, give any consideration to marginal utility and that our theory of marginal utility is wrong, after all? Certainly not! In every process of deliberation, even the most cursory, the object of evaluation is always the marginal utility, always what change in our well-being depends upon the good. In even the most inexact of estimations it can no more be said to cease to be the guiding principle of such estimation than the height of the column of mercury can be said to cease to be a guiding principle merely because the degrees are not read off the thermometer in tenths and hundredths, with the aid of a slide rule.

about the use value of a pound of meat, a dozen eggs, a loaf of bread. She merely calls upon her memory where the judgments of value with which she is concerned lie ready to hand.[97]

In fact, it is not even necessary that the judgments of value stored up in memory be derived from one's own experience. Advice and instruction are available, the judgments of others who have been active in similar economic situations are there to be looked at, there are old customs and habits that can be followed. The laboring man's child, before it can acquire first hand knowledge by forming its own judgment concerning the marginal utility of various things, finds that certain judgments have already been impressed on its memory. A dollar, a chicken, a pound of roast beef are valuable things; a nickel, a slice of bread are far less highly valued, but a house has infinitely greater value. The schoolboy in the elementary grades can use the rules of multiplication and division without having devised them himself; the student of history can absorb and convey historical facts without having performed the research that uncovered them in the original source material. In exactly the same way do we base innumerable judgments of value on what others have thought out before us and for us.

And finally there is another factor to ease our task and that is the organization of our economic life on the basis of division of labor and exchange. This factor serves us particularly in the instances in which otherwise the task of ascribing value would be the most difficult of all. I refer to the cases which involve estimating the value of goods of the remotely higher orders of production. Suppose a long series of intermediate members intervenes between the good to be appraised and the marginal utility that is applicable. Or assume that at each of the numerous stages of production there is an addition of complementary goods, the functioning of which complicates that of the good to be valued. How difficult it then is to retain a comprehensive oversight of such involved relationships and to say with even approximate certainty: "This much and no more of the ultimate marginal utility depends on our good." But we do not need to render this difficult decision at all. For division of labor has elevated almost every stage of the production process to an independent branch of production. For that reason anyone who possesses a good of higher order will almost never himself pass it through all the metamorphoses that it must traverse to arrive at the final form of the finished consumption good. Instead he simply advances it one step nearer to its final purpose and then sells it to the entrepreneur of the next stage of production. And for that reason he does not, even when estimating the subjective value that the good possesses for him, need to concern himself with the later stages of its functioning—stages which will eventuate quite outside the sphere of his interests. His only question is, "How many goods of the next lower order can I produce from the good? And how

---

97. It is, however, true that people who suddenly experience a complete change in their personal fortunes as, for instance, rich people who are suddenly reduced to poverty, are compelled to build up their judgments of value anew and "from the ground up." Before they succeed they have to learn through many a disadvantageous transaction and many a bitter experience that many of their long accustomed notions concerning the value of money, etc., have in their new situation become completely erroneous.

much value—and I mean exchange value—will they have?" Those are very simple questions, and every interested person can easily answer them within his own sphere.[98]

And so the intellectual labor that people have to perform in estimating subjective value is not so astounding as may appear after the description in the abstract of the basis for the valuation process. And incidentally, even if it were a considerably greater task than it actually is, one could still confidently entrust it to "John Doe and Richard Roe." Whenever there is a question of personal advantage, whenever any oversight incurs prompt punishment through the suffering of some loss or damage, the ordinary man becomes acute and sensitive. And the common people have furnished excellent proof of their sensitivity in economic matters by recognizing the essential nature of value long before the scientists did. Science was misled by confusing utility with value, and so it declared goods like air and water to be things of the greatest use value. The man in the street observed or sensed with greater accuracy and in spite of science treated air and water as they deserved to be treated, namely as things without value. And for centuries, long before science set up the doctrine of marginal utility, the common man was accustomed to seek things and abandon things, not in accordance with the highest utility that they are by nature capable of delivering, but in accordance with the increase or decrease in concrete utility that depends on each given good. In other words, he practiced the doctrine of marginal utility before economic theory discovered it.

---

98. I am quite well aware how easily this portion of my description can take on the appearance of argumentation in a circle. There is here some similarity to certain statements in Part A, in Chapter IV, on goods purchasable in any desired quantity. For this portion, too, seems to base the individual's valuation on socially established exchange values, whereas the latter themselves call for explanation on the basis of valuations by individuals. I therefore refer my readers at this point to the exposition in Part B immediately following, and more particularly to Chapter III of that Part. The material there is intended to fill a gap that has been left, up to that point, in my line of reasoning, and to meet the objection alluded to in this footnote.

Part B

PRICE

Part B—PRICE

Chapter I

Problems Confronting a
Theory of Price

FROM earliest times the actual problem confronting a theory of price was reputed to be the discovery and formulation of the laws which govern the conditions under which goods are mutually exchanged, which control their "objective exchange value," which determine the prices at which they are exchanged.[1]

We are speaking here of the *laws* of price. Can there really be such a thing?

1. Are There Really Laws of Price?

There was a time when that would have been an idle question. Early economic theory did not harbor a moment's doubt that there was a system of laws which applied to the prices of goods, nor that it was the office of economic theory to ferret out that system of laws and to announce what it should discover in the form of the "laws of price." The fruits of the indefatigable research which it transmitted to us were "the law of supply and demand" and the "law of costs." Later on there was a change. Methodological doubts arose which shook not only the prevailing faith in the traditional laws of price, but even the belief in the existence of any system of laws at all. This skepticism gradually trickled down from the specific writings on methodology until it reached the central system of the science of economics, where it has left its ineradicable marks. As is easily to be understood, the most distinct among those signs are discernible in the writings of German economists, whose enthusiasm for the methodological

Cross references by Böhm-Bawerk himself are based on original pagination of CAPITAL AND INTEREST, which are shown by these figures in the margin.

207

---

1. On the relation between objective exchange value and price, see the foregoing remark, p. 124. I wish to add here only the brief remark that I do not restrict the concept of price to the *money price*, as a number of English economists are in the habit of doing. On the concept of price cf. also my "Grundzüge der Theorie des wirtschaftlichen Güterwerte," pp. 478-480.

movement antedated and also exceeded that of all others.[2] Although the flood tide of methodological skepticism, if I am not mistaken, is ebbing, I should not care to ignore completely the question it has raised. And therefore I intend, without going into the question of methodology in general, at least to set down in unmistakable terms my own personal confession of faith as to what our duties of commission and omission are in the field of the theory of price.[3] The use of an analogy will make my task easier.

If we throw a stone into the middle of the glassy smooth surface of a tranquil lake we see the concentric waves spread out in perfect clarity and regularity in every direction. But if we are on the high seas we observe that the wind will blow in gusts which are perhaps approximately uniform as to velocity and direction, but never completely so. And that causes a movement of the waves which, observed as a large-scale, overall picture, reveals an unmistakably regular pattern but which, examined in detail, shows a multitude of minor deviations and irregularities. And if there is then a sudden change of wind, or if the ocean swell strikes a shore line of irregularly broken cliffs there results that wild confusion and that mass of crosscurrents which is known as breakers or surf, and which seems to have lawlessness as its only law.

If we seek the reason for this difference, we find it easily. In the first case only a single factor was responsible for the movement, and because it was the sole factor that was operative, it could achieve an entirely uncompounded result, completely in accordance with its own peculiar laws and undistorted by any disturbing factors. In the second case impulses of two different kinds were operative, but one was overpoweringly stronger and was thus able to lend to the composite result the approximate pattern of the effects peculiar to itself. And finally in the third case a highly variegated mixture of mutually antagonistic causes resulted in an equally variegated mixture of kinetic tendencies which impede and oppose each other in such a way as to destroy all semblance of regularity in the composite result.

---

2. On an earlier occasion I designated by name, as examples of such skepticism with respect to price laws, the treatment of the doctrine of price in Schönberg's *Handbuch der politischen Ökonomie*, as well as that presented in the well known textbook by Cohn, *Grundlegung der Nationalökonomie*, 1885, p. 487 ff.; see my *Grundzüge der Theorie des wirtschaftlichen Güterwertes*, p. 481 ff. But in very recent times Diehl, an author with a great liking for theoretical research and a long record of achievement in it, confessed to a very similar brand of skepticism. He writes in his *Sozialwissenschaftliche Erläuterungen* with respect to David Ricardo (1905, Vol. I, p. 141 ff.), "There is really no such thing as a *general* theory of price in the sense that the law of value furnishes a basic rule for the determination of price, and that individual prices constitute only deviations from this law of value. Quite on the contrary, it must be the province of the economic doctrine of price to investigate the tendencies observable in the setting of prices in individual important categories and groups of goods, and to become increasingly more conversant with them." And Diehl emphatically confirms this opinion when he writes, in the memorial publication which appeared in 1908 under the title *Die Entwickelung der deutschen Volkswirtschaftslehre im 19. Jahrhundert*, at the close of the chapter on the development of the theory of value and price, that he had "repeatedly pointed out the unsatisfactory character of the attempts to set up unified laws of value *and price*." The italics appear in the original by Diehl!

3. My general methodological confession of faith appears in its most concise form in my essay, "Zur Literatur der Staats- und Sozialwissenschaften" in Conrad's *Jahrbücher*, new series, Vol. xx (1890), p. 75 ff.

2. Over-Simplified Premise When
   Formulating a "Law" of Price, viz., Hypothesis
   Of Self-Benefit in Exchange as Sole Motive

It seems to me that completely analogous conditions bring about completely analogous results in the field of price phenomena.

Our human behavior is in general the result of the influence of causative factors, and our actions with relation to exchange are no exception. Depending on whether or not one aims at being precisely specific, the number of motives operative in the making of exchanges may be two or may be dozens and hundreds; the two will be egoism and altruism; the others will include such motives as, for instance, the quest of direct economic advantage, the quest of indirect advantage through attraction of clientele, or removal of competitors; disinclination to purchase of a personal enemy, of a political opponent, of nationals of a hostile country; anti-Semitism, vanity, vexation, stubbornness, vengefulness; the desire to bestow on another an economic advantage out of generosity or because of personal liking, the wish to punish someone, to impart a lesson, etc., etc. Any attempt to account for human behavior in the matter of setting prices by means of an explanation of men's motives may, perhaps, lead to a very instructive classification of numerous related motives into large groups, but it must inevitably entail a far-reaching specialization of those motives. For the injection of a slight additional element often signifies a complete reversal of behavior. The quest of selfish economic advantage, for instance, will bring about a radically different result according to whether the selfish advantage is the direct or indirect aim—let us say through underbidding a troublesome competitor. The seller's egoism will lead him to set his price high in the former case and low in the latter case. Or the basic motive "vanity" will effectuate diametrically opposite results when the vanity is manifested as a desire to be looked upon as a fine gentleman or "big shot" or as the wish to be looked upon as a particularly good business man and clever buyer.

209

Every motive tends to direct behavior in a given situation into certain channels. If we were always influenced in transactions involving price by a single uniform motive, for instance the motive of gaining for ourselves the maximum direct advantage in the exchange, then it would be possible at all times for the manner of functioning peculiar to that motive to develop untrammeled. And the price that became established under the exclusive influence of that motive would present an appearance no less clearly reflecting regularity and adherence to law than do the regular concentric waves set in motion by the stone thrown into the lake. And that is how economic science did, in actual fact, set up the hypothesis of selfish advantage in exchange as the sole governing motive, and thereon built the "law" of supply and demand which undertakes to predict with the precision of a mathematical formula the price that will be attained under any given relationship between demand and supply.

3. Reality Is Otherwise; There Are
   Numerous Intercrossing Motives for Exchange

But the situation is in reality otherwise. We very frequently, indeed even usually, act under the simultaneous influence of several or even numerous intercrossing motives, and the character of the resulting mixture varies greatly according to the number and the kinds and even the mutual intensity of the combining motivating forces. Naturally, then, their effects also intercross, with the result that the appearance of adherence to law which may be presented by our behavior is very materially distorted. That it is not completely destroyed would appear from the fact that in that case economists would never have been led to formulate a "law of supply and demand." Only in a portion of our cases do the determinations of price proceed exactly in accordance with the formula setting forth the law. In another portion the most that can be said is that a tendency to approximate some adherence to the law appears to struggle to manifest itself while leaving some margin for smaller or greater deviations. And finally, we encounter, for instance, acts of generosity which are disguised as a purchase, where the determination of price takes place in flagrant contravention of the "laws of price."

That is how the material is constituted, with which the price theorists have to deal. That constitution forces two questions upon our attention which must be answered at the very outset. The first is whether those cases which seem to conform only in approximate measure, or not at all to the rule, to the law, are really *sans* rule and *sans* law? And the second is, how can economic theory fulfill its explicatory duty with respect to them?

We shall find a useful hint toward the answering of these two questions if we consult our analogy. The layman may appear ever so well justified in saying that the welter of tumbling breakers and foaming surf is completely "without rule or regularity." But the physicist would only smile at the idea that any movement here could be the result of anything but the strictest adherence to kinetic law. He will, on the contrary, tell us that the extremely complex movement of the surf is the necessary and strictly regular product of the high degree of complexity evinced by the kinetic factors. He will say that when a wave strikes against such and such a sort of cliff, and then is traversed by the backlash or lateral impact of other waves at such and such an angle, then under the general laws governing the motions of waves no movement could possibly result other than that very movement which in its complexity must, to be sure, present to the layman's eye an external appearance of complete lawlessness. And if we will accord the matter some brief consideration, we will arrive at a completely analogous decision with respect to the apparently haphazard phenomena of price. If the "lawfulness" or regularity of human behavior consists in the fact that in the same situations the *same* motives result in the *same* actions, then it is entirely natural that *dissimilar* motives must result in *dissimilar* actions. If we know that in a sales transaction the buyer means to attain as a second objective the bestowal on the seller of a gift in disguise, then we shall certainly feel no astonishment, nor regard it as an abnormality if the price in this case turns out to be in excess of the usual market. That is no more a cause for astonishment than is the fact that a wave which breaks upon the shore behaves differently from a wave in the open sea; nor that a falling feather behaves differently in a vacuum from the way it does in the atmosphere; nor that a double charge of gunpowder imparts to a bullet a velocity different from that resulting from the normal charge. In the world of human behavior, just as in the physical world, when there is a difference of causative forces, the difference in the ensuing results is the normal consequence and no abnormality at all.

But how is economic science to perform its functions with respect to such cases which are apparently without rule, but in actuality only complicated?

4. First Step to Solve Laws of Price Is to Develop the Law of the Basic Phenomenon

Let us once more and for the last time, pattern our procedure after the physicist's. The first step he takes is to develop the *law of the basic phenomenon,* that is to say of the movement of waves, presupposing a single, simple causative kinetic factor. Once he has clarified that point, he proceeds to investigate the effect produced when the activity of other influences is added to that first and simplest situation. He studies the influence exerted by the interposition of an obstacle—say a firm wall—in the course of the wave, and further subdivides by determining the effect when it strikes the wall at right angles, and when it strikes it at an acute angle. He makes a further development of the laws of "interference phenomena" which result from the collision of several waves. And here again he makes an analysis segregating the various principal types that may eventuate, such as the case of waves pursuing a parallel course as against their following reciprocal transverse courses; the first case must be broken down into the parallel course in the same direction and the parallel course in opposite directions; further modifications may arise when the interfering waves are of the same length, and when of unequal length; or when crests and troughs coincide, or when they are half a "beat" apart, or have some other rhythmic difference, etc., etc. Of course, the physicist's research will not provide for a separate examination of each one of all the possible causes of interference, but he will select the 211 characteristic types in such number and with such variety as the nature of his general or specific explicatory problem makes it seem to him expedient. And so for instance, he will as a rule consider it sufficient to work out a law and a formula for the wave of an impact against a regular firm wall, without attempting to provide for every conceivable irregularity such as round arches, multiple interstices or cleft surfaces. However, some special circumstance may cause it to appear that some particular conformation assumes practical significance. There might, for instance, be a question of the method of construction to be employed in building a breakwater that required some unusual features. In that case the physicist would immediately establish the relationship existing between this one concrete conformation and the types of obstacle and resistance covered by his general investigation.

Our physicist, then, has clarified the modification resulting from one after the other of the typical causative factors which bring about a complication of the basic phenomenon of undulant motion. Now the effects which result when many or all of the several types interact simultaneously will also cease to be a riddle. He simply analyzes what appears at first sight to be a chaos of surf, his reason breaks it down into a multiplicity of individual movements each of which is now familiar, and the manifestation of a well-known system of law. But the same physicist would certainly consider it to be as absurd as it would be hopeless, to begin by attempting at the very outset to explain all the interference phenomena without previously reducing to a rational basis both for himself and for others, the law governing the simple motion of a wave.

5. Most Basic Motive in Exchange Consists of A Quest of a Direct Benefit Through Exchange

Now it is my belief that the price theorist has every reason to follow the same procedure. He, too, will have to begin by developing the law of the *simple basic phenomenon.* If he cannot succeed, before all else, in discovering a rational basis for the determination of price under the influence of only a single motive, then he will certainly labor in vain for a rational understanding of the complicated phenomena resulting from the simultaneous interaction of numerous heterogeneous motives. But what is here to be regarded as a basic phenomenon? On a purely psychological basis, each one of the hundred individual motives that are capable of exerting an influence in exchange transactions is co-ordinate with each of the others. Since, as a matter of pure psychology, there is no reason why the quest for selfish benefit, for instance, has no inherent claim to precedence over the desire to bestow a gift, it would be quite possible for a competitive struggle to arise—and one that could never reach a decision—as to which of the hundred possible motivating impulses should be considered a "basic force," the functioning of which should therefore be considered the "basic phenomenon." But though the intrinsic reasons cannot decide this issue, extrinsic considerations very definitely do. For there is an enormous difference in the scope and in the intensity of individual motives with respect to their influence on exchange transactions. One motive towers far above all others, and that one is *the quest for the attainment of a direct advantage through exchange.* And most naturally so. Exchange is a process by which one intends, for a consideration, to obtain something for himself. Hence it no less lies in the nature of things than it is the fruit of our experience that, save for purely nominal transactions, the desire to gain an advantage through exchange is almost never absent, and that in the enormous majority of cases it has the lion's share of the influence that determines our exchange transactions. That justifies the methodological choice of those price phenomena which take place under the exclusive influence of the quest for gain through exchange, as those to be regarded as the "basic phenomenon." We may, in consequence, look upon the laws governing them as the "basic law," and regard as mere modifications of that basic law such divagations as arise through the contributory influence of other motives. In doing so we act precisely as does the physicist who, for purposes of his research into the behavior of falling bodies, regards gravity as his basic force, and falling under the exclusive influence of gravity (in other words, in a vacuum) as his basic phenomenon, but the contributing influence of resistant media such as air, water, and the like, simply as "resistance," as obstacles, and so on.

6. Böhm-Bawerk Lists Almost a Score Of Secondary Factors Affecting Price; Two Approaches: General Law and Individual Cases

Accordingly, it seems to me expedient to divide the problem of the theory of price into two parts. The first part concerns the necessity for developing *the law of the basic phenomenon in its purest form*. That is to say, developing the system of law which manifests itself in the phenomena of price under the presupposition that all persons participating in an exchange are actuated by the one single motive of the quest for the attainment of an immediate benefit through exchange.[4] The second part of the problem consists in incorporating into the basic law the modifications which result from the contributory activity of other motives and factual circumstances. This will be the place to expose the influence of certain other motives, having due regard to what the situation demands and what may be expedient, and accordingly indicating mere approximations at certain times and at others making observations with complete accuracy. The typical and widely prevalent "motives" which will come in for treatment here will include such things as habit, custom, justice, benevolence, generosity, laziness, pride, national enmities, race prejudice. All considered, of course, in relation to their influence on the determination of price. But this second part is also the proper situs for revelations concerning the function performed by certain highly concrete institutions such as monopolies, cartels, coalitions, boycotts, governmental sales taxes, boards of arbitration, boards for the awarding of damages, labor unions and many other organizations which in modern times are fond of interposing socialization measures and a state-controlled economy as a "breakwater" to combat the force of the egoistic price waves.

7. Two Schools of Economists:
(a) General Theorists, Exemplified by English Classicists, and
(b) Researchers in Specific Cases, Exemplified by Historical School in Germany

The amount of attention devoted by economists to each of these two parts of the theory of price has varied with the prevailing phase in methods of research. As long as the abstractly deductive phase characteristic of the English school was in the ascendancy, the first part of the price problem was almost the only one to be treated, and much too nearly to the complete exclusion of the other. Later on, the historical method, originating in Germany, took over the lead. It was characterized by a fondness

---

4. The presupposition must be made in the exact terms in which they appear above in the text, if there is to be any guarantee of the pure character of the basic phenomenon. If we were simply to presuppose, as is often done, an impelling motive in such general terms as "quest for economic advantage" or, in still more general terms, as "selfishness," then some particularized motives would, as has been mentioned on occasion, have to be included here which have diametrically the opposite effect on human behavior. On the other hand, Neumann once said (in Schönberg's *Handbuch*, 2nd ed., p.

286) that it is necessary to restrict the presupposition to selfishness that is constantly of uniform intensity and power. That, in my estimation, is carrying the thing too far. For if there is in our psyche no room for any other motive than selfishness anyhow, then the weakest degree thereof will direct our behavior along the same lines as will the strongest. The degree of strength or intensity of the motive can exert an influence on the net resulting behavior only when it is a question of the overcoming of other competing motives.

213 for emphasizing not only the general, but the particular as well, for noting not only the influence of the broader types, but also that of national, social and individual peculiarities. During this phase there was indeed a zealous and praiseworthy retrieving of neglected duties in connection with the second part of the problem. But there was also a less praiseworthy and excessive zeal, attributable perhaps to an understandable tendency toward reaction, which manifested itself in according just as exclusive a preponderance of attention to the second part, as the first part had previously enjoyed. *

8. Böhm-Bawerk Opts to Follow British Classicists and Considers Price Determination Under the Circumstances That a Man Will Act in a Manner to Accomplish What He Prefers More to What He Prefers Less

It is my own intention to occupy myself here and now with the first part of the price theory exclusively. I am going to develop the basic law of the determination of price solely on the hypothesis of the singlehanded dominance of the quest for direct advantage through exchange. In order to prevent any misunderstanding from the very outset, I wish to declare explicitly that I make no claim that I am thereby offering a complete explanation of the phenomena of price. I acknowledge that what I am offering indubitably calls for complementary treatment of the second part of the theory of price with a content such as I have sketched for it above. The justification for my decision to restrict my treatment nevertheless to the first part is not difficult. Above all, the working out of the second part would be an extremely extensive and demanding task in itself, and one which, on purely physical grounds, the scope of this present work would not permit me to incorporate. That is all the more the case, in view of the utterly different method of presentation and procedure which would be demanded and which would make it impossible to fit it into the character of the present work. Moreover, a great deal of work has been done and is being done, with the energetic and successful care characteristic of the school of research which I described as the second phase, the school which emphasizes the study of the concrete and the particular. On the other hand, the general theory of price has for some time now suffered neglect and its very necessary development has faltered.† And finally, I cannot and will not deny that, although I respect the scientific importance of attention to the particular, I still consider consideration of the general to be the far more important study, because it is fundamental. I find a satisfactory situation with respect to the price theory inconceivable, unless that theory can find a basis in a satisfactorily clarified fundamental law of the determination of price. I am quite prepared to encounter a good deal of opposition to that statement even today, when a return to a

*PUBLISHER'S NOTE: In the United States economic schools of thought somewhat parallel to the Historical School in Germany would be the Institutionalists and the Econometricians.

†PUBLISHER'S NOTE: This has a cautious implication that the laws of price of Smith and Ricardo, Mill and Marshall needed fundamental improvement.

"propensity to theorize" has made undeniable progress in Germany. It seems to me to be neither appropriate nor possible to overcome that opposition by a formal proof, because of the highly subjective nature of the point at issue. There is just one point which I should like to commend to the attention of the contrary minded. It is a consideration which, to my mind, bears very important testimony in favor of the methodological importance of the fundamental law based on the hypothesis of individual advantage. I refer to the circumstance that even though in actual life that basic motive functions subject to the interplay of hundreds of other motives, such as benevolence, habit, the influence of special provisions of law, etc., the actual price structure nevertheless does not depart so very **214** far from the line it would take if it were subject to the exclusive influence of subjective advantage alone. I gladly concede that small differences in usefulness and rarity, or in costs of production can be buried and deprived of their effectiveness under the weight of those other factors. But the major differences will in all cases still exercise their effect. Or can it be denied that, by and large, the market price for a large landed estate will be higher than that of a smaller one? Or that an elegant house will sell for more than a miserable hut, a piano for more than a three-legged stool? Do not even the co-operatives sell high grade coffee for more than the common grades, sugar for more than coal, and caviar for more than sugar? Is it not "conventional" that the fee of a skilled physician or lawyer should exceed the daily wage of a day laborer or a porter? The rejoinder may be that all these are stale and self-evident platitudes. Granted. But they are so only because it is self-evident that individual consideration of benefit and of cost always remain paramount factors. And that is the very reason why we can go about developing that basic law which features the influence of the personal quest for advantage through exchange, knowing full well that in doing so we are developing that part of the price theory which, of all the parts, is the most indispensable to an understanding of price phenomena. And we may be especially sure that it is the most indispensable for accomplishing the particular purpose which was the aim of my interpolation at this point of a discussion of the theory of price. For that purpose was to establish the connection between the elementary phenomena of subjective value and the complicated phenomena of interest. *

---

*PUBLISHER'S NOTE: *A fragment,* as is this Extract *(Value and Price)* from Böhm-Bawerk's opus, *CAPITAL AND INTEREST,* will of course fail to reveal *fully* the excellent fabric of evidence and reasoning which Böhm-Bawerk eventually lays before his readers in explanation of "originary interest," that is, interest on loans, rent on land, and profits in business.

Part B—PRICE

Chapter II

The Basic Law of
The Determination of Price

Introduction

215   I SHOULD like to submit as a preface to this second chapter a few considerations that may make it possible to expose the content of that fundamental motive which constitutes the basic presupposition for all of the examination which follows.

1. Three Requisites to Exchange

The decisions that have to be made in any exchange transaction always revolve about two points, namely, (a) whether in a given situation one is to make an exchange at all, and (b) in case this is decided in the affirmative, on what terms one is to attempt to conclude the exchange. Now it is quite obvious that he who transacts an exchange with the aim of attaining a direct advantage, and with no other aim, will adhere to the following rules in arriving at the decisions mentioned above: he will make an exchange only (1) *if he can exchange to advantage;* (2) *he will exchange to greater advantage in preference to exchanging to lesser advantage;* (3) he will, finally, *exchange to lesser advantage in preference to not exchanging at all.*

It is probably unnecessary to clarify the proposition that these three rules are completely in the spirit of our basic motive and really constitute a translation of that motive into terms of practical behavior. But it is necessary to clarify one expression that recurs in each of them. What do we mean by "exchange to advantage"?

2. Necessity That There Be Inequality in Exchange

Obviously that means to exchange in such a way that in the goods he receives he gains a greater benefit for his welfare than he gives up in the goods with which he parts. Or, since the importance of goods for one's welfare is expressed in their subjective value, it means that the goods he receives have greater subjective value than those with which he parts. If *A* owns a horse and is to exchange it for ten barrels of wine, he can and will do so only if the ten barrels of wine offered to him have for him a greater value than his horse. Naturally the other party to the contract thinks likewise. He, for his part, is not willing to lose ten barrels of wine unless in their place he receives a good which, for him, possesses greater value. Therefore he will be willing to exchange his ten barrels of wine for *A*'s horse only if for him the ten barrels of wine are *worth less* than the horse.

216

From this we derive an important rule. *An exchange is economically possible only between persons whose valuations of the good and of the medium of exchange differ and, indeed, differ in opposite directions.* The potential buyer must ascribe to the good a higher value; the other a lower value to what he gives in exchange. And their interest in the exchange and also the advantage they gain from the exchange increases in proportion to the disparity between their valuations; as that disparity diminishes their gain from the exchange decreases; finally, if they do not differ at all, if their valuations coincide, an exchange between them becomes an economic impossibility.[5]

3. Fortunate Prevalence of Inequality of Evaluation

It is easy to see that the prevalence of division of labor must create infinite grounds for contrasting valuations, and hence infinite opportunities for exchange. For since every producer produces only a few kinds of commodity, but produces these in a quantity far exceeding his own need, he immediately faces a superfluity of *his own* product and a shortage of every other product. Hence he will ascribe to his own product a low subjective value and to the products of others a relatively high one. The producers of those other products will however, act just the other way around, and ascribe to his product, which they lack, a high value and to their own, of which they have a superabundance, a low value. Thus there results a situation favorable for the transacting of exchanges on a large scale, in that there are reciprocally contrasting valuations.

4. The Greater the Inequality, The Greater the Capability to Exchange

Let us pursue to its logical conclusions another idea which is implicit in the foregoing observations. We saw that an exchange is possible for an economizing individual pursuing his own advantage, only if he values the good to be acquired more highly than the good he himself possesses. It is patent that this relation will obtain the more easily, the lower anyone values his own commodities, and the higher he values the commodities of others. The owner of a horse for whom that horse has a subjective value of $50, and for whom a barrel of wine has one of $10, has a

---

5. If, for instance. *A* places the value of his horse at 5 barrels and *B* at 15 barrels, then the exchange at 10 barrels brings each a gain equivalent to the value of 5 barrels of wine. If *A* values the horse at 8 and *B* at 12 barrels, the exchange nets each one a gain of the value of only 2 barrels. If, final-ly, the valuations of both coincided at 12 barrels, then *B* to be sure, would be glad to acquire the horse for 10 barrels or for any price lower than 12 barrels, but *A*, of course, would not be willing to part with it.—Cf. Menger, *Grundsätze der Volkswirtschaftslehre*, p. 155 ff.

much wider possibility, economically speaking, of effecting an exchange, or as we shall hereafter phrase it, has much greater *capacity for exchange* than a man who values his own horse at $100 and a barrel of some one else's wine at only $5. The former can obviously still make the exchange if he is offered as little as six barrels for his horse, while the latter must forgo the exchange unless he is offered, at the least, something in excess of twenty barrels. If a third man should value his horse at even so low a figure as $40, and on the other hand place on a barrel of wine a value as high as $15, he would obviously be economically capable of making an exchange if the price went down even to *three* barrels of wine. That gives us the general principle that *that candidate for exchange has the greatest capacity for exchange who places the lowest valuation on his own good in comparison with the goods of others which he wishes to acquire. Another way of saying the same thing is that in comparison with the good of his own with which he is to part he places the highest value on the goods of others.*

217

Having made ourselves adequately conversant with the meaning and the content of our basic motive, we can now progress to our real problem. That problem is the development of the influence exerted, in accordance with regular laws, by the functioning of that basic motive on the determination of price. For this part of our problem I consider the methodological procedure of a few illustrious predecessors to be by far the most appropriate. They begin by demonstrating, in the case of selected typical examples, how under certain assumptions the determination of price will and must of necessity result. They then strip away such fortuitous trappings as may attach to the examples in order to leave what is typical and universally valid. That they formulate in laws. I shall begin with the simplest typical case, with the determination of price in an isolated exchange between a single pair of candidates for exchange.

A. Determination of Price in Isolated Exchange

FARMER *A* needs a horse, and his personal circumstances are such that his need for the horse represents an urgency of such degree that he attaches as much value to the possession of a horse as he does to the possession of $300. He goes to his neighbor *B* who has a horse for sale. If *B*'s personal circumstances were such that he too places a value on the horse as high as on the possession of $300, or higher, there would, as we know, be no possibility of an exchange between these two farmers. Let us therefore assume that *B* places a considerably lower value on his horse, say, a value of only $100. What happens?

In the first place it is certain that there will be an exchange. For under the conditions as assumed, each of the parties can make a considerable gain by effecting the exchange. If they make an exchange for instance, of the horse against $200, then *A,* for whom the horse he desires has a value of $300 will obtain a gain having a value of $100;

B obtains an equal gain, since for a good that was worth only $100 to him he now obtains $200. In accordance with the principle "better a lesser advantage than no exchange," the two will at all events agree on the exchange at a price which is advantageous to both of them. How high will that price be?

This much at least can be said with certainty: The price will certainly have to be lower than $300, otherwise *A* would have no economic benefit and hence no motive to effect the exchange. And the price will certainly have to be higher than $100, otherwise the exchange would entail a loss for *B* or at least be without benefit. But at what point between $100 and $300 the price will be fixed cannot be predicted with certainty. Every price between these two limits is economically possible, one of $101 being just as much so as a price of $299. This leaves a wide margin for bargaining. The price will be depressed or raised in the direction of the low limit or the high limit according to whether the buyer or the seller in the course of the transaction exhibits the greater cleverness, craftiness, stubbornness, persuasiveness, etc. If both parties   218 are equally proficient in bargaining, then the price will be determined at a point somewhere in the neighborhood of the midpoint of the gap, that is to say at around $200.

Let us briefly summarize whatever is here capable of being formulated as a law. *In an isolated exchange between two persons desiring to effect an exchange, the price will be determined within a range which has as its upper limit the buyer's subjective valuation of the good, and as its lower limit the seller's valuation.*

B. Determination of Price With One-Sided Competition Among Buyers

LET us now modify the conditions of our example to fit the next type of case by assuming that farmer *A* who wishes to buy finds that *B*, possessor of the horse, is already being visited by *Aa* who likewise has come with the intention of acquiring the horse that *B* is offering for sale. Now *Aa* is personally so situated that the possession of the horse is, in his estimation, to be valued as the equivalent of the possession of $200. What happens now?

Each of the two competitors wants to buy the horse, but of course only one can do so. Each of them desires to be that one. And so each will make an attempt to induce *B* to sell the horse to him. The means of doing so is to offer a higher price than does his competitor. That brings about the familiar situation where the bidders alternately overbid each other's offers. How long will that continue? Just as long as the rising prices that are offered remain within the valuation of the competitor with the lesser capacity for exchange, who in this case is *Aa*. That is to say, as long as the bids still remain below $200 *Aa* will be guided by the principle "rather a smaller gain than no exchange at all," and *Aa* will, up to that point, continue to raise his bids in order to win the competition for the exchange. Of course *A* will prevent that each time by raising his bid in turn. But *Aa* cannot go beyond the limit of $200, if the exchange is not to be a losing proposition for him. In this he is guided by the principle of the gaining of advantage but couched this time as the precept "better not to exchange at all than to exchange at a loss," and at that point he throws in the sponge.

All this does not necessarily mean that the price will finally be determined at exactly $200. It is possible that *B,* who knows how badly *A* needs a horse, will not be satisfied with $200 and that he may succeed through stubbornness or clever bargaining in exacting from *A* some price as high as $250 or $280 or even $299. The one thing that is certain is that on the one hand the price cannot exceed $300, the value placed on the horse by the willing buyer *A,* and on the other hand cannot fall below $200, the valuation of the competing and defeated bidder, *Aa.*

Now let us assume that in addition to *A* and *Aa* there are three more willing buyers—call them *Ab, Ac,* and *Ad*—who compete for *B's* horse. Their individual positions in life are such that they place a value on the horse amounting to $220, $250, and $280 respectively. In that case it can readily be perceived that in the competitive bidding that develops *Ab* will stop bidding when the price reaches $220, *Ac* when it goes to $250 and *Ad* when it reaches $280. Competitor *A,* however, will remain the one with the greatest capacity for exchange, and the price as finally determined will necessarily fall between $300 as the upper limit, and $280 as the lower limit, which is the value placed on the horse by the most pertinacious of the unsuccessful competitors.

Hence the results of this observation can be generalized in the following statement. *Where there is one-sided competition among willing buyers the competitor with the greatest capacity for exchange (that is, the one who values the good most highly in comparison with the consideration) will become the purchaser. And the price will fall within a range of which the upper limit is the valuation by the purchaser and the lower limit of which is the valuation by that one among the unsuccessful competitors who has the greatest capacity for exchange. This holds irrespective of the second subsidiary lower limit which is always the seller's valuation.* If we compare the foregoing statement with the typical case portrayed in Section (A), it becomes apparent that the effect of competition among buyers is to restrict the range within which the finally determined price will fall; and such restriction will be toward the upper end of the range. Between *A* and *B* alone the limits of the range of possible price were $100 and $300; through the addition of the competing buyers the lower limit of the range was raised to $280.

C. Determination of Price With One-Sided Competition Among Sellers

THIS case constitutes the exact counterpart to the preceding one. Entirely analogous trends lead to completely analogous results, except that the outcome is in the opposite direction.

Let us imagine farmer *A* as the only willing buyer and five owners of horses—let us call them *Ba, Bb, Bc, Bd,* and *Be*—each of whom, on a competitive basis, is offering to sell *A* one horse. We must further assume that the five horses are exactly equal in quality. Now *Ba*'s valuation of his own horse is $100, *Bb*'s corresponding valuation is $120, *Bc*'s is $150, *Bd*'s $200, and *Be*'s $250. Each one of the five competitors wants to exploit the sole existing opportunity for a sale to his own advantage. As in the previous case the means for assuring victory over one's competitors was overbidding, so in the present case it is underselling. But since no one is willing to offer his commodity for less than it is worth to himself, *Be* will stop underselling at $250, *Bd* at $200, *Bc* at $150. Then *Bb* and *Ba* will continue to vie with each other until at $120 *Bb* finds himself "economically excluded"[6] and *Ba* holds undisputed sway. The price at which he wins through to make the sale must exceed $100, otherwise he would gain no advantage and would therefore have no motive to make the exchange. But it cannot possibly exceed $120, otherwise *Bb* would have continued his competitive offering.

The case may be expressed in the following general terms. *When there is one-sided competition among sellers, it is again the competitor possessing the greatest capacity for exchange who consummates the exchange. That competitor is the one who places upon his own commodity the lowest valuation in relation to the buyer's good or medium of exchange. And the price must be determined within a range which has as its lower limit the valuation by the seller, and as its upper limit the corresponding valuation by the seller having the greatest capacity for exchange within the number of the unsuccessful competitors.*[7] In contrast to the case of the isolated exchange set forth in Section (A) where the price necessarily would be determined at some point between $300 and $100, in this instance the presence of competing sellers restricts the range of possible prices. And the restriction exerts its pressure downward.

D. Determination of Price With Two-Sided Competition

THE case of two-sided competition is both the most frequent occurrence in practical life and also the most important for the development of the law of price. We must therefore devote to it the most thorough attention.

6. Menger, *op. cit.,* p. 183.

7. Once more, of course, excepting and without prejudice to the second subsidiary upper limit which is the valuation by the buyer. But in the case of extensive competition among sellers this limit seldom has any practical significance.

The typical situation which this sort of case presupposes can be represented by the table below. That table conveys the picture of ten willing buyers and eight willing sellers each of whom wishes to buy or to sell, as the case may be, one horse. At the same time the table indicates the degree of subjective valuation applying to each of the candidates for exchange with respect to the commodity in question. The irregularity of the variation of the figures for those valuations is quite in keeping with the actualities of economic life. In actual fact the individual conditions of supply and demand which determine subjective value vary so widely that it is hardly possible that any two persons place exactly the same subjective value on any one thing.

The table is as follows:

Willing Buyer	Valuation of one horse	Willing Seller	Valuation of his horse
Aa	$300	Ba	$100
Ab	280	Bb	110
Ac	260	Bc	150
Ad	240	Bd	170
Ae	220	Be	200
Af	210	Bf	215
Ag	200	Bg	250
Ah	180	Bh	260
Aj	170		
Ak	150		

It is necessary to add to the foregoing description of the situation that all parties are present in the same market at the same time, that all the horses offered are equal in quality, and finally, that all the candidates for exchange are free from any misconception regarding the market situation which could prevent them from effectively pursuing their own interest.[8] Once more we ask, "What happens in this situation?"

5. Wise Buyers Exercise Restraint and Do Not Reveal Their Real Positions Immediately

Aa, whose individual circumstances cause him to value a horse at $300, would consider it to his advantage to buy even at a price of $290, and each of the eight sellers would certainly be most eager to sell his horse to *Aa* at such an advantageous figure. But obviously *Aa* would be acting most unwisely if he were to buy prematurely at so dear a price. For his interest demands not merely that he gain an advantage—any advantage at all—but that he gain a maximum advantage through the exchange. To that end he refrains from precipitately making the highest offer to which he could at the worst agree. He will prefer, instead, to

---

8. If, for instance, a buyer *erroneously* supposes that the supply delivered to market is materially smaller than actually is the case, then he may quite possibly concede a higher price than he would have needed to, if a correct knowledge of the situation had enabled him better to protect his interests. Of course, the theory of price cannot overlook the influence of such or similar mistakes, but this is not the place to consider them. It is our purpose at this point to develop only the simplest fundamental law.

begin with just as low offers as do his competitors of lesser capacity for exchange, and he will consent to raise his offer only at such time and to such extent as becomes necessary to prevent his exclusion from the exchange.

Similarly, *Ba* could, economically speaking, very well sell his horse for $110 and could very easily find buyers at that price. But he will carefully reserve the lowest offer that he *could* possibly accept, and will make his offer to sell only just low enough to remain in the competition at all for the sale. The transaction will therefore presumably begin with restraint, the willing buyers, on the one hand, offering low prices and the willing sellers, on the other hand, exhibiting the same restraint by demanding high prices.[9]

Let us assume the buyers begin with an offer at a price of $130. It is clear that in the absence of some gross error in the understanding of market conditions no sale will be concluded at that price. For all ten buyers place the value of a horse at over $130 and all ten would be willing to buy, while only two horses could, economically speaking, be offered at that price—the horses owned by *Ba* and *Bb*. It is clear these two sellers would be acting just as unwisely by failing to exploit the competition among the buyers to bring about a raising of the sale price, as would the buyers if they allowed the most advantageous purchase opportunities to be snatched away by two of their number without making an attempt to gain an advantage for themselves by offering a price somewhat higher, but still very advantageous. Hence, just as in the case described in Section B, there will have to be a sifting out of some of the large number of buyers through attempts on their own part to outbid each other. How long will that keep up?

At $150 all ten buyers can still remain in the bidding. From that point on the competitors with the least capacity for exchange must drop out, one after the other. At $150 *Ak* is forced to drop out, *Aj* likewise at $170, *Ah* at $180, *Ag* at $200. But at the same time, as prices rise there is an increase in the number of sellers for whom participation in the exchange becomes an economic possibility. From $150 up *Bc* can give serious thought to the matter of making a sale, at $170 *Bd* can do so, and at $200 *Be* can, too. Thus gradually there begins a shrinkage in the discrepancy, which at first yawned so widely, between the number of horses desired and the number effectively offered for sale. At $130 **222** there was an effective demand for *ten* horses and only *two* could have

9. The more experienced in business and the more familiar with the state of the market the people are who are seeking to do business on the open market, the more quickly do they terminate the preliminary "sounding out" by means of reserved or intentionally inadequate bidding. In a market where the action moves in "deep and well worn grooves" the participants will dispense entirely with extreme bids that have no prospect of acceptance at all; their very first offers will at least approach the zone within which the market price will ultimately fall. The extreme instance of abbreviated bidding is "fixed prices" which the sellers set by themselves. They represent a renunciation of all "sounding out" bids and are an attempt to predict with complete accuracy the exact zone into which market conditions will force the price. They *must* attempt to guess that zone accurately; for if they set the price lower, an opportunity for gain is lost, and if they set it higher, buyers will fill their needs in the market by patronizing other competitors, and the goods will not be disposed of. "Fixed prices" are concededly less customary in an open market than in shops. In the latter, sales are never made under the direct pressure of competition, and a miscalculation in the price asked is not quite so hazardous.

been economically offered for sale. Now, at a price of more than $200, there is an effective demand for only *six* horses and there are already *five* that can be offered for sale. The number of willing buyers exceeds by only one the number of competitors able to sell. Nevertheless, as long as the number of those desiring to buy is in excess at all, and this aspect of the market condition is correctly perceived by all parties, the business cannot be consummated. For one thing, the sellers still have the possibility of exploiting the excess in number of competing buyers to increase the price still more, and they have the inducement to do so. For another thing, the conflicting interests of the buyers compel them to continue to outbid each other. For *Af* would be making a poor defense of his interests if he supinely submitted to the action of his five competitors in buying the five most cheaply offered horses "from under his nose." For in that case *Af* would have absolutely no chance at all to make an exchange and hence to gain an advantage through such exchange.[10] At the same time none of *Af*'s competitors can permit him to acquire one of the five highest priced horses offered for sale. For if that happens, then the one who withdraws in *Af*'s favor, though he could still, to be sure, buy the horse he needs, would then have to get it from among the remaining less favorable exchange possibilities, the ones that are offered by the more stubborn sellers *Bf, Bg* and *Bh,* and then, too, at a price which *at the least* exceeds the subjective valuation that *Bf* places on his horse and hence exceeds $215. Thus the realization of their advantage impels all the buyers to continue to outbid each other above the $200 mark.

An important change in the situation takes place when the rising offers reach the $210 mark. Now *Af* is forced to drop out of the number constituting the "demand" and there are now only five making a demand aligned opposite five willing sellers. Since all the former five can be simultaneously satisfied, there is no longer any reason for them to drive each other out of the market by raising their bids. On the contrary, it is to their common interest, as against the sellers, to close their transactions at the lowest possible price. Hence the outbidding by the buyers which up to this time prevented a purchase being closed, now comes to an end, and *it is possible* to close at a price of $210.

6. Second Phase of Higgling on Price

But it does not follow that the closing *must* be at that price. It is possible that the sellers can be stubborn and that, hoping for still higher prices they refuse an offer of $210. What happens in that case? At first the willing buyers, in order not to fail after all to accomplish their purpose, will continue to bid. But they are getting close to their limit. For if the price demands of the sellers should exceed $220, then *Ae* would also have to forgo making a purchase and there would then be five willing sellers aligned opposite four willing buyers. In that case one of

10. Once the sellers *Ba* to *Be* inclusive have sold their horses, the seller with the greatest capacity for exchange that still remains is *Bf* whose valuation of his own horse is placed at $215, which is higher than the valuation of *Af*. Hence, as we already know, an exchange between them is economically impossible. The same is true in even greater degree of competitors *Bg* and *Bh* who have still less capacity for exchange.

the sellers would have to drop out. And since nobody wants to be the one to do the dropping out, motives will function that are similar to those that actuated the overbidding by the buyers when they were in the majority. Except that now there will be alternate *under*bidding by the sellers, who in number exceed the buyers until the fifth seller has found a buyer. And he finds him below the $220 mark.[11]

In fact, in our concrete example the price limit would have to be somewhat lower still. For as long as it were a question of a price exceeding $215, a sixth possible seller would arise in the person of *Bf*. His joining the ranks would put the sellers in the majority as against the five buyers and that would impose on those six sellers the necessity of taking measures to avoid being excluded from the exchange. And those measures would consist in under sell ing each other. Not until the weakest party to this competition meets defeat is the issue settled. And that defeat is the portion of *Bf* in the moment when the price demands of the competing sellers go below $215. At that moment the number of competitors in the group of sellers becomes equal to the number in the group of buyers, and that price is attained which constitutes the only one at which competition ceases. Hence we find in our example, (which presupposes economic behavior of all competitors and correct perception by them of the condition of the market) that the zone within which the price must of necessity be determined, lies between the limits of $210 and $215. For only within that zone do we have the only situation that meets the two conditions necessary to completion of the transaction. Firstly, all the parties who are still in a position to "talk business" can at that price gain an advantage. Secondly, all those who cannot at that price gain an advantage, that is to say, the excluded competitors, have no power to interfere in the business of the others.[12]

7. Four Crucial Questions

Let us cull from this long presentation of the facts those fruits which offer nourishment for our theory of price. We may deduce answers of broad validity to four questions. Two propositions concern the persons of the groups effecting an exchange, two concern the price at which the exchange is made.

8. Question and Answer No. 1

Our first question reads: "Among the competitors seeking to exchange, which ones actually succeed in doing so?" Our example gives

---

11. It is self-evident that the gradual "bidding up" by the willing buyers and the gradual "bidding down" by the sellers do not by any means necessarily take place as two separate and successive stages of the process. Rather is it to be expected that both activities as a rule, go on simultaneously.

12. It lies in the nature of things that the result derived in our abstract table eventuates with proportionately greater fidelity in actual practice, the more completely it is possible for all participants to be cognizant of the market situation as a whole —in short, the more concentrated the scene

of operations and the more complete the publicity. On the other hand, it is usually the case that the operations are carried on under such conditions that the respective groups, though able to communicate, are nevertheless separated in time or in space. In that case of course, within any one group the competitive conditions applying to *the market as a whole* are not fully operative. The result of that would be that the prices determined in the several groups would frequently only approximate more or less closely the ideal market prices derived by our table, without necessarily coinciding with them exactly.

us a completely precise answer; it is: *The competitors in both groups possessing the greatest capacity for exchange.* That is to say, it is the willing purchasers who place the highest value on the commodity (*Aa* to *Ae*) and the willing sellers who place the lowest value on it (*Ba* to *Be*).

9. Question and Answer No. 2

The second question is: "How many competitors on either side consummate an exchange?" The answering of that question is important, inasmuch as the definitiveness of the price laws we intend to set up must, as we shall soon see, depend on that answer. Let us begin by looking once more at our example. Five pairs effect an exchange. If we observe closely, we note that they are the same five pairs who, regarded individually, meet the economic requirements necessary to an exchange. That is to say, it is true of both members of each pair that each of them, as a contracting party, places a higher value on what he is to receive than he does on that with which he is to part. All those pairs of whom that cannot be said are excluded from accomplishing an exchange.[13] It is easy to convince ourselves that this is no mere fortuitous result, but rather a result based on inner necessity. There are two ways of so convincing ourselves—we can either multiply the number of concrete instances, or we can examine in detail the process by which the result came about. And in the course of doing so we shall also become convinced that the number of pairs is limited to such a number as we find meeting the required conditions when we pair them off in descending order of their capacity for exchange, first pairing together those with the greatest such capacity, next those with the second greatest such capacity, and so on.[14] We may therefore formulate the general rule as follows: The number of competitors of each class—buyers and sellers—who actually effect an ex-

---

13. In order for *Af*, in addition to his competitors *Aa* to *Ae*, to effect an exchange, it would have been necessary for a sixth seller to appear, one who would have been willing to offer a horse at a price economically possible for *Af*, that is, at less than $210. *Af* was excluded because there was no such *Bf*. And *Bf*, for his part, was excluded because there was no *Af* who would have been willing to pay a price economically possible for *Bf*, namely, one in excess of $215. If we should change the figures in our example so that *Af* also puts a higher valuation on a horse than *Bf*—say one of $216, then it can readily be seen that the "bidding up" would terminate between $215 and $216 and that then *Af* and *Bf* would become a sixth pair to be included among those actually effecting an exchange.

14. It would, to be sure, be possible to pair off the parties aiming to negotiate an exchange in such fashion as to have no fewer than eight pairs in which each willing buyer placed a higher value on the commodity than did the willing seller. Such a pairing would appear as follows:

Ak	$150	Ba	$100
Aj	170	Bb	110
Ah	180	Bc	150
Ag	200	Bd	170
Af	210	Be	200
Ae	220	Bf	215
Ac	260	Bg	250
Ab	280	Bh	260
Ad	240		
Aa	300		

But it is clear that economic behavior of all of the participants would preclude exchanges according to this pairing. If *Ba*, for instance, were to make an exchange with *Aj* he would have to be satisfied with a sales price well below *Aj*'s valuation, which he certainly will not do since he can get a higher price from any of the other willing buyers. Similarly *Ab*, if he made an exchange with *Bh*, would have to pay a price in excess of $260 which he would not be inclined to do, nor would he find it necessary to do so under prevailing market conditions. But as those willing to make an exchange refuse to deal with those who offer to trade only on unfavorable terms, the latter automatically suffer exclusion, and the number of pairs actually to consummate an exchange becomes restricted to that indicated in the text.

change may be determined by pairing off the competitors in descending order of capacity for exchange. The number of pairs making an exchange will then be equal to the number of pairs in which, in terms of quantity of the medium of exchange, the willing buyer places a higher valuation on the commodity than does the seller.

The third and fourth questions concern price directly.

10. Question and Answer No. 3

The *third* imposes the requirement that we establish that all exchanges effected under the influence of competition at any one given time are all consummated *at an approximately uniform price*. We did that in our example where we demonstrated that all five pairs would negotiate their exchanges at prices falling within the limits of $210 and $215.

11. Question and Answer No. 4

The most important question is the *fourth,* namely, *"At exactly what price is this uniform or 'market price' established?"* In no event may it be in excess of the valuation by *Ae,* and in no event inferior to the valuation by *Be.* For otherwise the price would have been so high, on the one hand, that the fifth buyer would have been excluded, or it would have been so low, on the other hand, as to exclude the fifth seller. And with either one excluded, no equilibrium would have been established. But it is also true that the price could in no event be higher than the valuation by *Bf,* nor lower than that by *Af.* For otherwise there would have been an addition, on the one hand, of a sixth bidder to the ranks of the willing buyers, or on the other hand, of a sixth competitor to the ranks of the willing sellers. And again the equilibrium would have been destroyed and there would have been no escape from a continuation of the over- and under-bidding until the price had been forced within the limits already noted.

Let us couch that conclusion in general terms. *Where there is two-sided competition the market price will become established at a point within a range having an upper and a lower limit. The upper limit is determined by the valuation by the last buyer to come to terms and the valuation by that excluded willing seller who has the greatest capacity for exchange. The lower limit is determined by the valuation by the last seller among those to come to terms, and the valuation by that excluded willing buyer who has the greatest capacity for exchange. The determina*tion of the limit by two valuations must be interpreted to mean that that valuation will prevail which in each instance makes narrower the range within which the price must fall.[15] Now in the above formulation let us discard the cumbersome and detailed description of the four persons described as the determining factors and employ the short and descriptive term of "marginal pairs." Then we arrive at the following most simple

225

15. In our example the deciding factor is furnished by the valuations by the excluded contracting parties *Af* and *Bf.* However, if the valuation by *Af* had been only $190 instead of $210, and if that by *Bf* had been $230 instead of $215, then the limits of the range within which the price would be set would have been the valuations by the last pair actually effecting an exchange. In other words, the price would have had to be set between $200 and $220.

formulation of the law of price. *Market price is established at a point within a range which is limited and determined by the valuations by the two marginal pairs.*

The result thus attained leads to a number of speculations which become significant for the total concept we must formulate of the process by which price is determined.[16]

12. Price Is Determined by Subjective Valuations

Pre-eminent among the objects of such speculation is the striking analogy between the determination of price and the determination of subjective value. The subjective value of a good is set up as a "marginal value" and is determined by the final utility which is situated at the very limit or margin of the economically permissible. And this is true quite irrespective of the more important uses to which certain individual examples of the total supply of the good may be devoted. In the same way every market price is a "marginal price" and is limited by the economic condition of those competing pairs who are situated at the very limit or margin of the "capacity for exchanging." Furthermore, it will be readily perceived that this analogy is not the caprice of coincidence, but rather a manifestation that related underlying causes in both cases bring about related results. In the case of subjective valuation the motive of economic advantage imposed the requirement that the available supply of a good must be utilized to satisfy wants in the descending order of their importance, whereby some particular want is satisfied last and thus designates the "marginal utility." In the case of determination of price the motive of economic advantage of the participants imposes the requirement that the pairs of contracting parties having the greatest capacity for exchange shall consummate exchanges in descending order of such capacity. The progression must reach one last pair which thus becomes the "marginal pair." In the former case there was assurance of the satisfaction of all

16. A few remarks of minor significance may well be assigned to this footnote. It is very easy to see that two-sided competition, in comparison with isolated exchange, tends to produce the result that the range within which the contracting parties are free to move becomes very much restricted; and that restriction takes place from both directions and to a very material degree. *Aa* and *Ba*, for instance, if they were dealing with an isolated exchange, could have come to terms anywhere inside the wide range of $100 to $300. But now they, and all the other contracting parties as well, are forced into that very restricted range which is all that remains open between the valuations by the marginal pairs.—Furthermore, it can now be perceived why we had to come to a definite decision, a little while ago, with reference to the question as to how many pairs of competitors actually consummate an exchange. For if that number were indefinite, or a matter of chance, then the persons who constitute our marginal pairs would also be indefinite and our whole law of price, which derives its formula for price from the economic situa-tion of those particular persons, would likewise be suspended in mid-air. There are critics who make that assertion even in the face of the complete exposition that I have presented. They include, for example, Zuckerkandl (*Zur Theorie des Preises,* 1889, p. 368 ff.) and in more recent times Bortkiewicz who took up anew the contention which Zuckerkandl had in the meantime abandoned. Bortkiewicz's contention appeared in Schmoller's *Jahrbuch,* Vol. xxxv, p. 432 in the course of his discussion of Davenport's *Value and Distribution.* Such critics probably fail to appreciate that my presentation of the answers to "the first question" and "the second question" on foregoing page 223 provides unequivocal definitiveness for my formula of the valuations by the marginal pairs. That part of my presentation seems to me to accomplish the very thing which Zuckerkandl quite rightly postulates as a requirement of any theory of price, namely, that it must indicate the natural location of the boundary line "which divides those desiring to make an exchange into two groups—those who succeed and those who fail."

wants surpassing the marginal utility in importance, even without the specimen which was being evaluated; and the only utility dependent on that specimen was the final or marginal utility. In the latter case there is consummation of exchange, even at higher or lower prices, on the part of all pairs surpassing the marginal pair in capacity for exchange; and the only pair whose fate is dependent on that exact price—neither higher nor lower—is the final or marginal pair. And finally, just as in the former case it is the importance of the last dependent want which, by virtue of this relationship of dependence, assigns to the good its value, just so in the latter case is it the economic circumstances applying to the last pair of contracting parties which assign a price to the good being exchanged —and again this takes place by virtue of that same relationship of dependence.

But the foregoing analogy by no means exhausts the relations between price and subjective value. It is of greater significance that *price is, from beginning to end, the product of subjective valuations.* Let us retrace our mental steps. It is the relation between the subjective valuations placed upon the good and its medium of exchange which determines who can entertain any idea at all of entering the competition to exchange the   226
one for the other—that is to say, it determines who possesses "capacity for exchange." That same relation determines the degree to which each competitor possesses that capacity. For each one of them it establishes with inexorable exactitude the point up to which his economic advantage demands that he continue to compete and just as exactly the barrier which forces him to concede defeat and to withdraw to the ranks of those whom his competitors have outbid and thus excluded. In further consequence, that relation determines who among all the competitors possessing the "greatest capacity for exchange" shall really consummate an exchange; it determines who shall occupy the position of marginal pair, and hence it ultimately determines how high shall be the price at which the actual exchange takes place on the market. Hence we may say that throughout the entire pricing process—insofar as it takes place on the basis of purely self-regarding motivations*—there is not a single phase, not a single feature which could not be traced back to subjective valuations as the underlying cause and, basically, it is entirely natural that that should be so. For we know that our subjective valuations indicate to what extent, if at all, our well-being depends on a given good; hence they are the natural, if not indeed the only possible guide for our actions whenever we acquire or relinquish goods solely in the interest of our well-being. We are therefore fully entitled to describe price as *the effect that results in the market from the reciprocal impact of subjective valuations of goods and of their media of exchange.*[17]

17. Sax, on the whole, builds on the same basic foundation with respect to a theory of value and price as that laid down by Menger. In his *Theoretische Grundlegung der Staatswirtschaft* (p. 276 f. and frequently elsewhere) he repeatedly and emphatically refers to market prices as "an *average* of individual values." Presented without amplification that description is infelicitous, to say the least, if not downright misleading. As my presentation in the foregoing text reveals (and in even greater detail, that on p. 522 ff. of my "Grundzüge") it is, quite on the contrary, a characteristic of the resultant price that it is not an "average" in the usual sense of that word.

* Consulting Economist's note: Of course, subjective valuations include altruistic motives and intentions as well.

13. Excluded Competitors Do Not Influence Price Except the Marginal Excluded Pair

It is, to be sure, a resultant of a peculiar kind. The measure of price does not derive merely from the sum or from the average of all the valuations that are made. These exert quite a variety of influences on the determination of the resultant price. A certain portion of them, namely the valuations of the excluded competitors, exert no influence at all, with the single exception of that excluded pair which possesses the greatest capacity for exchange. As to all the rest, it would make no difference if ten times as many of them were represented in the market, the result would not be changed one iota. In our own example the excluded competitors Ag, Ah, Aj, Ak might be present in the market or not; the category of those "excluded" might be represented by those four or by hundreds of additional competitors, all of them not in the position to bid more than $200 for a horse. In any case the resultant price will inevitably be determined, as before, at a point between $210 and $215, as can easily be demonstrated. The excluded competitors can swell the market crowd but they are not a factor in the market situation which governs the determination of price.[18]

14. Neutralizing Effect of Non-Marginal Buyers and Sellers

There is a second group which plays a very peculiar role, and that is the group of valuations made by all the pairs of contracting parties actually consummating an exchange, excepting the final pair. The effective influence exerted by that group of valuations consists entirely in the fact that they check and neutralize each other. Let us look once more at our typical example. If we seek to determine what contribution the presence of Aa, let us say, makes to the determination of price, we discover that it serves to offset one member of the opposing group, such as Ba; and it does this so effectively that the pricing process goes on in exactly the same way as if Aa and Ba were not present in the market at all. Similarly, one can easily convince oneself that the effectiveness of Ab, Ac and Ad consists solely in that they cancel the effectiveness of the opposing Bb, Bc and Bd. With all of them present in the market the resulting price is determined at a point between $210 and $215; if all of them together were absent from the market, then Ae and Be would effect an exchange between them at a price between $210 and $215. At the same time it should be pointed out and emphasized that, as far as this result is concerned, *the degree of the subjective valuations* which belong to this group is a matter of complete indifference. For instance Aa in our table makes a valuation which we placed at $300; but he would be no more and no

---

18. At least with the express reservation which accompanied our discussion that the competitors who appear in the market have an accurate understanding of the market situation. Without that express provision it would, to be sure, be possible that the presence of a hundred persons presenting ostensible demands might give rise to the mistaken notion that their number included a sizeable group possessing high capacity for exchange. Such a situation might mislead the few competitors present who actually possess such capacity into making premature price offers that would be excessively high.

less of an offset for *Ba* if that figure amounted to only $250 or even $220. And, on the other hand, even if the figure were $2,000 or $20,000 this fantastically high valuation would not benefit the resulting price at all. Its entire effectiveness would still be completely absorbed in its neutralization of *Ba*.

But even though we deny to the valuations by this group *any direct influence* on the determination of the resulting price, it can nevertheless by no means be maintained that they exert no influence whatever. For the valuations that belong to this group—in our table they are those by *Aa, Ab, Ac,* and *Ad*—by neutralizing the valuations by an equal number of the opposing group—our *Ba, Bb, Bc, Bd*—serve a double purpose. In the first place they prevent a stronger competitor than *Be* among the sellers from acquiring membership in the marginal pair which does directly determine price. And in the second place, they prevent a situation in which the strongest competitors among the sellers, being themselves no longer offset, can move along to neutralize the next strongest competing buyers and so bring it about that instead of *Ae* some still weaker member of the group of buyers acquire membership in the determinative marginal pair.[19] We can therefore most accurately formulate the role played by all those exchanging pairs whose capacity for exchange exceeds that possessed by the marginal pair. And we can do so in the following words. *They do not, by their valuations, exert any direct influence on the determination of the resulting price; but they do exert an indirect influence insofar as, by their reciprocal neutralization, they reserve the position of marginal pair to some other definite pair.*

15. Crucial Price-Determining Pairs

There is, finally, a third and very small group of valuations which play a conclusive and deciding role in the determination of price. That group comprises the valuations of the marginal pairs. They and they alone are the component forces the resolution of which exercises the directly effective influence which results in a market price of a definite magnitude. All weaker competitors attempting to effect an exchange, be it remembered, are *ipso facto* without influence on price; all stronger competitors neutralize each other; only the marginal pairs remain. At first glance it may well appear to be strange that so few persons, and particularly persons so lacking in prominence, should be able to swing the decision which governs the fate of the whole market. But a closer examination of   228

---

19. In order to demonstrate this let us omit competitors *Aa, Ab, Ac* and *Ad* from our example altogether. The position of the remaining parties would then be as follows:

Ae	220	Ba	100
Af	210	Bb	110
Ag	200	Bc	150
Ah	180	Bd	170
Aj	170	Be	200
Ak	150	Bf	215
		Bg	250
		Bh	260

It is apparent that now the last pair that represents a range within which an exchange is permitted by their economic condition is the pair *Ah* and *Bd*. The marginal pair now comprises a much weaker representative of the competing buyers than before and a much stronger representative of the competing sellers than previously. Accordingly the limits of the price range which formerly stood at $210 and $215 now move downwards so that they touch $170 and $180 respectively.

the situation will reveal this to be perfectly natural. For if all are to make an exchange at *one and the same* market price, then that price must be so set as to suit *all* persons who make the exchange. Now every price which suits the contracting parties possessing the least capacity for exchange, must naturally suit all persons with greater capacity for exchange in correspondingly greater degree. But we cannot add to that statement "and vice versa!" And for that reason the economic situations of the *last pair* to whom the price must be acceptable or of the first pair to whom it must be unacceptable, must necessarily set the measure of price.[20]

This furnishes us with the premise of a remarkable conclusion. For it is by no means ineluctably necessary that every disturbance in the reciprocal relation of both exchanging parties (or in what so many like to call "the relation between supply and demand") bring with it a disturbance of the market price. Quite on the contrary, all those changes are without effect which fail to disturb the situation of the marginal pairs. For they alone are determinant. Let us state that in greater detail. Any increase or decrease in the number of *excluded competitors* is irrelevant; every increase or decrease in the *intensity of valuation on the part of those persons* is likewise irrelevant, provided it is not of such magnitude that they cease to be "excluded" competitors. And, finally, every increase or decrease, (even a unilateral one), in the *intensity of the valuations on the part of competitors actually effecting an exchange*—except for the marginal pair—is also irrelevant provided only that such persons are not thereby removed from the ranks of effective buyers and sellers.[21] Only two kinds of change are really significant. One is a change in the valuations on the part of those persons who comprise the *marginal pairs;* the other is a unilateral change in the *number of persons whose capacity for exchange exceeds that of the marginal pairs*. For this last change brings about a disturbance of the equilibrium, it necessitates the exclusion of one or more competitors, and it introduces different elements into the factors determining the marginal pairs who, in turn, directly bring about a determination of price.

20. Those conversant with the literature of economics will not fail to observe the relationship that exists between the theory just presented and certain dogmas which long ago acquired full rights of citizenship in economic literature. Von Thünen, and after him virtually all theoretical economists, taught that the rate of interest is determined by the productivity of the "*last* bit of capital invested," and that the rate of wages is determined by the amount paid to "the *last* worker employed in the enterprise." And even before that the question arose as to which one among several costs of production governed the market price, and that question was settled in favor of "the highest production cost of material still required by the market," which is to say, in favor of "the last seller." It is not difficult for us now to recognize that these are all manifestations of one general principle which has in each case been expressed in terms of one particular application of it. And that principle is the one on which we have erected the structure of our theory of marginal utility and our theory of the determination of price. It is simply a matter of a failure at that time to become aware of the universal significance of the specific lines of thought which led to those conclusions. It was generally believed that no more had been accomplished than to set up a few special rules of limited significance. Actually they had sounded a dominating *Leitmotiv* which is typical of all the mechanics of investigation into the functioning of economic interests, and which is therefore a basic underlying motive of the entire determination of value and price.

21. It makes no difference, so far as determination of price is considered whether, let us say, among a hundred buyers of a commodity which is on sale in the market for $10 there are five or ten individuals who would, if the worse came to the worst, buy it even at a price of $100 or $1,000. Nor would it make any difference if those same persons were willing to go no higher than $20. Their readiness to do either is never put to the test.

16. Only One Law Determines Price, Not Four

All this brings us face to face with the question as to the relation which exists between the price law we have developed for cases involving two-sided competition and the three other formulations of law pertaining to the simpler cases of isolated exchange and one-sided competition. Must we deal with four independent laws governing no fewer than four different varieties of price phenomena? The answer is, that we do not. The formula last worked out includes all those applying to earlier cases. It is the most complete of the four formulations and expresses a conformity to a single law which just as truly underlies all the earlier cases. It is merely that those earlier cases represent a simpler, nay, what one might term a stunted combination of facts, and that the law therefore appears in a somewhat stunted form. For inasmuch as in the earlier cases certain elements, which the complete formulation declares to be price-determining, are entirely lacking, there is therefore quite naturally a smaller number of limits which fix the range within which the price must be set. But all those price-determining elements which are present at all, exert their influence in exactly the same way as they do in the case of the principal formulation.[22]

229

17. Summary of Psychology of What Happens in Price Determination

Let us review. Of all the results we have attained in this chapter, the one that is by far of greatest import is the fact that all the influences which function in the determination of price have been resolved into subjective valuations and a rational appraisal of their functioning. And I do really believe we have here hit upon the simplest and most natural, and indeed the most productive manner of conceiving exchange and price. I refer to the pricing process as a resultant derived from all the valuations that are present in society. I do not advance this as a metaphorical analogy, but as living reality. To begin with, in the pricing process there are genuine *forces* in action—not physical forces, of course, but psychological. They are the *desires* which those wishing to buy harbor for a good and which those wishing to sell harbor for the money to be obtained for the good. Naturally the intensity of this force is measured by the magnitude of the utility which the individual promises himself from the desired good in the furtherance of his welfare—that is to say by the (absolute) magnitude of the subjective *value* which his valuation accords it. Now the market is the place where reciprocal cravings for goods belonging to others may legally be translated into effective action. But those

---

22. Let us follow this through for one of the three cases, that of one-sided competition among buyers. In this case the only pair that consummates an exchange coincides with the "last" pair in the case of two-sided competition. In other words it coincides with the marginal pair at the upper range-limit. There is present only one-half of the other marginal pair (that at the lower range-limit), namely, the excluded buyer. Now, since the influence of the nonexistent excluded competing seller is entirely absent, there are three limits to the range within which the price may be set. These are (1) the value of the commodity to the effective buyer; (2) its value to the seller; and (3) its value to the excluded buyer possessing the greatest capacity for exchange. And that corresponds exactly to what we have demonstrated in the text above.

forces cannot go into action in untrammeled strength, for each is accompanied by a certain inhibition. That inhibition consists in the desire to retain possession of what is one's own. The exchange goods of others cannot be acquired without parting with something of one's own. The more difficult it is to persuade oneself to take the latter step, the more strongly is the impulse toward the former inhibited. The intensity of the inhibition, of course, is in proportion to the importance possessed by the good to be parted with, for one's own welfare—that is to say the magnitude of its subjective value. All that follows then becomes quite simple. Competitors who have the smallest capacity for exchange feel the inhibition to be stronger than the force and therefore the latter, being completely inhibited, can exert no effective influence in the way of external results. These individuals neither effect an exchange, nor can they exert any influence on the conditions under which others consummate exchanges. In the case of competitors with greater capacity for exchange the avidity with which the goods of others are coveted is stronger than the desire to retain what is theirs—the force is greater than the inhibition. There remains therefore an excess of force which in their case leads to an actual transfer of goods. Now this very excess of force, which is greatest in the competitors possessing the greatest capacity for exchange would in and of itself be capable of influencing the determination of price in direct proportion to its own magnitude. But this perfectly understandable interest of the competitors having greater exchange capacity does not by any means go so far as to induce them to offer as much as in the most extreme case they *can*. Rather does it move them to offer barely as much as they *must* in order to succeed. They "succeed" in this case if they force out supernumerary competitors and thus assure for themselves a place in the ranks of those effectively consummating an exchange. And so they deliberately refrain from setting in motion the full force of their superior power to force an exchange, and are content to do just so much as the least of their own number is capable of doing and is compelled to do in order to maintain his superiority over the competitor next behind him. And therefore it comes about as a perfectly natural result that the standard for the determination of price is derived from the economic situation of the last of the "ousters" and the first of the "ousted," or as we expressed it earlier, from the subjective valuations by the marginal pairs.

18. Extreme and Artificial Simplicity of Foregoing Exposition

It has been with deliberate intent that the foregoing exposition of the law of price has been developed by means of a market situation of extreme and artificial simplicity. It was a market composed of very few persons, both buyers and sellers, and each of them sought to buy or to sell just one single unit of a market commodity. Furthermore, that commodity consisted of a comparatively large and indivisible object—a horse. I think that enabled me to gain the advantage of offering an easy survey of the whole problem which made it possible to select what is essential and typical in the whole process, without being confused by complicating but inconsequential details. Once oriented as to essentials, we cannot find it difficult to advance, step by step, to an understanding of the situation as it changes by reason of the subject matter becoming more variegated and complex. We shall be able to appreciate what effect that complexity can have on the result and to perceive whether it can add anything—and if so, what it can add—to the basic framework of essentials. Of course it must be accepted from the outset that such complexity cannot alter the basic framework itself.

19. Advance, Step by Step, to Understand Variegated And Complex Situations: Increased Number of Participants Will Reduce Margins Between Prices

Let us begin by presupposing everything to remain unaltered except that we change our little market into a big one. Instead of eight or ten individuals on each side of the market, let there be eight hundred or a thousand. The increase in numbers cannot alter the nature of the machinery which separates the stronger competitors from the weaker, which finally sifts out the buyers and sellers willing to come to terms at the market price, and which aligns them in the equal numbers that must be arrived at if business is to be transacted. But there is a very high probability that because of the increase in numbers one particular detail will develop along a certain line. For if, on the sellers' or the buyers' side of the market, the interval between the highest and the lowest valuations is occupied, not by six or eight intermediate valuations, but by 798 or even 998, then it will be altogether probable that these intermediate valuations will vary from one another by very much closer margins. In the sparsely attended market of our typical example there was a sizeable difference of ten, twenty or even forty dollars between each competitive valuation and the one immediately above or below it. That is now no longer true. The interval between each valuation and its nearest neighbor will, on the average, be reduced to a single unit of monetary value, or even to some fraction of such unit. And the further result will follow that the range of valuations by the two marginal pairs will lie between narrower limits. Previously the two-sided competition forced the pricing process into a zone within which the market could establish a momentary equilibrium. Now that *zone* has been narrowed down to a *point*.

231

20. Consequences of There Being Quantity Buyers With Decreasing Marginal Utility

We made the further presupposition, in connection with our simplified example, that each person attending the market wished to buy or to sell just one unit of the commodity. In real life the situation is customarily far more complex in this respect. One and the same person may wish to acquire or to dispose of several or even numerous units of a single commodity. But that person will then as a rule not feel the same urgency to buy or to sell each of those units. Accordingly, the same buyer will then as a rule inject into the price-determining process quantitatively differing valuations with respect to the various portions of the total amount he desires to buy. (I limit this particular statement to buyers, since I intend later to add a special observation in this respect concerning sellers.) Assuming, for instance, that Aa wants to buy, not one but five horses and that he is in pressing need of the first horse but feels a successively decreasing degree of urgency with respect to his need for each subsequent horse. In that case he may well be inclined to offer up to $300 for the first horse, just as we have it in our table, but for the second he may be willing to offer only $280, for the third horse perhaps only $270, for a fourth only $250 and for a fifth only $200.

The effect of this sort of complication or variegation of the material dealt with is multiplied many times when the market commodity, instead of being a large indivisible object, is one that may at will be subdivided into minute quantities—a commodity, for instance, like flour or sugar or brandy. Now if we assume indefinite divisibility of the market commodity, we must make the parallel assumption that the total requirement of each potential buyer comprises the total of a number of wants for partial quantities. In conformity with the law of marginal utility these partial quantities will possess decreasing importance for the satisfaction of wants, and so will be the object of valuation. In such case, when the divisibility is in actual fact a complete one, the valuation never decreases in abrupt steps but becomes smaller only by a minimum decrease for each succeeding infinitesimal partial quantity.

That brings with it two results pertaining to the development of our abstract model. The first coincides, by its very nature, with one effect we have already noted as characteristic of "large" markets, except that it can be effectuated even in a small market. That is to say, there are no intervals between the valuations accompanying the competing attempts to buy. Every single rung on the ladder of valuations is occupied. Hence there is a shrinkage of the zone that is bounded by the valuations on the part of the last ones to come to terms and those of the first ones whom competition excludes from the realization of their efforts. That shrinkage reduces the zone to a point.

21. Any One Buyer May Have Different Ranking in Capability to Buy

Thus the designation "last buyer" and "first excluded competitor" ceases to describe a definite single *person* in the market. Indeed, one and the same person may simultaneously occupy several positions in the market with respect to the several parts of his desire to buy. With respect to the most urgently needed portion of his desire to buy he may occupy the position of "first" or "most capable" buyer. With respect to his last and least urgently required portion of the commodity, but which he nevertheless does just still buy at the market price, he may be the "last buyer." And with respect to still further partial quantities which he would willingly acquire at a still cheaper price but which there is no seller on the market willing to sell at that price, he is even the *"first* excluded buyer." Of course with respect to any further partial quantities at still lower prices he is simply an "excluded buyer." If there were an ideally perfect working out of our presupposition that the market commodity be infinitely divisible, then each competitive buyer would be faced with a uniformly graduated series of valuations, exhibiting no slightest gap in its continuity, and thus corresponding in its entirety to his own infinitely graded succession of desires to purchase. In that case *every* buyer would, with respect to the last small portion of the good which he actually purchases, occupy part of the position of the "last buyer;" with respect to the next small portion which he sees himself forced to forgo under prevailing market conditions, he would at the same time occupy part of the position of the "first excluded competitor." Hence our formulation of the price law would have to be couched in correspondingly less personal terms. There is, of course, no change in the fact that the decision proceeds from the subjective valuations placed on the good by both parties to the market activity, as those valuations are quantitatively expressed in the "bid and offered" figures. But these figures are assignable, not to *persons,* but to partial *quantities* of the good being dealt in on the market. Thus, in our simplified table the topmost position in buying offers made by the buyers' side of the market was occupied by "the valuation by *Aa.*" Now in our developed table we shall have to have that position occupied by all those valuations at a figure of "$300 apiece" no matter who represents that valuation on the market, no matter what persons it may be who apply that valuation to the most urgently desired partial quantity of the good. The second position will now no longer be occupied by "*Ab*'s valuation," but by any valuation at "$280 apiece" for the next most urgently desired partial quantity of the good. It will occupy that position no matter what competitive buyer represents it—it may even be *Aa.* And thus the series continues. And now the part played in our simplified formula by the valuations by "the two marginal pairs" is performed by the subjective valuations applied, within the ranks of the two sides of the market, to the last partial quantity of the good which is still the subject of a consummated sale, and by the first partial quantity which remains unsold. All this does not mean that we have to renounce the briefer and more expressive formula of "the last buyer," etc.; all that is necessary is that, when the more richly variegated market situation just described enters the picture, we must interpret that term of our formula to mean the valuations by the buyer or buyers who acquire the last or the least urgently desired partial quantity of the good which still is taken off the market via exchange.

233

22. Confession of Basic Preference for Discursive Explanations Rather Than Mathematical Formulae

And I suppose all that can be quite readily perceived in connection with our simplified table. But it would be a highly tedious and awkward assignment to demonstrate it by means of a completely worked out example, loaded down with hundreds of facts and figures. That is the reason why many economists are accustomed to employ in their presentations such mathematical symbols as will permit them to portray even composite and complex situations by means of simple forms and formulas. That applies even to economists who are not otherwise well disposed toward presenting economic science in the mathematical manner. Thus, when buyers and sellers make continuously changing valuations—upward or downward, as the case may be—and these valuations represent offers to buy or sell partial quantities of a market good, there is a special predilection for depicting them by means of continuously ascending or descending curves and for indicating, by their points of intersection, the price situation which the competitive offers based on those valuations are in the process of developing. Now that is a perfectly unobjectionable procedure. And yet I still find it questionable whether, with its resulting unavoidable suppression of any personal point of view, this method of presentation is really capable of completely supplanting and making superfluous a description by running commentary of the determination of price, such as I have undertaken to present. Because I do not think the question can be answered in the affirmative, it has been my personal opinion that such a running commentary should be retained. And I think so despite its admitted inadequacy in certain respects and even though I accord full recognition to the mathematical form of presentation. Accordingly I have presented an example of extreme simplicity which is amenable only to such a running descriptive commentary, and have subsequently pointed out the special considerations that must be taken into account when the simple situation is replaced by a more complicated development of the matter to be dealt with.[23]

23. Use of Term, Supply and Demand, Almost as a Meaningless Cliché

Orthodox economics has been teaching for centuries that the market price of all goods is determined by the relation between supply and demand. Up to this point I have conscientiously avoided the use of those two terms. My reason was not that the terms are of themselves objectionable or improper, but because the earlier stages of the development of the theory of price have handed these terms on to us with a great mass of ambiguities and obscurities adhering to them, not to say actual errors. And those I had no desire to see bestowed, as a gratuitous appendage to the terms themselves, upon my presentation of the question

23. In previous editions of *Positive Theory of Capital*, I had restricted myself, in the presentation of the general theory of price, to the use of the simplest type of transaction involving only large indivisible units—horses. That led to the following awkward situation. In subsequent discussions of the determination of price in the labor market and the capital market, I found myself dealing with markets and with commodities which were more complex than my original simple type, and which exhibited all the special characteristics that accompany the "most highly variegated complexities of the material to be dealt with." Since I had not treated these special characteristics in my general theory of price, I felt that I had to explain and support them by means of a special auxiliary device. It was my opinion that the material for such a device was to be derived from certain alleged peculiarities of the labor market. But in the meantime Professor Edgeworth has contributed an observation which is no less accurate than it is worthy of grateful acknowledgment. He has pointed out that the auxiliary device is quite superfluous and that the peculiarities allegedly characteristic of the labor market are to be encountered in any well developed market in which the commodities dealt in are divisible to any desired degree, and the object of an elastic demand. Therefore, says Professor Edgeworth, the development of these typical phenomena is already a matter which should be included in the general theory of price. Hence that theory should not be limited in its presentation to the rarer type of an indivisible market commodity. ("Theory of Distribution" in the *Quarterly Journal of Economics*, Vol. xviii, No. 2, February, 1904, p. 189 ff.). I am grateful for his hint and have attempted to follow it in my present exposition without sacrificing the advantages which, from the instructional point of view, seemed to me to accrue from beginning with the presentation of the simplest type of market.

of price. I therefore preferred first to complete that presentation in complete independence of those equivocal and much abused terms, and thereupon to clarify the relation between the conclusions I reached and the traditional "law of supply and demand."   234

Those conclusions comprise, to put it briefly, the sound and definitively worded essential truth of that law. Supply and demand have from the outset been exceedingly broad and vague shibboleths. They have been broad enough to include by implication the correct concepts they connote; they have been sufficiently vague to preclude their imposing any compulsion to accuracy, and to leave room for all manner of uncertainties, ambiguities and errors. In certain earlier stages of the theory, stages which preceded the development of the theory of subjective value, that situation led to the following peculiar dilemma. If you restricted yourself to entirely general terms which designated the relation between supply and demand as the regulator of the market price of goods, you expressed a proposition of unquestionable verity and which anyone must concede to be convincing. But because of this very universality the proposition furnished the mind with too little content. The proposition was necessarily—and not unjustly—exposed to the criticism that it amounted to nothing more than a catchword, that it was hardly anything more than an empty and meaningless formula. If, on the contrary, you made an attempt at complete precision with respect to the meaning of those shibboleths, and more particularly precision anent the manner in which the "relation" between them brings about conformity to the provisions of the laws of price, you ran into error. For without the intensifying conception of the whole problem which became possible only through the theory of subjective value, it was only too easy to go astray and arrive at incorrect interpretations and formulations. Supply and demand were too mechanically conceived of as mere quantities. And even when it had become habitual to take their "intensity" into account, that intensity was erroneously attributed to all sorts of disparate and secondary causes, simply because of the still prevalent ignorance of the central motivating factor which is to be found in subjective valuations. Thus the economists sometimes came quite close to the truth and sometimes wandered quite far from it, depending on the rhythmic beat they happened to hit upon. And so the old theory of supply and demand oscillated, as it were, between the Scylla of a vacuous and unsatisfying vagueness and the Charybdis of an equally unsatisfying erroneousness.[24] *

It is now my opinion that the problem finds complete organization

---

24. I refer the reader expressly to my "Grundzüge der Theorie des wirtschaftlichen Güterwerts," Part II, Chap. v ('Wahres und Falsches am Gesetz von Angebot und Nachfrage') appearing in Conrad's Jahrbücher, New Series, Vol. XIII, pp. 524-534, where I expressed myself in detail on the question of the inadequacies of the old theory of supply and demand.

---

*PUBLISHER'S NOTE: For an illustration of how barren the term "supply and demand" is, versus how rich it can be made by invention, see Supplement II; the idea there is that buyers and sellers make markets by their subjective valuations, and not that brokers make markets. That brokers "make" markets is a common fallacy.

and solution if we introduce into the traditional frame the simple thought that price is completely and entirely the product of men's subjective valuations. That thought explains in the simplest and most unified manner, why people offer a commodity for sale or desire to buy it, explains the intensity with which they do so, the pertinacity and stubbornness with which they at times persist in supplying or demanding commodities, as well as the ease and rapidity with which at other times they cease to do so. Everything that was right and correct in the old formula thereby finds explanation and confirmation, the multitude of objectionable interpretations that intruded is corrected and removed. It even becomes possible to express with impeccable precision the final conclusion concerning the collaboration of those economic forces which are apparently in opposition to each other in the guise of supply and demand, but which actually bring about a resolution of those forces which constitute the counter influences which determine price. It becomes possible to avoid both the Scylla of vagueness and the Charybdis of incorrectness. *

235

And now there is no reason any more timorously to avoid those two traditional and deeply rooted catchwords. The newly won knowledge concerning the laws of price can now perfectly well be expressed in terms of the popular old names, provided only their precise and correct interpretation be established beforehand. Let us then place beside our first formula the one that now results.

24. Final Last-Word Summary of the Law of Price

Market competition forces the pricing process into a zone which, as we have seen, is characterized by the fact that it lies between the subjective valuations by the border pairs. And it is from this characteristic feature that we derived the formulation of our law of price as it appears above. But that same zone exhibits another characteristic feature. We find the amount of a commodity which is offered for sale exactly equals the amount there is a desire to buy. Or if we are now to use the traditional catchwords, it is in that zone that *supply and demand are quantitatively in exact equilibrium*. In the case that was set forth in our table there was a demand for more horses at every price lower than $210 than there were horses offered; at every price above $215 there were more horses offered for sale than were sought to be purchased. Only in the zone which our law of the marginal pairs designated as the zone between $210 and $215 was the situation achieved which is required for a cessation of competition in the matter of price. That is to say, only in that zone was the supply of horses exactly equal to the demand for them.

It is quite correct, if so desired, to base the formulation of the law of price on this second characteristic. In that case the law is expressed

---

*PUBLISHER'S NOTE: In no market in the world has there ever yet been "perfect competition." But unprecedented changes *can* be made to progress in the direction of "perfect competition"; see again Supplement II.

as follows: *The market price is established in that zone in which supply and demand are quantitatively in exact equilibrium.* This formula, so well known ever since the days of John Stuart Mill, is in its content exactly as correct as the one we enunciated above—it is merely a different set of words to designate identically the same zone. To be sure, this formula, if it is to preserve its correctness, requires commentary of a very definite sort. I have just attempted to indicate what that commentary calls for, generally. What it demands specifically, I intend to set forth in the more detailed analysis which follows under the title of "The Individual Determinants of Price."

PUBLISHER'S NOTE: The third assumption of Böhm-Bawerk on page 120 (middle of the page) that "all the candidates for exchange are free from any misconception regarding the market situation which could prevent them from effectively pursuing their own interest" was not realistic, and to this date has not yet been attempted. Böhm-Bawerk *assumes* a perfect matching of buying and selling orders; further, he does not suggest anything that specifically will accomplish that; he does not provide even for a posting board for buy and sell orders to be *ranked;* no one person *combines* all the bid and asked prices, or sorts them out by magnitude. To-date such requisite applications have apparently not been thought of, and certainly there is no record that they have been attempted. However, see Supplement II.

Part B—PRICE

Chapter III

The Individual Determinants Of Price

236   THE preceding chapter established for us that price is determined by the range within which the valuations fall which are made by the marginal pairs. But we must still inquire into the circumstances which determine whether that range of valuations is itself at a high or a low level.

1. Extensiveness and Intensiveness of Demand and of Supply

It is easy to make a beginning of the task of answering that question. For it is immediately obvious that both the *number* of valuations and the *intensity* of the wants manifested by the respective parties will exert the determining influence on the situs of the marginal pairs. It will work out in the following manner. The location of the marginal pairs will be at a high level when valuations on the part of buyers are very high and relatively numerous, while at the same time those on the part of the sellers are low and relatively few in number. For in such case the small number of low valuations on the part of the sellers will be reciprocally neutralized by a part of the more numerous high valuations on the part of the buyers; hence among the buyers there will still continue to be persons with high valuations and in the group of sellers only such persons exclusively. Therefore the individuals from either group who finally constitute the marginal pairs must necessarily be persons whose valuations are high. For entirely analogous reasons the valuations will be low when high valuations on the part of buyers are relatively few in number, while at the same time very low valuations on the part of the sellers occur in relatively great numbers.

If, in accordance with what has just been said, we extract the individual factors which combine to determine the high or low degree which the marginal pairs will attain, we will derive the following four "determinants" of price.

1] *The number of wants that apply to the commodity.* This is what is traditionally called "extensiveness of demand."

2] *The figures expressing the valuations on the part of the buyers.* This is the so-called "intensiveness of demand."

3] The quantity of the commodity that is *for sale*. This is called   237 "extensiveness of supply."

4] *The figures expressing the valuations on the part of sellers.* This is known as "intensiveness of supply."

2. Böhm-Bawerk's "Theory of Relativity" As It Pertains to Price Determination

At this point we can appreciate the full significance of one circumstance which I have mentioned in preceding expositions. But I did not emphasize it because such emphasis was not required. I refer to the fact that our "valuation figures" are not mere simple quantities. They are by no means simple expressions of the absolute magnitude of the subjective value which the commodity possesses for the evaluating person. Quite on the contrary, they are merely *figures expressing relativity* and are derived from the comparison of two different valuations—one that is applied to the commodity and one that is applied to the good or medium of exchange. Let us refer to our schematic example again. When we said there that one buyer valued a horse as equal to $200, we did not say, nor did we establish, anything at all concerning the absolute significance which the possession of a horse possesses for the well-being of that buyer; we did no more than express the relativity between the value to him of the horse and the value to him of the money, its medium of exchange. What we said was that *A* values a horse two hundred times as highly as he values a dollar. If, therefore, we are to attack our present problem, which is to set forth the *elementary* factors of the establishment of price, then we shall have to eliminate the complex quantities which our "valuation figures" represent and substitute for them the elements of which those figures are composed. There are two such elements. The first is the absolute magnitude of the subjective value possessed by the commodity for the person ascribing the value; the second is the corresponding absolute magnitude of subjective value possessed by the good of exchange. These two elements quite clearly combine their influences in such a manner that the higher the absolute value of the commodity and the lower that of the good of exchange, the higher will be the valuation figure. And vice versa, of course.

3. Explanation of Price Movements When The Subjective Valuations of Money Decline

One circumstance implicit in the foregoing statement deserves at least passing mention. A high valuation figure does not by any means necessarily permit us to infer that a high valuation is placed upon the commodity. It is possible that it results from such high valuation of the commodity; but it is equally possible that it results from a low valuation of money. And that leads us to a further fact—and one very well worth noting. The competing buyers with the greatest capacity for exchange, who place the "highest valuation" on the commodity, do not at all of necessity coincide with the persons for whom the desired commodity possesses the greatest effective significance for their well-being. Indeed, our company of buyers is merely an aggregation composed partly of persons actually in great need of the commodity and partly of persons whose need is not at all pressing but for whom money, its good or medium of exchange, has but very small value. The converse may obtain among the sellers. The competitors in that group who have the greatest capacity for exchange may include not only persons who can very easily dispense with the commodity to be parted with, but also persons for whom the commodity itself has a high value but whose need of money, the good to be exchanged for it, is still more pressing.[25]

4. The Six Price-Determining Factors

Let us therefore set up a schedule of price-determining factors which eliminates the composite nature of a figure which simultaneously expresses the valuation of the commodity and the consideration. If we then substitute each time the two elements of which that figure is composed, we derive the following *six* determinants of price.

1]   *The number of demands that are directed toward the commodity.*

2]   *The absolute magnitude of the subjective value of the commodity for the buyer.*

3]   *The absolute magnitude of the subjective value of the good of exchange for the buyers.*

4]   *The quantity of the commodity offered for sale.*

5]   *The absolute magnitude of the subjective value of the commodity for the sellers.*

6]   *The absolute magnitude of the subjective value of the good of exchange for the sellers.*

Now this framework has to be filled in, to some extent, by a more or less detailed commentary to be devoted to the individual determinants. This is necessary, partly in order to elucidate the determinants themselves in greater detail, and partly to expose the remoter and more concrete causes which become effective through them. At the same time the theory of subjective value constitutes a background to all of them and may be said to accompany the discussion of them in the guise of a general commentary, as it were. The theory of subjective value, that is to say, constitutes the indispensable foundation for the theory of price. What we learned in our treatment of the former need not be repeated here. But it would be well to select and to examine more closely certain features that are particularly conducive to an understanding of the determination of price.

Let us then consider our determinants seriatim.

---

25. We have here a point of departure for further observations touching upon a well-known and much-discussed topic of dispute, namely, whether, as has often been maintained, establishment of price under completely free competition will bring about, as a consequence peculiar to itself, the great- est possible benefit for society as a whole. As I proved in detail in my "Grundzüge" (p. 510 ff.), the answer to that question *is in the negative.* For later discussion of this same question see Wicksell's *Wert, Kapital und Rente,* Jena, 1893, p. 48 ff.

5. First Determinant of Buyers:
Mere Wishes Are Not Effective Demand

1] *The number of demands that are directed toward the commodity.*
Little can be said concerning this factor that would not be self-evident.
Obviously it is affected on the one hand by the extensiveness of the market and on the other by the character of the want, that is to say, whether
or not the commodity is the object of wide and general want and whether
or not consumption of it is of such a nature that the commodity calls
for a very large number of examples thereof. Articles of clothing are
always required in greater number than are Sanskrit grammars; bread
and meat which are needed anew from day to day, are the subject of
more numerous demands than are pen knives which last several years.

Furthermore—and this is the only observation of theoretical interest
called for at this point—not every person whose want engenders the
wish to possess a commodity becomes a potential buyer thereof. What
is requisite is not only the wish to possess, but also the wish to inter-
change possession of the commodity for possession of the good of exchange. And that wish, as we know, comes into existence only in the
presence of a certain relationship between two intensities, namely the   239
intensity of the desire to acquire the commodity and the intensity of the
inhibiting desire to retain the good of exchange. Countless persons who
need a good and wish to possess it, nevertheless voluntarily stay out
of the market because their valuation of the good of exchange, under
the presumptive price conditions, so far exceeds their valuation of the
commodity, that from the outset any economic possibility of consummating a purchase is out of the question for them. The roster of those desiring a commodity constitutes, so to speak, our broadest original register
of prospects. A preliminary sifting takes place, based on the first two
determinants of price, namely, the valuations of the commodity and of
the medium of exchange. The resulting and much reduced classification
of persons seriously intending to buy is now subjected to a second sifting
which takes place in the exchange contest itself and out of which comes
the still more reduced classification of effective buyers.

Although the presence of persons who never had any serious intention of becoming buyers has at the start no influence at all on the determination of price, yet their existence cannot be ignored by economic
theory. For they are not set apart by any firm barrier from the serious
potential buyers, and both groups are constantly merging into each
other. Let us bear in mind the factors that promote the mere "I wish I
had" to a serious intention to buy—the valuation of the commodity, the
corresponding valuation of the medium of exchange, the presumptive
market situation with respect to price. These three factors are highly un-
stable quantities and often a very slight displacement among them can
attract new masses of active purchasers into the market. Many a man
who goes to the stock market in the morning to sell securities, switches
and becomes a buyer if it suddenly appears that the prospects for a bull
market are bright!

6. Second Determinant of Buyers: A Man Will Buy If the Marginal Utility Exceeds His Lowest Final Utility Among All Extant Demands. His Demand is Not Finally Based on Price, But Utility

2] *The valuation of the commodity by the buyers.* As we know, the magnitude of value is in general determined by that of the marginal utility which the buyer derives from the good to be acquired. And that marginal utility is in turn determined by the relation between want and satisfaction. More explicitly, it is determined, on the one hand, by the number and importance of the wants that demand satisfaction and, on the other hand, by the number of available specimens of the good.

But at this point a certain confusion becomes apparent, or at least that *appearance* of confusion to which I have made reference on previous occasions and which we must now clear up completely.[26] In our discussion of the theory of subjective value we came across numerous cases in which the value of a good was determined, not by its own immediate marginal utility but by the marginal utility of goods of a different kind that can be drawn upon as substitutes. And one outstanding example of that kind of substitution is substitution by way of exchange. In an earlier illustration, let us recall, I placed a value on my one and only winter overcoat in accordance with my assumption of the existence of an open market. And so I do not value it in accordance with the extremely high marginal utility which it delivers as a preserver of my health and my life. Not at all. But, providing I can count with certainty on buying a replace- 240 ment at any time for $80, I place a value on it of those very $80, or of the marginal utility that its price of $80 can furnish me.[27] Now is it possible that this doctrine involves us in the toils of an explanation that goes around in a circle? At this point we are explaining the magnitude of the market price by the subjective valuations on the part of the two parties constituting the market; some time ago we explained people's subjective valuations—at least in a considerable proportion of the cases—by the magnitude of the market price. Are we not arguing in a circle?

No, we are not. And for the very simple reason that valuation on the basis of "cost of acquisition" is not made unconditionally and without exception, but is undertaken only in the light of certain assumptions; and for the further reason that because of a lack of such assumptions the market is the very place where we do not undertake such valuations. If we survey the situation in its entirety we find the course of action proceeds as follows.

In the confident expectation that a winter overcoat can certainly be bought for $80, a man ascribes its value in accordance with that presumable cost of acquisition rather than in accordance with its direct marginal utility, which may amount to ten times that much. In doing so he bases his valuation on a provisional assumption, which cannot become a reality until he gets to market. That of course, makes his valuation a conditional and hypothetical one which stands or falls according to the

26. See foregoing pp. 153 ff., and Note 98 to Book III, Part A.   27. See foregoing p.151 ff. as well as p. 182 f.

correctness and soundness of the assumption underlying it. But despite its conditional character it is perfectly reasonable and is suitable in the most varied economic situations that require us to render a decision as to value—*with one single exception*. That exception is the situation which concerns the realization of the assumption itself.

And the situation on the market is just such a situation.[28] I cannot, for the purposes of acquiring the overcoat, make my calculations and direct my behavior as if I already had the coat. I must decide how much I am resolved, if worse comes to the worst, to assume in the way of trouble and sacrifice in the market, for the sake of acquiring a winter overcoat. Now would it not be a crazy world indeed, if I took my measure of trouble and sacrifice from the intensity of my need for that coat, not *before* but *after* success had crowned my efforts? In other words here is the situation. When I come to market as a potential buyer it is not permissible for me to be governed by a valuation which presupposes the coat has already been acquired at a definite price. Instead, I must apply what under these circumstances is the only reasonable valuation, namely, that at direct marginal utility. I must direct the intensity and the persistence of my demand by weighing the risk to my well-being which would result from a failure to acquire the coat. And then such considerations as the preservation of health and of life itself—in short, consideration of the higher direct marginal utility of the desired good—will exert a definitive influence on my deliberations.

Probably no careful observer of every day life will doubt that this is the manner in which we actually reason and behave. It may certainly happen often enough, that we go to market with the very definite anticipation that we can buy a desired good at a certain price, such as the winter overcoat for $80. But we will by no means so regulate our own behavior in the market that we adopt as a standard this preconceived opinion as to the ultimate determination of price—especially not as a *final and definitive* standard. If we do get the commodity at the anticipated price, then we are exempt from being put to further test.[29] But if it is not to be had at that expected price, no reasonable person will without ado forgo all attempts to acquire the urgently needed overcoat. Instead, he will simply discard the anticipation which reality has proven to be ill founded and

241

28. A second case of this same type arises when we are called upon to decide whether we are to give precedence to the replacement of the winter overcoat at all, rather than to satisfy other wants which can be met by an equal expenditure. In this instance too, it would be nonsensical to assign to the overcoat from the outset only the lesser importance of the wants which are displaced by that of the overcoat. The overcoat can obviously displace them only if it has *greater* importance than they, and then it does so for that reason. And it is just that greater importance which is the deciding factor that causes the verdict to be rendered in favor of the coat and against the other wants. Incidentally, this instance reveals the same organization of its logical structure as is evident in the one discussed in greater detail in the first half of my Essay VIII (which appears in Volume III, *Further Essays on Capital and Inter-*

est). And so I request the reader to take into consideration the points made in that essay.

29. To be quite exact, we must say that we are at this point testing whether the desired commodity is ascribed a value, *not equal to* but *higher than* that of the prospective purchase price. For if we placed on the desired overcoat a value only exactly equal to the purchase price asked for it, we should have no incentive to change the *status quo*; there would be an absence of that minimum of advantage through exchange which could impel us to overcome inertia and consummate the exchange. The situation would be completely analogous to the case which I present in greater detail in my Essay VIII, and which I compare to that of Buridan's ass which, placed between two absolutely equal attractions, is condemned to abiding inactivity!

will reflect whether or not, in view of his circumstances he should persist, and up to what limit he is going to persist in his demand, and in spite of the higher price that is being asked.

These reflections will pursue a course that varies according to whether or not the market in which he happens to be is the only one that offers him an opportunity to provide himself with the needed good. If it does constitute the only market, then he will certainly continue to "raise his bid" and will even, if it becomes absolutely necessary, go as high as the full direct marginal utility which he expects to derive from the good he is purchasing. For if he does not buy here and now, he will not acquire the good at all and will be forced to forgo its entire direct marginal utility. The one who neglects this only opportunity to buy the needed overcoat will freeze and perhaps get sick. Under those circumstances he will act in accordance with the motto "better exchange to lesser advantage than not at all," and will sooner consent to any price short of the direct marginal utility than forgo the purchase entirely. The result of all this in terms of our price theory can be expressed as follows. He contributes to the determination of price, not in accordance with a lower, indirect marginal utility based on the presumption of a definite market price, but in accordance with the higher direct marginal utility of the good.

To be sure, the course of events may be somewhat different if the market which the prospective buyer enters is not the only one that is open to him. In that case, even if his expectation of buying at a certain price meets with disappointment in the first market, that expectation may persist with reference to another market. Such an expectation can then move the prospective buyer to abandon the first market without accomplishing his purpose, in preference to exceeding the price he had anticipated paying. In that case his behavior in the first market is admittedly influenced by his hypothetical valuation. But only his behavior in the *first* market, be it well observed, and not his behavior *in the market as a whole*. For it is clear that, rather than leave the second market empty-handed—or if there are several available, then the last market—our purchaser would prefer to extend his competitive bidding up to the full amount of the direct marginal utility. The effect of his hypothetical valuation can therefore be that he transfers his patronage from one partial market to another, but it cannot prevent the reception, by some part of the market as a whole, of the impact of the full force of valuation that will, if it must, rise until it attains the full amount of the direct marginal utility. Such a valuation effects no more and no less than does any mere generalized hope of making a purchase at a cheap price, and it does so even if it does fall short of taking concrete form as an expressed valuation. And a hope of that kind can, and hundreds of times does bring about one result, namely, that a purchaser who is not satisfied with the price demanded at one shop will go on to another. But if the hope proves false there too, the purchaser will accede to a higher price than originally contemplated, rather than forgo the purchase altogether.

That leads us to the following result. Subjective valuations based on the supposition that the good so valued can be purchased at a certain price furnish a rule of conduct for us in that market in which we hope to see the supposition become a reality. But the rule is at best only a psychological guide for our preliminary behavior, and never the standard for definitive action. That standard is derived from a consideration of the amount of the good's direct marginal utility. Thus we reach a conclusion that is important for the inherent logicality and consistency of our theory. That conclusion is as follows. The determinant of price which I defined as the valuation of the commodity on the part of the buyer proves, when analyzed in detail, to be a factor genuinely attributable to the originary subjective evaluating activity of the potential buyers, and not a result of the process itself by which price is determined. Hence it is not the mere fruit of reasoning in a circle.

There is another by no means infrequent type of case which reveals a certain kinship with the one just discussed. That is the case of the purchaser who does not value the commodity at its use value at all, but rather at its (subjective) exchange value. This always applies when any commodity is bought for resale. The grain merchant, for instance, who buys wheat from the farmer or the banker who buys securities on the stock exchange places a value on them solely in accordance with what he hopes to realize from them in another market (after allowing for whatever shipping and handling charges he has incurred). In transactions of that kind the determinants fall into the following causal sequence. To begin with, the market price is influenced by the dealer's appraisal of the commodity's exchange value; the latter is based on the presumptive market price in a second market; and the latter of these, in turn, is based on the originary valuation on the part of the potential buyers in the second market area. Hence through the agency of the dealer, the valuations on the part of the public pertaining to a second market, or the conditions applying to the relation between supply and demand in that second market, exert an influence on the price that prevails in the first market. Nor should that occasion surprise. For the appearance of a dealer in a market is in actual fact nothing more than a form by which the demand on the part of persons who, physically, are situated in a different market area can be economically brought to bear on the first market. The function of the dealer may be compared to that of a business agent without directions or orders. He considers the demands of a few dozen or a few hundred absent clients, computes what price they would, under the prevailing conditions, be likely to agree to, and then without their knowledge, but for the conduct of their economy, consummates the purchase within the maximum price as set by his own supposing. As far as the determination of price in a given market is concerned, it simply makes no real difference whether a dealer removes 500 pieces of a commodity at $40 each for customers in another market and at his own risk, or whether those 500 customers have directly and expressly commissioned him to buy the 500 pieces for their accounts at $40 each. In both cases there is a demand to purchase 500 pieces at $40 each, and the physical basis of the demand is in each case the wants of 500 persons who are not physically present but who are economically represented. The only difference is that in one case they are represented of their own knowledge and act for their own account, while in the

243

other case, though the dealer acts as their representative, he does so without their knowledge, and for his own account and at his own risk.

Now the dealers' estimates of exchange value go back to the judgments as to use value on the part of their absent clients as final determinants. And the absentees' judgment as to use value as well as those of the buyers who are physically present are all based on the magnitude of the direct marginal utility. Hence these cases involving exchange value which we have just considered do not in any way vitiate the result which we previously formulated, and it remains true throughout all variations of our problem that everything depends ultimately on the direct marginal utility that the commodity has for the buyer.[30]

7. Third Determinant of Buyers: Varying Marginal Utilities of Rich and Poor, etc.

We may now continue to point number

3] *The subjective value of the good of exchange for the buyers.* Where the medium of exchange for one commodity is some other commodity, as in the case of barter, then what was said under point 2 with respect to the valuation is equally valid. But goods of exchange are ordinarily in the form of money, and since money can be made to serve equally well in all classes of want, its marginal utility and its value do not depend on the relationship between want and satisfaction in any single class of want, but rather on how well the persons concerned are able to provide for the totality of their wants. As we already know,[31] the subjective value of a unit of money is smaller for the rich and greater for the poor. At the same time it should be noted that the important point here is not the absolute amount of wealth or of income, but rather the relationship of these to the wants of the persons concerned. But there are in addition some special circumstances which can influence the sub-

---

30. The essential point, with respect to this question of arguing in a circle, is always that those subjective valuations which are founded on the presumptive determination of a concrete market price are not the same ones as those on which the actual determination of that very market price is itself founded. And vice versa. Any appearance of circuitousness is due solely to the dialectic repetition of the words "subjective valuation." That is deceptive unless it is made clear that this one expression does not in both cases denote one and the same phenomenon, but rather two different concrete phenomena both of which are denominated by the name of the one category into which both fall. The relationship that exists here can perhaps be better and more briefly clarified by an analogy than by any direct and detailed exposition. A convention whose constituent personnel consists of the members of a number of delegations, operates under a form of parliamentary compulsion known as the "unit rule." That is to say, all the members of each delegation cast their individual votes in the meetings of the convention in accordance with the decision previously arrived at by a majority of that delegation sitting by itself. Now it is manifestly perfectly correct to argue that the decision of the delegation is based on the votes of the individual members; it is equally correct to argue that the subsequent vote of the members in the convention is based on the decision of the delegation. And yet there is not the least ground for maintaining that those who advance the two arguments are arguing in a circle. The dialectician may say, "You argue that the decision of the delegation is based on the vote of the members, and also that the vote of the members is based on the decision of the delegation," and thus create the appearance of a circuitous argument. But he does so only so long as he fails to reveal that it is a question of two different votes on two different occasions. In quite analogous fashion the determination of market price is, to begin with, based on the totality of originary subjective valuations on the part of the parties to the market, and thereupon this determination of market price —be it supposititious or anticipated—forms the basis of further *different* subjective valuations which, upon *other* occasions than in that same market itself, are decided upon and used to guide our actions.

31. See foregoing, p. 150.

jective value of money. Frivolity and prodigality depress it, the urgent necessity of making important payments makes cold cash more precious. Even the richest merchant, confronted by the necessity for meeting pressing obligations when his till is depleted, will certainly practice retrenchment in the matter of luxuries such as, let us say, costly oil paintings.[32]

8. First Determinant of Sellers: Their Number Is as Variable as the Number of Buyers, for Parallel Reasons

Let us proceed to point number

4] *The number or quantity of the commodity that is for sale.* In order to exhaust the determinants that are involved, we must first go back to the quantity in which the commodity in question is present at all within the whole market area. Or, indeed, is going to be present, since it is no uncommon thing to conclude purchases of commodities not yet in existence, such as grain to be gathered in the next harvest, or commodities to be delivered upon completion of manufacture at some future time. If we pursue the causal chain one link further backward, we perceive that the quantity of commodities available in a market area is itself determined by a variety of factors. These may include purely natural conditions, as in the purchase and sale of land, or in transactions involving natural produce, where the abundance of supply depends on how harvests turn out. Or they may include conditions that are purely social or juridical, such as monopolies, cartels, coalitions and the like. Or they may include the magnitude of costs of production, a factor that finds particularly wide applicability. For the higher the cost of producing a commodity, the smaller, comparatively, is the number of units of that commodity which production will offer for the satisfaction of demand, and vice versa. This is true for a number of readily understandable reasons which, incidentally, we shall later examine more closely. At any rate this matter of what influences the available quantity of a given commodity constitutes the starting point of any attempt to determine why costs exert their generally recognized influence on the price of goods. The total number of units of a commodity that are in existence constitutes the primary basic material that the market may be called upon to deal with. What portion of it is actually brought to market is a question the answer to which depends on the subjective valuation of commodity and good of exchange on the part of those who own them, and as such the question involves matters we are about to consider as our points 5 and 6. But we can say here and now that the situation is analogous to the one pointed out in connection with the quantities of a commodity that are desired by potential buyers. That is to say, there is no fixed barrier between that part of the total supply which its possessors regard as being for sale, and that part which they consider as not for sale. Any alteration in the rela-

244

---

32. Earlier theory used in place of "subjective valuation of the good of exchange" the term "ability to pay" on the part of prospective buyers to designate this determinant of price. Because of the connection pointed out in the text between wealth and valuation of money, the term is not appropriate to the great majority of cases; indeed, it is in some cases positively incorrect; and in any event it is a much too narrow formulation. Cf. the more detailed exposition in my "Grundzüge," *op. cit.,* p. 527 ff.

tion of those subjective valuations, or even in the presumptive situation with respect to the market price can convert a quantity of goods, which, the moment before, its owners described as "not for sale," into goods that are thrown into the market as part of its "effective supply."

9. Second Determinant of Sellers:
Sellers Subjective Valuations Are Usually Low,
Making the Last Buyer the Significant Personage

We proceed to point number

5] *The subjective value of the commodity for the sellers.* The determination of this value takes place, in general, in accord with the familiar law of marginal utility, but it very frequently manifests one very notable peculiarity. For most of today's sales are made by those who are in the business of producing or trading commodities and who possess them in such quantities as constitute an unusable superfluity, as far as their personal utilization of them goes. Hence the subjective use value[33] of their goods is usually very close to zero for these persons and therefore their "valuation figure" which, as we know, embraces subjective use value as a determining element, likewise falls to practically zero. And the final result of that is, that the last seller, as far as any practical significance goes, no longer exerts the limiting influence which, in the case of such sales, our theoretical formula attributes to his valuation figure. And so price is actually limited and determined by the valuations on the part of buyers exclusively. Commodities once produced, and therefore present in such quantities that, for their personal needs, the possessors have no use for them, must certainly be disposed of. In order to insure a sale it becomes necessary to descend the scale of price until the point is reached where the whole quantity that must be disposed of will find buyers. In the case of 1000 units of a commodity that will be a price which is just below the valuation of the thousandth buyer and just above that of the thousand and first. If production and selling conditions are normal, the whole quantity offered will almost always be absorbed by the demand at a price which far exceeds the minimal use value which the commodity possesses for the seller himself, and will ordinarily reimburse him for his costs completely and leave him a business profit. On the other hand, if conditions are unfavorable, it may very well happen that failure to sell will force the seller to seek considerably lower levels of the demand in order to dispose of the goods; he may have to be content with prices which in comparison with his cost of production cause him a loss. But even these emergency sales and give-away prices still exceed the subjective use value possessed by the commodity for the seller. Even at that point then, this use-valuation does not yet exercise its function of determining the low limit of price. Only if the price had fallen to nearly zero would it have been prevented from falling still further by the limiting action of the buyer's valuation which would now finally become operative. But things practically never reach that stage,

33. It is this use value rather than the subjective exchange value which we must here relate to the determination of price, if we are to preserve our analogy to our exposition of point 2.

because the competition among buyers itself almost always brings the descending prices to a halt at some higher point on the scale.

The effect of this is to bring about a great simplification of the law of price as it applies to the large-scale market. There are four valuations which constitute the "valuations of the two marginal pairs;" of these the valuations of the sellers, under the conditions first described, are entirely eliminated.[34] Moreover, if the buyers are extremely numerous, the gap as we noted earlier, between the valuation figures of any two buyers in juxtaposition ordinarily tends to become so small that the margin between the last buyer and the first defeated buying competitor virtually shrinks to a point. Hence it is sufficiently accurate, for purposes of the great numbers involved in a market economy, to state that market price *is determined by the valuation figure of the last buyer.*

10. Third Determinant of Sellers: Varying Marginal Utilities of Sellers, Rich and Poor, etc.

We conclude with point number

6]   *The subjective value of the good of exchange for the sellers.* What is to be said on this point is similar to what has already been stated above with reference to point number three, the subjective value of the good of exchange for the buyers. And here again it will be appropriate for us to draw several distinctions. Wherever the exchange constitutes barter, primary attention is usually directed toward the use value which the particular good of exchange possesses for the economy of the sellers. More frequently however the medium of exchange is money, the value of which in the eyes of the seller who is to receive it can of course be only an *exchange value.* Now the subjective exchange value of a good, as we pointed out on page 159, is at all times identical with the value of the consumption goods which are to be exchanged for it. Hence, it will be the greater, the more consumption goods can be exchanged for it, and the more highly the individual values the marginal utility of the consumption goods acquired through the exchange. And consequently it will vary, on the one hand, with the objective exchange capacity of the good to be valued (the money in this instance), and on the other hand with the evaluating individual's general position with respect to wants and the satisfaction of them. The last named factor furnishes the basis

246

---

34. That is to say, no competitor among the sellers will allow himself to be excluded *for the reason that* the market price which the "last purchaser" is willing to pay is less than his own subjective estimate of the use value of the commodity. There may be many a seller who, on a given market day allows himself, provisionally, to be excluded. But that is done only for tactical reasons and as employment of speculative delay because he is waiting for more favorable market conditions to develop on some later market day. But it is certainly an extremely rare occurrence for a producer or seller who operates under division of labor to allow himself to be definitely shut out of the market. If we watch the course of commodities produced for the market, we will observe that they are actually sold, right down to the last one. They all find a sale sooner or later, at normal prices or at prices resulting in a loss, possibly not until a referee in bankruptcy disposes of them—but they do get sold. As a rather rare exception, and one to be ascribed to a different and more technical cause, certain commodities do remain unsold if they are subject to spoilage and so go to waste. And as a still rarer genuine exception, commodities do remain unsold if the producer, failing to receive an offer to purchase at a price exceeding his own subjective estimate of use value, retains the commodity for his personal use.

for the factual situation repeatedly pointed out in previous passages, including the discussion of point 3, namely, that as a rule money has less subjective value for the rich than it has for those who are less affluent.

With respect to this sixth point too, we shall see that this factual situation will frequently play a significant part. That is especially true when the purchase price received by the seller is intended to serve a purpose in the household or the private life of the seller. Consider the case of an oil painting which is a really valuable work of art. If the owner of it is a poor man, it is quite likely even if he is fully aware of its artistic merit, that he will be disposed to part with it for a considerably smaller sum of money than will a millionaire. That is because the use value which the oil painting has for the poor man is counterbalanced by a much smaller sum of money than in the case of the millionaire. There is also a further very delicate aspect of the matter which has not so far been mentioned but which deserves to be explicitly brought out. That is the fact that there are many cases in which the effectiveness of a difference in affluence is cancelled out by a sort of compensation because it appears as a factor "on both sides of the ledger" as it were, and so constitutes a "contra item" that offsets itself.

This applies, let me point out briefly, to business purchases which are transacted as part of the constantly recurring activities of a going concern. We shall, in actual fact, find no evidence that the greater or lesser wealth of the entrepreneur exerts an influence on the prices he pays in the course of his regular business. Normally he will make his computations in terms of money and will weigh the money that the commodity is scheduled to bring in by its sale against the money that production of the commodity costs him. The money realized from the sale of a quantity of his output is not spent on expenditures incurred in his private household, but is expended—certainly for the most part, by far —to continue the going business. It is presumably used to purchase the means of production needed for production of the next quantity of salable commodities. Whether a unit of this money, even had it been used for purposes of consumption, would then have had a high or a low marginal utility is completely immaterial as regards determination of price, so long as it is not actually devoted to consumption purposes in his personal household. A higher or lower valuation used in entering this money on the ledger account would always be exactly compensated by the same higher or lower valuation at which it is later removed from the account. We have here a companion piece to the well-known case of the small farmer who produces a quantity of grain sufficient only for the needs of his personal household. For him the market price of grain is a matter of indifference. Now just as it is immaterial to the farmer whether he calculates the grain that he raises and consumes in his own home at a high or a low figure, since it is merely a counterbalancing entry on both sides of his ledger, just so is it immaterial to the entrepreneur whether he calculates at a high or a low figure the money which, nominally, he receives and expends, but which actually does no more than pass through his hands.

11. Potency of Subjective Exchange Value
In Personal Needs Superseded in Many
Cases by Objective Exchange Value of Money

With regard, then, to the subjective exchange value of the money, we note that its potency as a determinant of price is nullified in those very numerous cases which involve provision for the personal needs of the economic subject concerned. But with regard to the objective capacity for exchange possessed by money, it is to be observed that in these cases as well as all others its potency as a determinant continues unaffected. We said earlier that the subjective exchange value of a good will always be greater or smaller in proportion, first, to the greater or smaller number of consumption goods for which it can be exchanged and, second, to the marginal utility those goods possess for the economizing individual. Now the second is nullified through self-cancellation in the causal sequences just mentioned, but the first continues to apply. The more consumption goods (which means in this case goods specifically required for the continuation of production such as labor, raw materials, machinery, etc.) that can be obtained per unit of money, the fewer can be the units of money which the entrepreneur can be content to receive in the sale of the commodity he produces. And vice versa. Here is the principle which enables economic theory to assign a place in the schematic organization of determinants of price to the familiar effect on price of any depreciation of money. And at the same time it provides a niche for the factor of "costs" which I have advisedly refrained from listing in my schematic organization of the general determinants of price.

If, finally, there occurs in the regular round of business activity any disruption which causes the proceeds of the sale of commodities to be devoted to ends lying outside that regular round, and which allows differences in personal needs to make themselves felt, then the influence of the latter on the determination of price once more achieves potency, even in sales of a purely business nature. In this category belongs, for instance, the following phenomenon. There are times when manufacturers or merchants are obliged to meet very pressing money obligations, or indeed are tottering on the brink of bankruptcy. At such moments they place a specially high value on the medium of exchange, money, and for that reason are compelled to reconcile themselves to accepting small amounts of money for the commodities they offer for sale. Herein lies part of the explanation of the inordinately low prices which obtain at a forced sale or which prevail generally in a panic.[35]

35. The *Verein für Sozialpolitik* held a general convention in 1909 at which Wieser read a report under the title "Geldwert und seine Veränderungen" (Vol. 132 of the publications of that society, particularly pages 501 and 509). Wieser made particularly apt and keen observations on the subject of the elimination of personal valuations of money in business computation. It can readily be seen that not only in the case of business *sales* but also in the case of business *purchases* for resale there can be this very kind of elimination of the "personal valuation of money," and for entirely similar reasons. If a dealer wants to buy a commodity for the sole purpose of resale at a profit, then in the normal course of business his own personal valuation of money will constitute only a self-compensating item on "both sides of his ledger." For that reason I could have brought up this special feature of the causal sequence when I was discussing point 3, subjective value of the medium of exchange for the buyers. I deferred its treatment until I reached point 6 because there it finds much more extensive and more important application. For in the field of demand the deciding influence is exerted, directly and indirectly, by the individual need for purposes of consumption. In the field of supply, on the other hand, the decisive factor is mass production for sale in the market under division of labor.

Part B—PRICE

Chapter IV

The Law of Costs

1. It Is a "Good Half of Economics" To Understand That Costs Do Not Essentially Determine Prices!

THERE is a "law of costs" which is as deeply rooted in economic literature as it is in practical experience, and just as we met it in treating the theory of subjective value, so do we encounter it in the field of the theory of price. This law tells us that the market price of goods that are reproducible in any desired quantity tends in the long run to equal the cost of production. It is customary in support of this contention to advance the following completely sound argument. The market price of these freely reproducible goods cannot long be maintained materially higher or materially lower than its cost. If at any time the price does rise considerably above cost, then the production of that article becomes exceptionably profitable for the entrepreneurs. That not only supplies an incentive for them to expand their flourishing establishments, but it also encourages new entrepreneurs to enter this profitable line of business. The quantity of that particular product that is offered on the market is thereby increased, with the ultimate result that, in conformity with the law of supply and demand, the price begins to fall. Conversely, if at any time the market price falls below cost, continuation of the production of the good in question becomes a losing proposition and consequently the entrepreneurs abandon or restrict its production. That decreases the supply of that commodity in the market, as a result of which, again in conformity with the law of supply and demand, an increase in the market price must necessarily ensue.

There is an inordinate quantity of theoretical detail that attaches to the law of costs.[36] For our purposes such detail may all be safely ignored. Our entire interest is centered on the question of the position

36. Such details include the question whether, in computing costs, we must figure *cost of production or of reproduction,* whether in the case of differing costs we are governed by the highest, the lowest, or something in between, and also the question just which elements constitute costs, etc., etc.

which the law of costs, empirically so well attested, occupies in the system of the theory of price. Does it conflict with our law of the marginal pairs, or not?

It does not. Our marginal pairs are no more irreconcilable with it than they are with either of the two principles laid down in the theory of subjective value. Those are, first, that marginal utility determines subjective value, and second, that costs determine that value. The steps in the thought processes which reconcile the apparent contradiction in the case of subjective value find their counterparts, as to every detailed feature, in the corresponding process which applies to price. There is but the one exception to be noted, that in the present case each step is surrounded by more intricately involved complications. That is due to the fact that the element of exchange is now interposed and the whole phenomenon is transferred from an individual economy to society. In the succeeding pages I will attempt to describe as briefly and clearly as I can the interaction of price, value and costs. And it is in my opinion no exaggeration to state that to understand their connection is to understand a good half of economics.

2. To the Contrary, Prices Are Finally Determined Solely by Consumers' Subjective Valuations of Finished Goods

The determination of value and of price originates in *the consumers' subjective valuations of finished products.* They determine the demand for those products, and that demand is confronted at the outset by the producers' stock of finished goods. The intersection of the valuations by the two groups or in other words the magnitude of the valuations by the "marginal pairs," determines price, as we have seen. And such price is individually determined for each particular kind of product. Thus the price of iron rails is determined by the relation between supply of and demand for *rails,* the price of iron nails by the relation between supply of and demand for *nails.* And likewise in the case of all other products that are manufactured out of the raw material iron, such as spades, ploughshares, hammers, sheet iron, kettles, machines etc., their price depends on the relation that happens to obtain between supply and demand with respect to those special kinds of product. In order to make the matter very clear, let us assume that conditions with respect to the needs for and the available stocks of different iron products vary very widely and that as a result their prices initially vary very widely too. And let us further assume that the price of a quantity of the several commodities requiring a given unit of raw material[37]—say a hundredweight of iron—varies between *one* dollar for the cheapest class of commodity and *ten* dollars for the most expensive. These prices are the result of the momentary market situation, and we are beginning by regarding as a constant quantity the stocks of finished products which constitute the supply. However, they are only momentarily constant, becoming a variable quantity as time goes on and as production continually

---

37. For the sake of simplicity I am for the present ignoring the contributions of other complementary means of production.

keeps adding to those stocks. Let us examine the relations of this production. In order to manufacture finished ironware, the producers need raw iron.[38] In a specialized economy with its division of labor they have to buy that iron in the market. It is they who represent the demand there. As far as its extensiveness goes, obviously each manufacturer will want to buy just so much iron as he needs for producing such quantity of his commodity as he anticipates he can sell to his own customers. But what of the intensiveness of the demand? Obviously no manufacturer will pay more for a hundredweight of iron than he can realize from it[39] in the purchase price that his customers will pay him. But he can and, if need be, he will bid as high as that rather than allow his factory to stand idle for lack of raw material. The producer, therefore, who can make profitable use of the iron he gets in the market at ten dollars a hundredweight will be a willing buyer in the iron market, even up to that maximal price. But the producer who can make profitable use of it only if he can buy at 250 eight dollars a hundredweight, will of course be willing to pay only eight dollars at most, and so on. In this manner the participation in the market demand for iron on the part of each producer depends on his own estimate, and that he derives from the market price of his own special kind of ironware. (Where applicable, this means of course such portion of its market price as is assignable to iron, in conformity with the law of complementary goods.)

To meet this demand the owners of the mines and smelting works offer a supply in the form of their stocks of iron. As we know, the latter come into the possession of those competing buyers who have the greatest capacity for exchange, and at a price that coincides approximately with the valuation of the last buyer.[40] Assuming that the stocks of iron available in the markets are just sufficient in quantity to satisfy the requirements of those buyers whose valuations of a hundredweight of iron run from $10 down to $3, then the valuation of the last buyer will be *three* dollars and that will be the market price.

3. Examination of the True Causal Sequence of Prices

Let us examine the causal sequence that brought about this market price. It most definitely leads in an unbroken line from the value and price of *iron products* to that of the component of cost, *iron,* and not in the opposite direction. The subjective valuation of iron products on the part of consumers stands as the first link in the causal chain. It begins the process by helping to determine the valuation figures, in terms of money,

---

38. Again for the sake of simplicity I am disregarding other requirements necessary for production.

39. It must be noted that we are here continuing to ignore the contributions made by other complementary means of production, as for example, labor, tools, fuel, etc. If I did not do that, I should of course have to act in accordance with the fundamental principles I myself set forth on a previous page (p. 161 ff.), I should then have to assign a portion of the value of the product to each of the remaining collaborating goods and accord to iron only its *quota* of the value of the product. In that case, however, I should establish that the same relation which has been shown in the text to arise between the value of iron and the value of the complete product would then be established between the value of iron and its quota of the value of the complete product.

40. Cf. p. 242 f.

that enable the consumers to participate in the demand for iron products. Then those money valuations, following a pattern now familiar to us, determine the price that results in the iron products market. This resulting price of the products in turn indicates to the producers how high an estimate of (exchange) value they, for their part, can place upon the raw material iron, and so furnishes them with the valuation figure at which they can enter the buying competition. And from that there finally emerges the market price of *iron*.

But we can elicit from all this still another deep lying principle. *This is simply another instance of the operation of the great law of marginal utility.* That law provides that the available supply of goods always finds utilization in the order of profitability, and that the last utilization dependent on a good determines the value of it. Where this is worked out within the framework of an individual economy, the most profitable uses manifest themselves to be those which correspond to the most intensive subjective wants. The value, then, that results as the fruit of these individual circumstances, is a purely personal or individual subjective value. But if it is worked out within the broader framework of the market, then it is no longer a matter of direct relation to individual subjective wants, but of relation through them, by indirection, to money. Money furnishes, as it were, the neutral common denominator for the otherwise noncomparable needs and emotions of different individuals. The most profitable uses no longer manifest themselves to be the ones that correspond to the absolutely most intensive wants, but the ones that correspond to the highest valuations in terms of money, that is to say the *best paid uses*.[41] And the value which emerges is objective exchange value. And that is what happens in the case of iron products. In the various markets they are transferred to the buyers who pay the most, and the valuation of the last buyer determines their market value and their price. The same thing happens in the case of the raw material iron itself, though by a slightly roundabout course. In the iron market it is sold to the producers who pay the most and the estimate of the last producer determines its price. But they are here merely agents. Since they hand on the iron to the best-paying consumers, the stocks of iron are in reality devoted to *the most profitable consumer uses,* and the *last of the latter* that can still be provided for determines the market price of the element of cost, iron, through the estimate of the last producer in his function as buyer. It is not the iron which, on the basis of an originary and determined price, dictates a price for the products that emanate from it. On the contrary, iron has its price placed upon it through the agency of the price of its products. And that is set in conformity with the great law of marginal utility which provides that the available supply force its way into the most profitable uses and receive its price from the valuations of the latter.

251

---

41. In my "Grundzüge," pp. 510-513 in Conrad's *Jahrbücher* I pointed out in detail and by submission of the causes and consequences of this fact, that both do not necessarily coincide, unfortunate as that may be.

4. Resultant Phenomena Which Can Seduce People to Have Erroneous Ideas Regarding "Costs" as Being Determinative of Prices

Now this leads us to a group of resultant phenomena that evidently gave rise to the opinion that costs exert a causative influence on the price of products. For so long as the price of the various products made out of iron fluctuates between $10 and $1, while the price of iron becomes fixed at $3, we have an indication that there has not been complete fulfillment of one requirement which economic principle demands. It is the principle that the stocks of iron be devoted to the most profitable uses. On the one hand, iron is being used for purposes to which a value of only one dollar or two dollars is ascribed, and which therefore are situated *below* the level of the "last" economically permissible use. On the other hand, there are numerous uses valued at more than three dollars which are not yet provided with iron. For if, for example, the market price of an iron product still stands at ten dollars, that proves that only those consumers of that product can buy it, who place its value at $10 or more, while other consumers who have unsatisfied opportunities for utilization of iron at prices of $9, $8 and downward to $3, cannot be provided for in the market. Similarly as regards products of which the market price is $8, there will be a stratum of demand not provided for which offers opportunity for utilization at prices from $7 down to $3, and so on. That situation has to be corrected. And ordinarily the business sense of the entrepreneurs will quickly effect the correction which economic principle here demands. With the incentive of reward that is supplied by the difference between cost and price, there will inevitably be an increase in the production of such ironware as commands a market price in excess of $3. And that increase will go on to the point where all forms of utilizing iron which have a utility exceeding $3 will still be able to satisfy their demand. The resulting increase in the supply of ironware naturally has the result that even the stratum in which the "last" buyer is to be found gets to be a lower and lower one. That means the market price keeps falling until finally the valuation of the last buyer, and hence the market price, reaches the normal rate of $3. Conversely, the penalty of loss to be incurred will unfailingly inhibit any offers to utilize iron for purposes that are valued at less than $3. The means to that end consists in suspending or curtailing for a time the production of such ironware as commands a market price of less than $3. The resultant shrinkage in supply will soon cause an increase in price up to $3, and now the commodity is again attainable for any buyers who have use for it at the figure of $3, and thus the situation is brought into conformity with economic principle. The prices of all iron products have now come down from above or come up from below to meet at $3 which is "cost." But the reason why that takes place is obviously not because the element of cost, iron, is able to impose upon its products its independently established price. It takes place because all the participating products and also that element of cost called iron, obey the law of marginal utility and insinuate themselves, one after the other, into the most profitable uses, and the last of these determines the price of all of them.[42]

There is no lack of illustrations of this principle to be culled from practical experience. It is a well-known fact that when there is brisk activity in the field of railroad building there will be a rise in the price of iron rails and consequently in the price of iron. Then again, today's great need of copper wire for transmitting electric current has caused the price of copper to go up. In these cases it is clear that the upward movement of price arose in the end products and progressed from there to the raw materials. But some people, including perhaps many a reader, will raise the objection that we can imagine cases in which a fluctuation in price has its origin in raw material. The supply of iron, for instance, of which we were speaking throughout our example, is not a fixed quantity, they will aver, but may be larger or smaller according to what goes on in the field of iron production. Supposing then, that by virtue of increased production there is an increase in the supply of iron, then the price of iron will fall because of a reason that applies peculiarly to *iron itself,* and that fall in the price of iron will bring with it a fall in the price of ironware. Is it not true then after all, they will ask, that the path of the causative process leads from cost to price?

This doubt, too, can be laid to rest. We need but follow to its beginning the course of the causative process which we have as yet exposed for only a portion of its length. It is quite correct to say that the supply of iron is not a fixed quantity, but only the variable result of the production of iron which can at will be expanded or contracted. For the production of iron we need iron mines and—to put it briefly—direct and indirect labor. The iron mines are a fixed quantity and not capable of being devoted to any other purpose than the production of iron. However, though the total amount of labor which is available in an economy is a fixed quantity which depends on the size of the population at a given time, nevertheless the amount of labor that is devoted specifically to producing iron is not such a fixed quantity. Labor is of course a productive force that can be used in very many ways, and all the branches of production that are carried on in a country compete with each other for that labor. Who decides how much of the two originary productive powers, labor and use of land, which are available in an economy, shall be devoted just to the production of iron? And who decides on the value and the price of those productive powers per unit?

253

---

42. Possibly the amount of the costs can itself be altered by the corrective process which I have described and can, for example, be made higher. For the following might take place. In order to meet the demand, as yet unsatisfied, which desires to buy iron products at a figure even higher than $3, so much iron must be withdrawn from the market that the supply is no longer sufficient to meet the demand at $3. Then of course the latter demand is excluded by the stronger competition and the market price is determined at more than $3. And thus we get another proof that it is not "costs" which are the fixed point to which the prices of products accommodate themselves, but just the other way around.

5. Originary Productive Powers Are Forced Into Use in the Order of Profitability, and Receive Value and Price From the Last of Them. How Profitability and Demand in Lower Orders of Goods Suction-Pump From Higher Orders.

Here we have the ultimate repetition, in the case of the basic elements of all economy, of what we have previously been observing in the case of final and intermediate products. *Even the originary productive powers of the nation are forced into uses in the order of profitability and receive their value and their price from the last of them.* They possess no *a priori* established value any more than does any other good—perhaps even less so—and receive their value only from the use to which they are put. Whether a day's labor is worth $1 or $10 depends on the price of the product that labor can produce. And indeed the "product" must here be understood to be that "last," cheapest product for the production of which there is still labor of corresponding quality left over, after all better paid uses of labor have been provided for. Production may be compared to a vast pumping station. Every branch of demand has its suction pipe let into the reservoir of originary productive powers; it attempts, in competition with all other branches, to suck up what it needs for its own requirements. Furthermore, all branches exert suction with varying strength; that strength being the greater, the more numerous and the more remunerative are the uses which it serves, or in terms of exchange activity, the higher the valuation they enjoy in terms of money. There are differences too, in the construction of the suction pipes. Some of them are quite simple, others are provided with independent compartments through which the suctional pressure that originates in the want is transmitted from station to station, as it were, and through which the productive powers which are to be supplied to that want are likewise pumped up from each stage to the next. Now let us apply our analogy to the matter in hand. Such wants as require for their satisfaction the performance of personal services attract labor directly and in proportion to the remuneration that they are willing and able to give for it. However, such wants as require for their satisfaction *goods in kind* first suck them up by giving a sufficiently well paying market price for them. And the sufficiently well paying market price of the products must then continue to attract the productive powers necessary to create them. Sometimes this requires one or two stages, sometimes twenty or thirty. In our example the want demanded and was prepared to pay for the ironware; the market price of ironware made the purchase of iron attractive; the price of iron, finally, attracted the originary productive powers into production of iron. In the case of other consumption goods there may be twice as many, or ten times as many intermediate steps or, to remain faithful to our analogy, the number of intermediate compartments in the suction pipe may be twofold or tenfold as numerous. But the principle of progression and—what is of prime interest to us—the result always remain the same. No matter whether the intermediate members are few or numerous, the effect can neither be enhanced nor diminished, although it may be accelerated or retarded. But in the end every want will attract the productive powers it requires, directly or

indirectly, and in proportion to the powers of attraction inherent in its   254
"valuation figures." There are always numberless productive powers
active in the cause of the wants of the rich, even though the economy may
at the same time experience a shortage of goods and manpower at other
points. Why? Because the high money figure which the rich man is
capable of offering for the satisfaction of his wants never fails to make
its powers of attraction felt through all the stages of the productive process and right on down into the reservoir of the originary productive forces.

Thus all wants apply suction in proportion to the power indicated
by their valuation figures. That stratum of want which is willing and
able to pay a high rate, such as $10 a day and more, for a day of
labor devoted directly or indirectly to the satisfaction of that want will
soon have sucked up its fill. After and beside it those strata that can
and will pay lesser amounts for a day's labor devoted to satisfying them,
will be filled in the order of their daily rates of $9, $8, $7, $6, and so
on down to, say, $5, $4, $3, $2. If, through a descent to a limit of
$2, the entire supply of originary productive powers has found employ-
ment, then a twofold result has been attained. First, all wants that cannot or will not remunerate a day of labor devoted to satisfying them at
the rate of at least $2 will remain unprovided for. And second, the
market price of a day's labor is established at $2, that being the valuation
figure of the last purchaser of labor. But if we make the further assumption that the amount of available labor is greater, then the provision for
wants can descend to still lower strata. It then becomes possible, for
example, that the last wants to be directly or indirectly satisfied are those
which carry a remuneration of only $1 for a day's labor. In that case
the market price of labor will accommodate itself to that situation and
be established at only $1 a day. And that market price will be uniform.
We shall not find the topmost stratum of wants paying $10 and at the
same time the lowest stratum paying $1 for the same commodity or the
same work, but the one market price will be the same for all buyers.

And now one of the doubts that was raised by our earlier example
can be resolved. Let us assume the price of a day's labor to be $1, and
that of a hundredweight of iron, the production of which has heretofore
required three days, to be $3. And now suddenly iron mines are discov-
ered that yield very rich ore, or some invention brings about a marvelous
improvement in the production process, so that as a result it becomes
possible to produce a hundredweight of iron in *two* days. What happens now?

As long as iron and iron products maintain their former price of
$3, then throughout the iron industry only those wants will be provided
for which now are willing and able to pay $3 for the product of *two*
day's labor and hence $1.50 for a day's labor. At the same time, in all
other branches of production and of wants, provision is still to be had
for all strata down to that stratum of wants inclusive, which pays only
one dollar for a day's labor. Now the principle of economic behavior, by
virtue of the opportunities it offers for profit, always finds very eager
exponents in the entrepreneurs of production. In accordance with that
principle it is inevitable that any heretofore unexploited opportunities   255

which remunerate a day's labor at a rate *in excess* of $1 will be taken advantage of and hence, that more originary productive powers will be invested in the production of iron, and that there will be an increase in the supply of iron and iron products. That will continue up to the point where, in the iron industry as everywhere else, the satisfaction of wants extends down into the stratum which is willing to remunerate a day's labor with no more than $1 and hence to pay for a hundredweight of iron, which takes two day's labor to produce, no more than $2. The parallel phenomenon which takes place is then, naturally, that the price of iron and iron products[43] falls to $2. All this takes place, not in violation of our law of marginal utility but in strictest conformity with it. And the law of costs, correctly understood, is really only a special way of stating the law of marginal utility in order to adapt it to a special group of phenomena.

6. There Are Two Factors Delaying Price Adjustments to Changed Circumstances

It is inconceivable that in actual practice production should pursue an ideally perfect course, untrammeled by limitations of time or space, free of any friction, with perfect foreknowledge of future wants, without any disturbing dislocations in demand, supply and the technique of production. But if such perfection were attained, then ideal mathematical accuracy would also characterize the investing of originary productive powers in the most profitable uses, and then the law of costs would have ideally complete validity in any sense in which it has validity at all. All groups of complementary goods (from which, after all, any consumption good must arise) would at all stages in the progress of production maintain an exactly uniform value and price. The consumption good would then at every stage exactly equal its costs, those in turn would at every stage equal their costs, and so on back up the line to the very last originary productive powers which are the ultimate source of all goods. However, this ideal symmetry is thrown awry by two disturbing factors.

7. One Factor Consists of "Frictional Obstacles"

One of these I should like to designate by the comprehensive term of "frictional obstacle." At almost all times certain obstructions prevent the prompt investing of originary productive powers in the consumption uses that happen to be most profitable at the moment. These obstructions may be great or small, temporary or of long duration, but in any event they result in a certain inequality or asymmetry in the provision for wants and in prices. This manifests itself partly in the relatively more abundant provision for wants in individual fields. Thus woolen goods,

---

43. It must not be forgotten that for the sake of simplicity we are ignoring the contributions of other complementary goods to the production of iron products. Suppose we did want to take them into consideration and made the assumption, for instance, that the transformation of iron into the iron product required the expenditure of two additional days of direct or indirect labor. In that case the $2 price of iron would correspond to a *$4* price of iron product, and of that price the law of complementary goods would then require that a quota of $2 would have to be assigned to the productive good, iron.

for example, may be so plentiful that wants are provided for which are so low on the scale that they remunerate a day's labor indirectly at the rate of only $.95; at the same time it may be true in the field of copper goods that the industry is unable to satisfy demands that offer remuneration lower than $1.50 for a similar day's labor. Or the asymmetry may manifest itself in the classes of goods which constitute means of production and which are successively transformed from each class into the next in order finally to become consumption goods. There the asymmetry consists in the fact that these classes are not uniformly valued at each stage of their progress. The stream of the means of production does not maintain uniform breadth on its course toward the final stage where they become consumption goods. Instead, because of some disturbing cause or other, the stream at some points is dammed up and it broadens, while at others it falls and the stream narrows. Consequently there are asymmetrical deviations in price as between earlier and later stages of the production process or, as it is customarily conceived and expressed, the price of a product (or of an intermediate product) deviates from its cost. Thus in our example of the iron industry there is a change whereby production suddenly becomes much cheaper and falls from $3 to $2. As a result there is at first an increase in the amount of iron produced, and that depresses the price of pigiron although iron *products* are able for some time to maintain their price which exceeds their cost. But gradually the "bulge" in the supply moves on into the later stages of production as well, progressing from the production of raw material right on to the manufacture of the finished products, where it depresses the price to the same $2, thus once more restoring the lost symmetry of price and costs.

In actual practice such "frictional obstacles" are infinite in number. There is no moment of time and no branch of production which could boast a complete absence of them. And that is what gives the law of costs its well known character of a law which has only approximate validity and which teems with exceptions. And those numberless big and little exceptions are the inexhaustible source from which flows the constant stream of entrepreneurs' profits—and of entrepreneurs' losses as well.

8. Second Factor Consists of Lapse of Time
— Which Is the Explanation of "Originary
Interest," the Comprehensive Term for the Three
Categories of Unearned Income — Profit, Rent and
Also Interest (in Narrow Sense) on Borrowed Money

The second disturbing factor however, is the *lapse of time*, the passing of weeks, months and years which must intervene between the investment of the originary productive powers and the presentation of their end products ready for consumption. While difference in time exercises a profound influence on our valuations of goods, it also causes a regular difference in value between those groups of the means of production which stand at the various stages in the course of that production process which all of them alike must traverse. And that regular difference must be carefully distinguished from those asymmetrical deviations which are attributable to frictional obstacles. It is this second disturbing factor which gives rise to *interest*. It will now be our further task to fit the theory of interest into the framework which we have up to this point constructed in the process of devising a theory of value and of price.[44] *

44. I request friends of economic theory to consult, in the guise of a commentary to this chapter, as it were, my far more detailed exposition in the essay entitled "Der letzte Masstab des Güterwerts" which appeared in the *Zeitschrift für Volkswirtschaft, Sozialpolitik und Verwaltung*, Vol. III, 1894. It was published in English under the title "The Ultimate Standard of Value" in *Shorter Classics of Böhm-Bawerk* as Essay V (Libertarian Press, South Holland, Illinois 60473, U.S.A.).

I call particular attention to the second chapter on the various meanings of the word "costs" and to the sixth chapter which sets forth what the law of costs actually states and then announces my final conclusions. Here I believe I am entitled to restrict myself to the positive exposition of my own views; there I have set down in addition such clarification and elucidation as seemed to be called for by the fact that I found myself in opposition to interpretations of the "law of costs" by other economists, differing from and in contravention of my own. I further request a comparison with the essays I contributed to the controversy between Dietzel and myself which appeared in Conrad's *Jahrbücher*. My essays were entitled "Zwischenwort zur Werttheorie" (New Series, Vol. XXI, 1890) and "Wert, Kosten und Grenznutzen," (Third Series, Vol. III, 1892). Finally, I wish to make reference to Essay VIII in *Further Essays on Capital and Interest*. It is pertinent insofar as the questions treated there, even though they arise from a treatment of the theory of subjective value, nevertheless contain important applications which have bearing on the position of costs in the theory of price.

*PUBLISHER'S NOTE: Interest in italics in the third from the last line is a term now customarily changed to "originary interest." *Interest* can be used in a narrow sense, but also in a broad sense. In the narrow sense the term means return on borrowed money. In the broad sense interest includes rent on land, profit on business as well as interest on borrowed money. In the threefold sense, originary interest refers to all so-called *unearned* income, one of the most controversial subjects in the history of mankind. That is the subject of the remainder of the volume entitled, *Positive Theory of Capital*, which is the title of the book from which this publication, *"Value and Price,"* was abstracted.

Location of Definitions of
New Terms by Böhm-Bawerk

Capital and Interest

Volume I
History and Critique of Interest Theories

APPENDIX

Recent Literature on Interest
(1884 to 1914)   *355*

Capital and Interest

Volume II
Positive Theory of Capital

THIS PART ALSO APPEARS IN THIS BOOK

Capital and Interest

Volume III
Further Essays on Capital and Interest

for Means of Subsistence" in *Positive Theory of Capital,* especially p. 316 ff.)

Experiments with Matching Buy and Sell Orders in Different Ways

With Preliminary Reflections on the Problem of "Just Prices"

Publisher's Preface to Supplement I

An attempt to analyze whether Böhm-Bawerk, although he made great improvements, had not attained the best solution — that an equal or better market can be obtained by other ways of matching buy and sell orders — is presented in this Supplement; but every other variation in matching fails and should be rejected. Pondering that fact leads to the conclusion that a *free* market — with no coercion, theft, or fraud — is a beneficent institution, and should be a bulwark to prosperity, contentment, and economic, social and political stability.

PUBLISHER'S NOTE: This material has been taken from a monthly publication, *First Principles in Morality and Economics* (Libertarian Press, South Holland, Illinois 60473, U.S.A.), and the numbering of Charts and Tables has not been made continuous nor "reconciled," but this does not affect a reader's ease in following the analysis. The original Charts I and II are omitted.

Experiments with Matching Buy and Sell Orders in Different Ways

With Preliminary Reflections on the Problem of "Just Prices"

Böhm-Bawerk's ideas of "value" and "price" were different from those of earlier schools of thought, whether ancient or even as recent as English Classical. Daily communication with business-men can make it clear that the ideas of Böhm-Bawerk and his associates on those subjects are still unknown; those ideas are not referred to, nor quoted as thoughts clarifying in themselves, nor fertile for also reaching associated and derivative ideas of significance. Therefore, some graphical presentations will be made of Böhm-Bawerk's price-determining ideas.

We live in an intricately organized *exchange* society, which requires that most goods and services must be priced in order to be bought or sold. Because there is extreme inequality in obtaining the goods and services men need and want, there has developed a considerable interest, much mistrust, and some hatred against the free market pricing system, under which the more prosperous segments of the world operate. One searching question is: What is the effect of competition within the price-determining mechanism; or at least in a mechanism as the horse market that Böhm-Bawerk postulated? A second question is: Does the price-determining mechanism that Böhm-Bawerk considers yield a "just price," which is a common ideal in present day society?

A "free market" is traditionally identified with non-coercion of the participants by each other. They do not strike blows, nor intimidate; each participant remains free to act or not to act; to raise or lower his ideas on what he wishes to pay or to receive.

Further, misrepresentation of the merchandise or services is considered to be dishonest, and therefore deceiving fellow partici-pants in a market is taboo; when Böhm-Bawerk *assumed* that all the horses were equal he really *assumed* fraud out of his village horse market.

And, of course, by definition a horse market is a place for trading and not for stealing; and so Böhm-Bawerk has also in effect removed *theft* from his market.

A "free market" therefore by its implicit assumptions excludes violence, fraud and theft. With such a definition of "justice" the following charts were prepared. (Brief sections of Böhm-Bawerk's presentations are repeated to enable the reader to obviate the necessity of referring back repeatedly to earlier pages.)

Determination Of Price In Isolated Exchange

Böhm-Bawerk considers first "Determination of Price in Isolated Exchange."

By "isolated exchange" he means *one* buyer and *one* seller (not two or more buyers and not two or more sellers). As will become apparent later, isolated exchange is the kind of transaction most susceptible of "injustice." Böhm-Bawerk writes:

> Farmer A needs a horse, and his personal circumstances are such that his need for the horse represents an urgency of such degree that he attaches as much value to the possession of a horse as he does to the possession of $300. He goes to his neighbor B who has a horse for sale. If B's personal circumstances were such that he too places a value on the horse as high as on the possession of $300, or higher, there would, as we know, be no possibility of an exchange between these two farmers. Let us therefore assume that B places a considerably lower value on his horse, say, a value of only $100. What happens?
>
> In the first place it is certain that there will be an exchange. For under the conditions as assumed, each of the parties can make a considerable gain by effecting the exchange. If they make an exchange for instance, of the horse against $200, then A, for whom the horse he desires has a value of $300 will obtain a gain having a value of $100; B obtains an equal gain, since for a good that was worth only $100 to him he now obtains $200. In accordance with the principle "better a lesser advantage than no exchange," the two will at all events agree on the exchange at a price which is advantageous to both of them. How high will that price be?
>
> This much at least can be said with certainty: The price will certainly have to be lower than $300, otherwise A would have no economic benefit and hence no motive to effect the exchange. And the price will certainly have to be higher than $100, otherwise the exchange would entail a loss for B or at least be without benefit. But at what point between $100 and $300 the price will be fixed cannot be predicted with certainty. Every price between these two limits is economically possible, one of $101 being just as much so as a price of $299. This leaves a wide margin for bargaining. The price will be depressed or raised in the direction of the low limit or the high limit according to whether the buyer or the seller in the course of the transaction exhibits the greater cleverness, craftiness, stubbornness, persuasiveness, etc. If both parties are equally proficient in bargaining, then the price will be determined at a point somewhere in the neighborhood of the midpoint of the gap, that is to say at around $200.
>
> Let us briefly summarize whatever is here capable of being formulated as a law. *In an isolated exchange between two persons desiring to effect an exchange, the price will be*

determined within a range which has as its upper limit the buyer's subjective valuation of the good, and as its lower limit the seller's valuation.

In Chart III we have drawn a line four inches long, and we have shown on that line the range in which "injustice" can occur.

CHART III
Justice and Injustice in
ISOLATED EXCHANGE

| Injustice | | J u s t i c e | | Injustice |

| 0 | $100 | $200 | $300 | $400 |

(Dollars as price for a horse)

If *A* and *B* are *free* (uncoerced) buyers and sellers, then they cannot suffer "injustice." But if either is a *coerced* buyer or seller, the seller will suffer injustice below $100 or the buyer above $300. The range of injustice is zero to $100 for *B*; and $300 to $400 (or more) for *A*.

The "range of justice" is between $101 and $299. Some may declare that $200 is the only really just price. But if justice and injustice still play a role within the limits set by $101 and $299, then this observation should be made: so wide a range exists only in *isolated* exchange.

Determination Of Price With One-Sided Competition Among Buyers

By definition, *isolated exchange* precludes the phenomenon of competition being part of the situation. Böhm-Bawerk next moved to one-sided competition, namely, on the buying side.

What competition does to price is illuminating. Böhm-Bawerk writes about one-sided competition among buyers as follows:

Let us now modify the conditions of our example to fit the next type of case by assuming that farmer *A* who wishes to buy finds that *B*, possessor of the horse, is already being visited by *Aa* who likewise has come with the intention of acquiring the horse that *B* is offering for sale. Now *Aa* is personally so situated that the possession of the horse is, in his estimation, to be valued as the equivalent of the possession of $200. What happens now?

Each of the two competitors wants to buy the horse, but of course only one can do so. Each of them desires to be that one. And so each will make an attempt to induce *B* to sell the horse to him. The means of doing so is to offer a higher price than does his competitor.

That brings about the familiar situation where the bidders alternately overbid each other's offers. How long will that

continue? Just as long as the rising prices that are offered
remain within the valuation of the competitor with the lesser
capacity for exchange, who in this case is Aa. That is to say,
as long as the bids still remain below $200 Aa will be guided
by the principle "rather a smaller gain than no exchange at
all," and Aa will, up to that point, continue to raise his bids
in order to win the competition for the exchange. Of course
A will prevent that each time by raising his bid in turn. But
Aa cannot go beyond the limit of $200, if the exchange is not
to be a losing proposition for him. In this he is guided by
the principle of the gaining of advantage but couched this
time as the precept "better not to exchange at all than to
exchange at a loss," and at that point he throws in the sponge.

All this does not necessarily mean that the price will
finally be determined at exactly $200. It is possible that B,
who knows how badly A needs a horse, will not be satisfied
with $200 and that he may succeed through stubbornness
or clever bargaining in exacting from A some price as high
as $250 or $280 or even $299. The one thing that is certain is
that on the one hand the price cannot exceed $300, the value
placed on the horse by the willing buyer A, and on the other
hand cannot fall below $200, the valuation of the competing
and defeated bidder, Aa.

Now let us assume that in addition to A and Aa there
are three more willing buyers—call them Ab, Ac, and Ad—
who compete for B's horse. Their individual positions in life
are such that they place a value on the horse amounting to
$220, $250, and $280 respectively. In that case it can readily
be perceived that in the competitive bidding that develops
Ab will stop bidding when the price reaches $220, Ac when
it goes to $250 and Ad when it reaches $280. Competitor A,
however, will remain the one with the greatest capacity for
exchange, and the price as finally determined will necessarily
fall between $300 as the upper limit, and $280 as the lower
limit, which is the value placed on the horse by the most
pertinacious of the unsuccessful competitors.

Hence the results of this observation can be generalized
in the following statement. *Where there is one-sided competition among willing buyers the competitor with the greatest capacity for exchange (that is, the one who values the
good most highly in comparison with the consideration) will
become the purchaser. And the price will fall within a range
of which the upper limit is the valuation by the purchaser
and the lower limit of which is the valuation by that one
among the unsuccessful competitors who has greatest capacity for exchange. This holds irrespective of the second
subsidiary lower limit which is always the seller's valuation.*

If we compare the foregoing statement with the typical
case portrayed in . . . [the preceding case], it becomes apparent that the effect of competition among buyers is to
restrict the range within which the finally determined price
will fall; and such restriction will be toward the upper end
of the range. Between A and B alone the limits of the range
of possible price were $100 and $300; through the addition
of the competing buyers the lower limit of the range was
raised to $280.

What has now happened to the "range" in which the price
must fall is shown in Chart IV.

CHART IV
Justice and Injustice in
ONE-SIDED Competition Among BUYERS

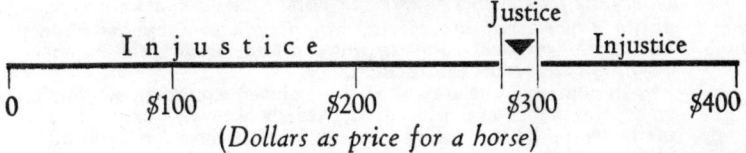

Justice

Injustice   ▼   Injustice

| 0 | $100 | $200 | $300 | $400 |

(Dollars as price for a horse)

By the existence of competition among buyers the range of injustice has been narrowed from $200 to only $20.

It is now becoming apparent how competition is a "reducer" of "injustice."

Higgling about the price for the horse will now have a relatively narrow range. The *skill* of each buyer — the *power* of each buyer — has been reduced by competition. But the *power* of the lone seller has increased.

Determination Of Price With One-Sided Competition Among Sellers

Having considered the case of one seller and five buyers, Böhm-Bawerk next turned to consideration of the case of five sellers and one buyer. It is interesting to note what happens in this case. He writes:

> This case constitutes the exact counterpart to the preceding one. Entirely analogous trends lead to completely analogous results, except that the outcome is in the opposite direction.
>
> Let us imagine farmer *A* as the only willing buyer and five owners of horses—let us call them *Ba, Bb, Bc, Bd,* and *Be*—each of whom, on a competitive basis, is offering to sell *A* one horse. We must further assume that the five horses are exactly equal in quality. Now *Ba's* valuation of his own horse is $100, *Bb's* corresponding valuation is $120, *Bc's* is $150, *Bd's* $200, and *Be's* $250. Each one of the five competitors wants to exploit the sole existing opportunity for a sale to his own advantage.
>
> As in the previous case the means for assuring victory over one's competitors was overbidding, so in the present case it is underselling. But since no one is willing to offer his commodity for less than it is worth to himself, *Be* will stop underselling at $250, *Bd* at $200, *Bc* at $150. Then *Bb* and *Ba* will continue to vie with each other until at $120 *Bb* finds himself "economically excluded" and *Ba* holds undisputed sway. The price at which he wins through to make the sale must exceed $100, otherwise he would gain no advantage and would therefore have no motive to make the exchange. But it cannot possibly exceed $120, otherwise *Bb* would have continued his competitive bidding.
>
> The case may be expressed in the following general terms. *When there is one-sided competition among sellers, it is again the competitor possessing the greatest capacity for*

exchange who consummates the exchange. That competitor is the one who places upon his own commodity the lowest valuation in relation to the buyer's good or medium of exchange. And the price must be determined within a range which has as its lower limit the valuation by the seller, and as its upper limit the corresponding valuation by the buyer having the greatest capacity for exchange within the number of the unsuccessful competitors.

In contrast to the case of the isolated exchange set forth in . . . [the second preceding case] where the price necessarily would be determined at some point between $300 and $100, in this instance the presence of competing sellers restricts the range of possible prices. And the restriction exerts its pressure downward.

Chart V shows what has happened to "justice" in this instance; this time the just price has moved far down to between $100 and $120.

CHART V
Justice and Injustice in
ONE-SIDED Competition Among SELLERS

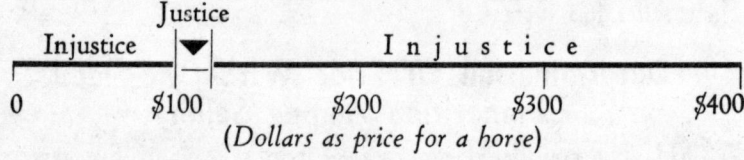

(Dollars as price for a horse)

Determination Of Price With
Two-Sided Competition

Price Formation And Justice

Most exchanges take place under circumstances involving several buyers, competing with each other to buy; and several sellers, competing with each other to sell. *Reality* in price-formation in the modern world is represented by two-sided competition in exchanges of goods and services.

Böhm-Bawerk, in regard to two-sided competition, writes:

Bohm-Bawerk's Eight Sellers Of Horses And Ten Buyers

The case of two-sided competition is both the most frequent occurrence in practical life and also the most important for the development of the law of price. We must therefore devote to it the most thorough attention.

The typical situation which this sort of case presupposes can be represented by Table I. That table conveys the picture of ten willing buyers and eight willing sellers each of whom wishes to buy or to sell, as the case may be, one horse. At the same time the table indicates the degree of subjective valuation applying to each of the candidates for exchange with respect to the commodity in question. The irregularity of the variation of the figures for those valuations is quite in keeping with the actualities of economic life. In actual fact the individual conditions of supply and demand which determine subjective value vary so widely that it is hardly possible that any two persons place exactly the same subjective value on any one thing.

The table is as follows:

TABLE I
Buyers And Sellers Of Horses In Two-Sided Competition

Ten Willing Buyers		Eight Willing Sellers	
Designation	Each Man's Valuation Of One Horse	Designation	Each Man's Valuation Of His Horse
Aa	$300	Ba	$100
Ab	280	Bb	110
Ac	260	Bc	150
Ad	240	Bd	170
Ae	220	Be	200
Af	210	Bf	215
Ag	200	Bg	250
Ah	180	Bh	260
Aj	170		
Ak	150		

It is necessary to add to the foregoing description of the situation that all parties are present in the same market at the same time, that all the horses offered are equal in quality, and finally, that all the candidates for exchange are free from any misconception regarding the market situation which could prevent them from effectively pursuing their own interest. Once more we ask, "What happens in this situation?"

The reader's awareness of the difficulties and his pleasure in solving the problem, will be enhanced if he takes pencil and paper, and sets himself the task of solving the problem by his own method.

I. BAFFLING AND CONTRADICTORY RESULTS FROM VARIOUS COMBINATIONS OF PAIRS OF BUYERS AND SELLERS

His first inclination will be to make a quick effort to "match" buyers and sellers, and provide a snap answer.

When he examines the data in Table I, he soon realizes that he can "match" several ways:

(1) High-price buyers matched to low-price sellers. (In this case, he works down the two columns, pair by pair.)

(2) Low-price buyers matched with low-price sellers. (In this case, he works up the buyer column and down the seller column.)

(3) High-price buyers matched with high-price sellers. (In

this case, he works down the buyer column and up the seller column) ; and

(4) Low-price buyers matched with high-price sellers. (In this case, he works up the two columns, pair by pair.)

Matching High-Price Buyers With Low-Price Sellers. Method No. 1

The way the buyers and sellers are listed in Table I makes it natural to begin by trying to match buyers and sellers simply by working down both columns; that is the way we read, and so we endeavor to solve as we read.

Buyers and sellers are listed with high-price buyers first and low-price sellers first. *Aa* is the first buyer listed, a buyer willing to pay $300 for a horse; *Ba* is the first seller listed, a seller willing to sell for $100. And so on down the columns.

When the reader comes to buyer *Ae* willing to buy at $220, and to seller *Be* willing to sell at $200, he realizes that these two can make a deal between $200 and $220.

From that point on, it appears no more exchanges can take place, because the sellers want more than the remaining buyers are willing to pay. On that basis, five horses will be sold, and no more.

And what will the price be? The first question to consider in that connection is whether these horses, all equal, are to sell at the same price, or different prices. Should *Aa* pay $300 and *Ae* $220? Should *Ba* sell for $100 and should *Be* get $200? Or should the price be *equal* for all buyers and sellers? There are, then, three questions: (1) who is to be included in the deals, (2) should the price be equal, and (3) what should the price or prices be?

Chart VI shows the possible "range" of prices for each pair of buyer and seller.

CHART VI
Range Of Prices For Each Pair Of Buyer And Seller, When High-Price Buyers Are Matched With Low-Price Sellers

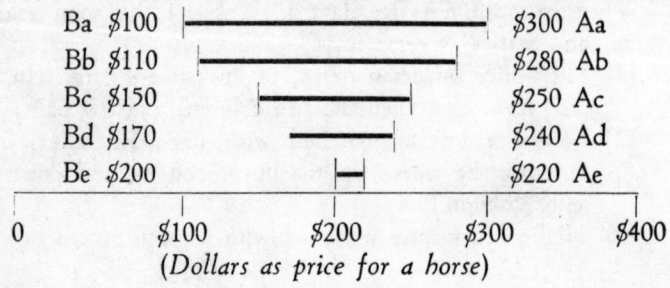

(*Dollars as price for a horse*)

Under this matching system there can be five different prices. The market will be chaotic.

The first pair can "horse-trade" between $100 and $300; the fifth pair can "horse-trade" in a much narrower range, between $200 and $220.

Obviously, if there is to be uniformity of price, on the ground that uniformity of price is a requirement for justice, then the foregoing way of matching buyers and sellers is inappropriate, and will have to be abandoned.

Further, this system "isolates" each pair, and lets the bargaining strength of each buyer and each seller, *uninhibited by competition,* have free rein within the limits set by their respective subjective valuations. This is really not a *market,* but purely isolated trading.

A conclusion may be reached: Method No. 1 is not desirable.

(Note: Other combinations of pairs, affecting details somewhat, can be arranged in this and in the following cases as well. But these variations were not considered worthy of the space required.)

Matching Low-Price Buyers With Low-Price Sellers. Method No. 2.

In this case, we work up the original data in the buyer column and down in the seller column, in Table I. So that we can *conveniently* work down both columns again, we rearrange the data appearing in Table I to get Table II; the buyer column is inverted.

TABLE II
Buyers and Sellers of Horses in Two-Sided Competition

Ten Willing Buyers		Eight Willing Sellers	
Designation	Each Man's Valuation Of One Horse	Designation	Each Man's Valuation Of His Horse
Ak	$150	Ba	$100
Aj	170	Bb	110
Ah	180	Bc	150
Ag	200	Bd	170
Af	210	Be	200
Ae	220	Bf	215
Ad	240		
Ac	260	Bg	250
Ab	280	Bh	260
Aa	300		

In this case, all eight horses can be sold. There can in this case be eight different prices, depending on the skill of the eight sets of traders. Chart VII shows the situation in this case, in a manner parallel to the situation shown in Chart VI.

CHART VII
Range Of Prices For Each Pair Of Buyer and Seller, When Low-Price Buyers Are Matched With Low-Price Sellers

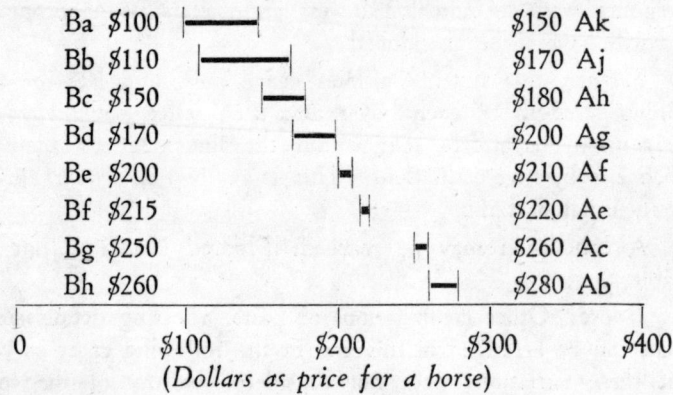

Ba $100	$150 Ak
Bb $110	$170 Aj
Bc $150	$180 Ah
Bd $170	$200 Ag
Be $200	$210 Af
Bf $215	$220 Ae
Bg $250	$260 Ac
Bh $260	$280 Ab

0     $100 $200 $300 $400

(Dollars as price for a horse)

This case has an added peculiarity, to wit, two buyers who were willing to pay much, *Aa willing* to pay $300, and *Ad,* $240, are both excluded. (However, the pairing could be different; instead of excluding the high-price buyers, the pairing could have excluded two of the low-price buyers.)

Justice? How can the sellers have had justice when the best and fourth-best buyers, ready and willing and able to pay $300 and $240 respectively, were excluded?

Method No. 2 must be adjudged inadequate and unacceptable.

Matching High-Price Buyers With High-Price Sellers. Method No. 3.

In this case, again for easy analysis, we arrange the figures, originally shown in Table I, by reversing the seller column and beginning with the high-price sellers. This gives us Table III.

TABLE III
Buyers And Sellers Of Horses In Two-Sided Competition

Ten Willing Buyers		Eight Willing Sellers	
Designation	Each Man's Valuation Of One Horse	Designation	Each Man's Valuation Of His Horse
Aa	$300	Bh	$260
Ab	280	Bg	250

Ac	260	Bf	215
Ad	240	Be	200
Ae	220	Bd	170
Af	210	Bc	150
Ag	200	Bb	110
Ah	180	Ba	100
Aj	170		
Ak	150		

It is quickly obvious that when this system of pairing is employed all eight horses will be sold. The only buyers left are *Aj* and *Ak*, who were willing to pay $170 and $150 respectively for a horse. There were, in fact, two sellers who would have been willing to sell for $100 and $110 respectively, but they were able to get more than $170 from the buyers with whom they were paired.

Chart VIII shows the range of prices for the eight trades.

CHART VIII
Range Of Prices For Each Pair Of Buyer and Seller, When High-Price Buyers Are Matched With High-Price Sellers

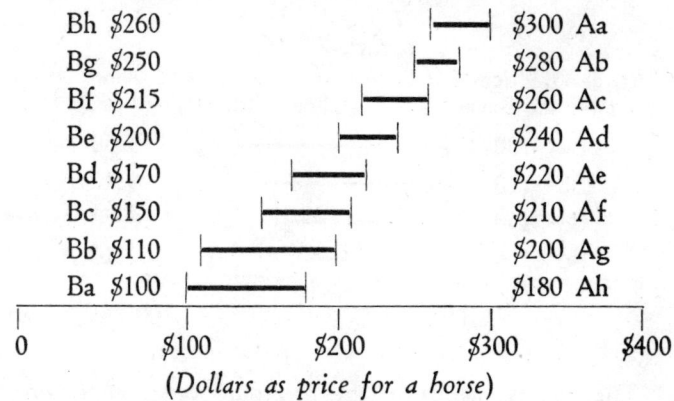

(*Dollars as price for a horse*)

Again, this is not a *market*, but a number of isolated sales. Each pair is uninfluenced by other buyers or sellers. The pairs are, as it were, in water-tight compartments. Almost surely, the eight horses, of equal quality, will nevertheless have eight different prices, determined by the pairing and the trading skills of the men in each pair.

Matching Low-Price Buyers With High-Price Sellers. Method No. 4

In this case, the figures in both columns in Table I are reversed, and we get Table IV, as follows.

Four horses will be sold. Excluded buyers will be *Ab*, willing to buy at $280; and *Aa*, willing to buy at $300; the excluded sellers will be *Be*, *Bf*, *Bg* and *Bh*.

Graphically, the situation is portrayed in Chart IX.

TABLE IV
Buyers And Sellers Of Horses In Two-Sided Competition

Ten Willing Buyers		Eight Willing Sellers	
Designation	Each Man's Valuation Of One Horse	Designation	Each Man's Valuation Of His Horse
Ak	$150	Bh	$260
Aj	170	Bg	250
Ah	180	Bf	215
Ag	200	Be	200
Af	210	Bd	170
Ae	220	Bc	150
Ad	240	Bb	110
Ac	260	Ba	100
Ab	280		
Aa	300		

CHART IX
Range Of Prices For Each Pair Of Buyer And Seller, When Low-Price Buyers Are Matched With High-Price Sellers

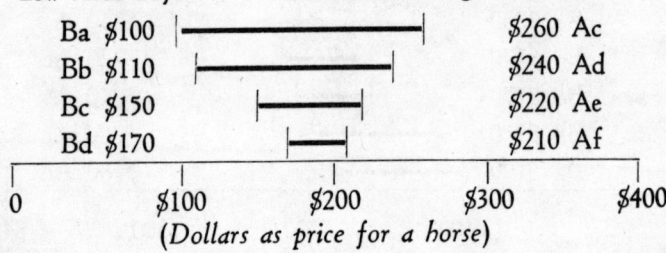

Ba $100		$260 Ac
Bb $110		$240 Ad
Bc $150		$220 Ae
Bd $170		$210 Af

0        $100 $200 $300 $400

(Dollars as price for a horse)

The remarks made in the preceding cases, apply one way or another here, too.

Conclusions, From Foregoing Attempted Quick Solutions

It is apparent from the foregoing that the solutions attempted are invalidated by eager and superficial over-simplification. Individual pairs of buyers and sellers are matched *arbitrarily* just to get a quick answer. But by that process the answers can be so varied that they are worthless.

In the foregoing, *four* patterns of solutions were attempted; we began with high and high, or low and low pairs, etc., but what was to prevent us from selecting *any* pair on a different basis? Nothing. Answers that might be obtained are as numerous as the permutations mathematically possible.

The deficiency consists in that a solution has been attempted without assuming a *market*. A market at least requires that buyers begin by underbidding and finally bid what they are willing to pay, and that sellers begin by over-asking and finally ask what they are willing to sell for. They *compete* with each other.

The existence of a *market* assumes in addition to the foregoing that *each* buyer endeavors to play his need off against *all* sellers, and that *each* seller endeavors to play off his wish to sell against *all* buyers. Every man in the situation is motivated by his own peculiar motivations, by the "pursuit of his self-regarding interests." His basis is his own individual *subjective* evaluation. Those valuations differ more or less for every person.

Each man begins by disclosing a little of his subjective evaluation. As the bidding and asking proceeds, each man is compelled to reveal, to all the others, more and more what his evaluation is. The market, however, does not reveal *everything* about the evaluations of the buyers and sellers.

The "struggle" of the participants in the market is to *find one single price for all*. Probably most people would agree that that is "justice." If that is not justice, then the question is: what is justice *otherwise?* a *varied* price? and *how* should it be determined?

The Range Of Justice In Two-Sided Competition

A chart can now be drawn similar to Charts III, IV and V, but in this case of two-sided competition, to show where "injustice" ends and where "justice" exists.

CHART X
Justice And Injustice In Two-Sided Competition

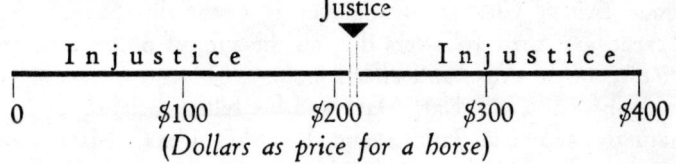

Justice

Injustice   Injustice

| 0 | $100 | $200 | $300 | $400 |

(*Dollars as price for a horse*)

The higgling of the market has been narrowed by competition to a range between $210 and $215. Bargaining strength and skill has, by competition, been restricted to this limited range.

But below $210 and above $215 the price will be "unjust"
because then either some seller or some buyer will be *coerced*. Justice is assumed to be not compatible with coercion.

Confusing Cause And Effect In
Price Formation

Parents of an adolescent son may marvel at his appetite,
and they may "explain" the situation by saying that "John has
a big appetite, because he is growing fast." On reflection, they
might reverse the statement and say, "John is growing fast, because he has a big appetite." Clearly, the *effect* which John's
parents have in mind is his "growing fast," and the immediate
cause is his big intake of food.

In the sciences, cause and effect have frequently been "reversed" erroneously. This has happened conspicuously in the science of economics. One writer has written:

> Malicious persons have been prone to describe [British
> Classical Economics], the system of political economy which
> Ricardo formulated and Mill made popular, as the cart-
> before-the-horse system, . . . according as they were struck
> by the [frequency] with which that system mistakes cause
> for effect.

Ricardo, for example, taught that *costs determine prices*. It is instead the other way around, because the prices obtainable for finished merchandise determine which costs are tolerable; that is,
demand determines prices. One way to formulate the difference
between British Classical Economics and Austrian Neoclassical
Economics is that the former says *costs determine prices,* and
the latter says *demand determines prices.*

There can be no real doubt that the statement just quoted
about British Classical Economics is essentially correct; Smith,
Ricardo and their followers did, on the subject of price determination, confuse cause and effect.

Unfortunately, Karl Marx and his fellow-socialists undiscrim-
inatingly accepted Smith's and Ricardo's ideas. Marx asserted
aggressively that a cost factor—*one* important cost factor, namely
labor—was the determinant of prices, or should be.

In confusing cause and effect in the crucial field of prices,
Smith, Ricardo and Marx made the same basic error.

Justice And Injustice In Price Determination Under Four Different Circumstances

Prices Under Four Different Circumstances

In isolated bargaining the price of a horse (under Böhm-Bawerk's assumptions) can vary in a wide range, between $100 and $300.

Under one-sided competition among buyers, the prices will fall in a higher and narrower range, between $280 and $300.

Under one-sided competition among sellers, the price will fall in a lower and narrower range, between $100 and $120.

Under two-sided competition, the price will fall in a middle and very narrow range, between $210 and $215.

Chart XI shows the foregoing, graphically.

CHART XI
"Just" and "Unjust" Market Prices For Horses Under Four Circumstances

(1)   Isolated Exchange
(2)   One-Sided Competition Among Buyers
(3)   One-Sided Competion Among Sellers
(4)   Two-Sided Competition

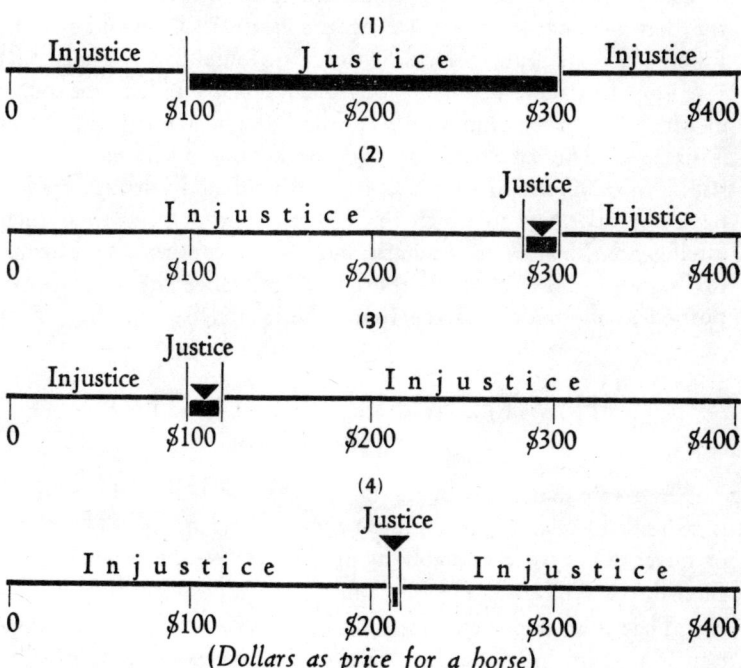

(*Dollars as price for a horse*)

1. When there is one buyer and one seller, the range in which the bargaining takes place can be very wide. The trader who is better, or bolder, or more ruthless, can force the price far in the direction of his own idea of what the price should be, and far away from what the other man would like the price to be. (See the heavy portion of the first horizontal bar in Chart XI, which shows the range in which the price can fall.)

2. When there is *one* seller but *many* buyers, the seller has a heyday. He easily obtains a higher price, not because he is a better, bolder and more ruthless trader, but *because the buyers compete with each other by outbidding each other*. To get a high price is not evidence that a man is an extortionist and hardhearted; it often is nothing more than evidence that buyers consider it to be for their own good to outbid each other. It is not so much the seller who extorted for himself the higher price; instead he received the higher price effortlessly because of the eagerness of the several buyers. (See the heavy portion of the second horizontal bar in Chart XI.

3. When there are *many* sellers and *one* buyer, the situation is reversed. The sellers under-sell each other. A low price is not conclusive evidence of skillful and heartless pricing by the buyer; it may instead be evidence of eagerness of sellers to sell. It is for that reason that the price of the horse that is sold will be lower. (See the heavy portion of third horizontal bar in Chart XI.)

4. When there are *many* buyers and *many* sellers, the range in which the buyers and sellers can be "tough" toward each other is narrow. The range in our example became a trifling $5 compared to $200 in isolated trading. Skillful and ruthless traders have no real range in which to "extort" from another what their intelligence, wealth or strength might induce them to attempt to "extort." The "market" restricts them. (See the small heavy portion in the middle of the fourth horizontal bar in Chart XI.)

How The Market Protects The Individual Trader

In a free market, with enough buyers and sellers so that there is two-sided exchange, is the inexperienced and nonpowerful seller or buyer *protected* reasonably against others — the powerful, the shrewd, the veterans?

That is an important question, because the customary assumption is that an inexperienced, uninformed, nonrich buyer or seller is at a grave disadvantage, and needs to be protected against others by a paternalistic bureaucrat. Such a buyer or seller is thought to be "on his own," unassisted by others, and consequently exploitable.

If the reader turns back to page 120 where Böhm-Bawerk first set up his Table of buyers (ranked downward in their valuations), and sellers (ranked upward in their valuations), and if the reader has understood the text matter following (in which Böhm-Bawerk explains the critical marginal pairs), then if he (the reader) will examine Table V he will discover that its designates the marginal pairs with whom Böhm-Bawerk was concerned.

TABLE V
Buyers And Sellers Of Horses In Two-Sided Competition

Ten Willing Buyers		Eight Willing Sellers	
Designation	Each Man's Valuation Of One Horse	Designation	Each Man's Valuation Of His Horse
Aa	$300	Ba	$100
Ab	280	Bb	110
Ac	260	Bc	150
Ad	240	Bd	170
Ae	220 (a)	Be	200 (a)
Af	210 (b)	Bf	215 (b)
Ag	200	Bg	250
Ah	180	Bh	260
Aj	170		
Ak	150		

(a) "First" marginal pair.
(b) "Second" marginal pair.

Böhm-Bawerk's idea may be given a final summary as follows:

1. Note the two marginal pairs. One of the pairs is the last to make an exchange; he calls them the first marginal pair; see items marked (a) in Table V. The other is the first of the pairs not to make an exchange; he calls them the second marginal pair; see items marked (b) in Table V. The first pair determines the participants. The second pair determines the range of prices. In regard to actual trading, it is the first pair that is ultimate. In regard to price, it is the second pair that is ultimate.

2. In two-sided exchange, no individual buyer or seller sets the price: the second marginal pair determines a (narrow) range for it. See pages 120-123. Everybody who makes an exchange makes a good deal *for himself* by exchanging. Even the two mem-

bers of the first marginal pair (Ae and Be) gain from the exchange; what they get is subjectively more valuable to them than that with which they part. But all the others who are in the pairs which have a still greater capability for exchange than the first marginal pair have an even bigger spread between their subjective valuations and the price range set by the second marginal pair.

3. Those with still smaller capacity for exchange than the first marginal pair, simply are not willing to make a deal to which others will agree. They are outside of the market, but they hover on the edge, and when their valuation and that of others change, they may be able to participate.

4. Böhm-Bawerk is meticulous and detailed in regard to the marginal pairs in his exposition; see page 125ff. If the answer in regard to price determination is to be further simplified, then it would read this way: *the price range is determined by the would-be buyer and the would-be seller who come the closest to making an exchange but fail.* The price will fall between the bid of that would-be buyer and the offering of that would-be seller. (In Böhm-Bawerk's illustration that buyer was Af bidding $210 and the seller was Bf offering a horse at $215).

Böhm-Bawerk, by his ideas on *value* and *price* revolutionized thinking on those subjects; he brilliantly clarified the definition of the new terms he used; but he did not propose a single improvement; he relied on men's voices; their capability of hearing; their memory; and their presumed knowledge of when everybody had reached his best offer to buy or sell. He then indicated that they would all act simultaneously.

In fact, Böhm-Bawerk, although he *outlined* a perfect market, made amazing assumptions about it. He made provision only for *individual matchings;* he did *not* make provision for comprehensive over-all matching. He either assumed individual trades (commonly known by the denigrating term of "horse trading") or else he *assumed* that *all* buyers and *all* sellers had *mysteriously* sorted out all their bids, at an imaginary simultaneous instant. No auction market in the world operates according to Böhm-Bawerk's horse market, or ever has, or will, unless certain aids are devised that Böhm-Bawerk did not trouble himself to develop. There is no evidence that Böhm-Bawerk thought of specifying that every broker in an auction market should or did sort his bid and asked quotations according to one single principle, as in Table V on page 203.

Frederick Nymeyer

ABC Optimum Price Computator

For Attainment of Perfect Competition
in Auction Markets of Stocks,
Bonds, Foreign Exchange, Fungible Goods, Etc.

Publisher's Preface to Supplement II

Which Describes a New Method of Establishing a Perfect Auction Market

Böhm-Bawerk published his *CAPITAL AND INTEREST* more than eighty years ago. A horse market in a rustic village may not have an image that appears relevant in the late twentieth century. The Supplement which follows will reveal how it should be possible to make the most complex and intense of present-day auction markets become operative on the basis of Böhm-Bawerk's ideas.

Böhm-Bawerk never published a "method" or a "procedure," nor specified facilities or mechanisms to make his "market" a reality and/or more effective. He relied on the intentions, memories, and the sorting-out of quotations in each of the minds of the buyers and the sellers. He does not once refer to an agent or broker. Nobody was suggested to sort out the "capable" buyers and "capable" sellers in the Böhm-Bawerkian sense of capability. His *mechanism* consisted of no more than men's voices bidding and asking, men's ears hearing, and each man's mind separately comparing quotations but without a common rule of how to match bid and asked quotations.

Supplement II outlines a novel system for a new era of making Auction Markets perform *perfectly*. This kind of a market is a genuine antithesis of any socialist price-setting system and/or its social-planning derivatives.

ABC Optimum
Price Computator

For Attainment of Perfect Competition in Auction Markets of Stocks, Bonds, Foreign Exchange, Fungible Goods, Etc.

To explain the functioning of this Computator in auction markets the simplest thing to do is (1) to describe the present method of "price determination," (2) to outline the new method of price determination by the Computator, and (3) then to call attention to the significance of the differences.

In a general way, this Computator (1) greatly reduces the labor involved presently in "making a market"; (2) can result in commission charges being reduced, but brokers continuing to make as much or more profit; (3) can realize that elusive vision of economic theorists of a price based on "perfect competition" which most of them consider to be unattainable; (4) will make some functions, now considered necessary or at least helpful, superfluous; and (5) permit regulatory agencies to be able facilely to research the goings-on in the "market."

This Computator is revolutionary; it permits doing what hitherto has been considered to be impossible to do. Brokers describe their many functions (as brokers) to be an art, not a science. Understanding the operation of this Computator suggests one conclusion: That which has been designated as "art" is only a bungling way of doing poorly, slowly and at high cost what can be reduced to exact, speedy and low-cost scientific method.

The explanation of what determines prices, namely, *supply and demand*, is a meaningless cliché which people use as an explanation of "price determination," but which they are invariably unable to explain in turn, and, in principle have never been able to explain, thoroughly. Their explanation consists only in a phrase which they are unable to demonstrate mathematically. In other words, the explanation consists in a generality and in vagueness.

In this Computator *every* buyer and seller capable of making a transaction is enabled to do so at *one* ideal price for all. Contrarily, all would-be buyers or sellers, who are in their pricing ideas too high as sellers, or too low as buyers, are excluded. Sellers and buyers of stocks, bonds, foreign exchange and fungible goods have a potential future which will be revolutionarily better than their own past experience, or any experience of the previous generations of mankind.

When several years ago the idea of this ABC Optimum Price Computator was intimated in a general way to several economists, their answer was, "It can*not* be done."

I ‑ Present Method of Price Determination

The functions of a broker can be described in various ways and in more or less detail, namely, he receives orders to buy and orders to sell; he transmits the orders to the floor of the Stock Exchange; he offers the stock for sale or endeavors to purchase and makes the commitment at what price to buy or sell; he reports back to his customer; he makes arrangements to deliver the stocks sold or to receive the stocks bought; etc.

A *broker* is essentially different from a *salesman*, in that a broker merely executes what the customer wants done; a salesman endeavors to tell the customer what he ought to do. Therefore, a broker, in his function as broker, merely posts on his "book" what securities the customer wants to buy or sell; at what price; for how long the sale or purchase order is good; if the sale is to be permitted at higher or lower prices from the last sale recorded, then the buyer or seller will instruct the broker how far he may go.

For example, a customer may say that he wishes to sell at the "market," but if the broker asks him what to do if the market goes lower, the customer may respond by telling what the limit is that he will accept. On the other hand, if he is buying stock, he will probably say, "Buy at the present market or lower"; and then if the broker asks him how high he may go, the customer may put a limit somewhere above the present market. There are, of course, many variations of buy or sell orders (too many to outline here).

If a man has been designated as a Specialist in a particular stock, he may get an order from one customer to sell a stock at a particular price, but he may already have an order to buy such a stock at that same price; or he may get it shortly thereafter. In a sense, therefore, a specialist has many opportunities for "matching" buy and sell orders. The principal function of a specialist is to do just that, to "match"orders, whether the buy or sell orders are both in his hand (or book), or he learns about them when given quotes in another specialist's book. In a sense, therefore, a specialist can make a number of deals using only his own "book."

On Friday, August 11, 1972 XYZ Corporation stock closed on the New York Stock Exchange at $11\frac{1}{4}$. On that Friday, there were 26,000 shares sold. The market opened at $11\frac{1}{8}$; the high was $11\frac{3}{8}$; the low was 11. The net change for the day was $\frac{1}{4}$ up. Furthermore, the high and the low for the year, thus far, was 14 high and $8\frac{3}{8}$ low.

It is impossible for a broker to retain all the orders and their prices in his memory, and so he has a "book." Description of this "book" and how it is used is reproduced on the following pages from *Now, About the SPECIALIST*, put out by the New York Stock Exchange. Readers are referred to the reproduced pages, especially page 4.

Now, about the Specialist...

New York Stock Exchange

who he is

The average Specialist on the Exchange is in his mid-fifties. He is one of 350 Members engaged in the same business and associated in about 110 separate units — mostly partnerships and joint arrangements. On the average, each unit specializes in about eleven stocks.

144 Specialists, or about 41% of the total, have been in this profession for more than 20 years; 226, or about 65%, have been Specialists more than 10 years.

his place of business

Every Specialist works at a particular location at one of the Trading Posts on the Floor of the Exchange at the only point where the stocks in which he specializes may be traded.

how he becomes a specialist

He makes application to the Exchange and receives formal approval. But before approval is granted, he must show that he can meet the capital requirements prescribed by the Exchange, and demonstrate his ability to perform the Specialist function after serving for a designated training period as an "associate" Specialist with an established Specialist group. He must also agree to conduct his business under an extremely rigid set of prescribed rules and policies and must observe a high standard of business ethics.

capital requirements

In general, the Exchange requires that each Specialist be able to carry an over-night position of 400 shares of each 100 share unit stock in which he is registered. That is the bare minimum, however, and many Specialists employ a great deal more capital in servicing the stocks which they handle. Some use only their own funds; others augment this with financing arrangements with other Exchange Member organizations or banks.

2

his functions

He has two big jobs. . . .

He must effectively execute orders entrusted to him by other Members of the Exchange. These orders are left with him when the current market price is away from the price of the orders. The Specialist represents them when the market level reaches those prices. Thus he makes it possible for other Members to conduct business elsewhere on the Trading Floor.

and

He must maintain, insofar as reasonably practicable, fair and orderly markets in the stocks which he services. When there is temporary disparity between supply and demand he buys or sells for his own account to narrow the price changes between sales. By doing this, he keeps price continuity more orderly than would otherwise be the case and contributes to the liquidity of the market. He thus makes it possible for investors' orders to be executed at better prices.

executing orders

The Specialist enters orders on his "book" under each price category in the order of their receipt. He indicates for each order the number of shares and the Broker from whom it was received. He represents those orders in the market, frequently competing against other Members who are representing their customers. As he is successful in executing the orders on his book, he sends reports of executions to the Members for whom he acted in the order of listing in his book under the particular price category. When he makes a transaction for another Broker, or when an order is cancelled, he crosses it out on his book. Some pages from a typical Specialist's book might look like this:

3

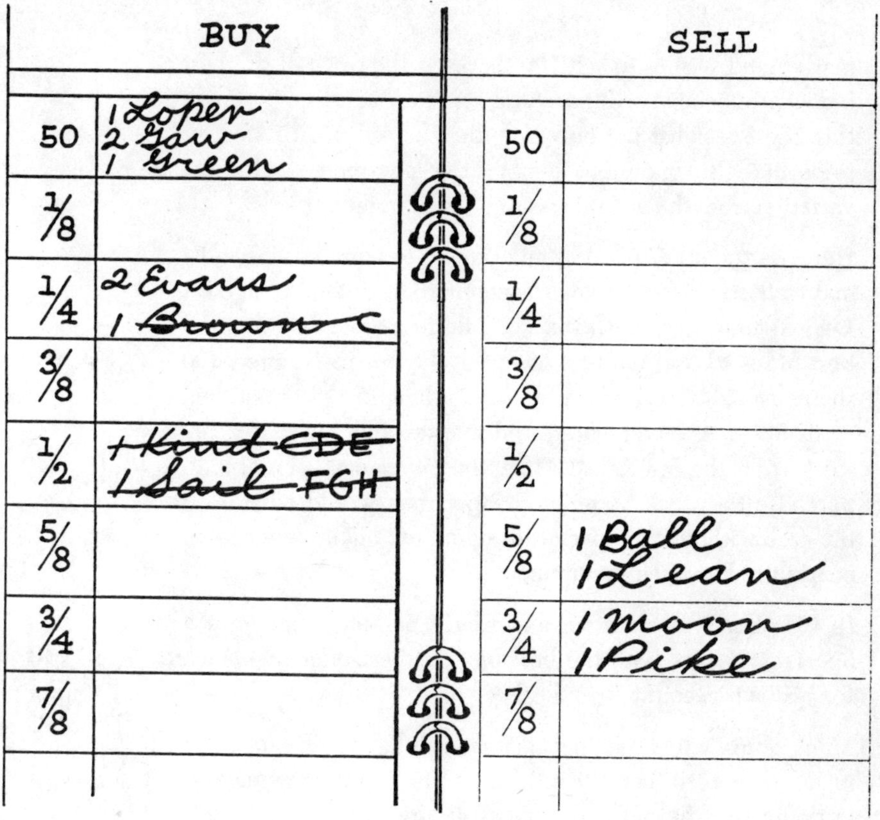

BUY			SELL	
50	*1 Loper* *2 Gaw* *1 Green*		50	
⅛			⅛	
¼	*2 Evans* *1 ~~Brown~~ C*		¼	
⅜			⅜	
½	*~~+ Kind CDE~~* *~~1 Sail~~ FGH*		½	
⅝			⅝	*1 Ball* *1 Lean*
¾			¾	*1 Moon* *1 Pike*
⅞			⅞	

(The orders to buy at 50½ have been executed and notations made indicating the selling Brokers. The order to buy 100 at 50¼ has been cancelled.)

maintaining a market

The Specialist maintains markets by purchasing stock at a higher price than anyone else is willing to pay or by selling stock at a lower price than anyone else is willing to take. For example, let's assume that a stock has just sold at 55. The highest price at which anyone is willing to purchase more of the stock is 54¼ (the best bid), and the lowest price at which anyone is willing to sell is 55¼ (the best offer). The Specialist, acting as a dealer for his own account, may now decide to bid 54¾ for 100 shares, making the quotation 54¾-55¼, which narrows the spread between the bid and offer prices to ½ point. Now, if a prospective seller enters the

4

market and wishes to sell 100 shares at the price of the best bid, the Specialist will *purchase* his stock at 54¾. By doing this, the Specialist not only provides the seller with a better price but also maintains better price continuity, since the variation from the last sale is only ¼ of a point.

Here, on the other hand, is an example of how the Specialist may *sell* stock for his own account to maintain a market: Let's assume that, with the last sale in a stock at 62¼, the best bid is 62 and the best offer 63. The Specialist offers 100 shares at 62½ for his own account, changing the quotation to 62-62½. A buyer enters the market and purchases the stock from the Specialist. Thus, the buyer has been able to purchase the stock ½ point cheaper than would have been the case without the Specialist's offer, and again better price continuity has been maintained.

In his efforts to maintain an orderly market, sometimes a Specialist makes both the best bid and best offer in a stock for his own account.

Many times, when the Specialist doesn't have sufficient stock in his inventory, he will sell "short" to maintain a market; in doing this, he must observe all the rules and regulations governing "short" selling.

a "fair and orderly" market

The Specialist is not expected to prevent a stock from declining nor is he expected to keep it from going up. He is, however, expected to make every effort to keep rises and declines fair and orderly, insofar as is reasonably practicable under the circumstances.

Obviously, a single, specific formula cannot be applied to markets in individual stocks to determine whether they are fair and orderly. What is considered fair and orderly in one stock may be regarded as completely inadequate in another. It depends on such things as market conditions, the price level of the stock, the normal volume of transactions, the number of outstanding shares and how closely the stock is held.

5

[Pages 6 through 11 not relevant; therefore omitted.]

arranging the opening

Most of the orders received by Brokers on the Floor before the opening of the market are left with the Specialist. Using these orders and also dealing for his own account in varying degrees, the Specialist arranges the opening price in each stock as close as possible to the previous close. In arranging the opening he must consider general market conditions and market circumstances in the particular stock.

Sometimes unusual situations arise which demand special treatment. Let's assume that XYZ Oil Company Common Stock closed at $39\frac{7}{8}$. However, after the close of the market, announcement is made of a new oil strike on land owned by the XYZ Oil Company. This leads to a heavy influx of buy orders the following morning.

A Governor of the Exchange is called into the "crowd" to supervise the situation. All orders to buy and sell are given to the Specialist.

Let's say that, after a count is made, the Specialist finds himself with orders to purchase 15,000 shares at the market and orders to sell 3,000 shares at the market. (Usually there are also limited orders to *buy*, but for purposes of simplicity, they are eliminated from this example.) The Specialist also has limit orders to *sell* at the following prices:

$$
\begin{array}{r}
700 \text{ at } 40 \\
100 \text{ at } 40\frac{1}{8} \\
400 \text{ at } 40\frac{1}{4} \\
600 \text{ at } 40\frac{1}{2} \\
200 \text{ at } 40\frac{3}{4} \\
1{,}500 \text{ at } 41 \\
300 \text{ at } 41\frac{1}{2} \\
500 \text{ at } 42 \\
100 \text{ at } 42\frac{3}{4} \\
200 \text{ at } 43
\end{array}
$$

Thus an additional 4,600 shares are offered at prices ranging from 40 to 43. If it were decided to open the stock at 43,

12

selling orders, including the market orders to sell, would supply only 7,600 shares of the 15,000 wanted — and at a price over three points higher than the previous close. This might be considered too great a variation, and so an attempt would be made to narrow the gap between the large demand and the small supply.

To do this, the opening of XYZ Oil Company's stock is delayed. Floor Brokers who had left orders with the Specialist, and others, ask, "How's XYZ?" The Specialist replies that there are "buyers" in the stock. The Floor Brokers then relay this information to their Member Firm offices so that customers will know that XYZ is probably going to open at a substantially higher price than the previous close.

Similar information is also passed along by the Specialist to those firms that he knows have been interested in the security. Floor Traders might also be consulted to see whether they wish to sell stock.

After the Governor in charge feels enough time has passed to permit the situation to crystallize, a quotation is established even though there may be a wider than usual spread between the bid and offer prices.

As a result of all this let's assume that 1,000 of the 15,000 shares to buy at the market are cancelled. Sellers, however, are attracted by the bid price. They put in orders to sell totalling an extra 1,500 shares.

The Governor and the Specialist now reappraise the situation and find that there are 14,000 shares to buy at the market and 4,500 shares to sell at the market, leaving 9,500 shares to buy on balance. The Governor notes that there are limited price orders in the Specialist's possession to sell 3,500 shares up through 41. In other words, if the stock opens at 41, 3,500 shares could be sold on the orders limited at 41 or lower, reducing the on-balance amount to buy to 6,000 shares. The Governor learns that the Specialist is "long" 2,200 shares of

13

..XYZ.OPD 14.000.s.41¼..

stock, which, if sold, would reduce the on-balance amount wanted to 3,800 shares.

At this point, the Specialist and the Governor decide on a quotation of 41 bid, offered at 43. This quotation is published on the ticker tape. It results in only one extra order being received — 500 to sell at 41¼. The Governor then discusses the situation with the Specialist to see at what price he would be willing to supply the balance by going "short." As a result of this discussion then, 14,000 shares of XYZ Oil open at 41¼, up 1⅜ points from the previous close. 4,000 shares are sold on behalf of the orders held by the Specialist to sell at limits of 41¼ or lower; 4,500 shares are supplied by the market orders to sell, and 5,500 shares by the Specialist (his inventory of 2,200 shares and 3,300 shares sold "short.")

matched and lost

Exchange rules govern trading on the Floor where there is more than one bid at the same price, and it is not possible to determine the order in which the bids were made. The bids are then considered to be on a par with one another provided they are as large, or larger, than the amount which may be offered in the market at the particular price. (The same principle applies to offers.) In such instances, the Brokers who are on parity "match" coins to determine who makes the transaction. For example, let's say that three Brokers all bid for stock at a price of 50 at the same time, two of them bidding for 200 shares each and the third bidding for only 100 shares. Then another Broker with a sell order decides to sell 200 shares at 50. The two Brokers bidding for 200 shares each would "match" to see which one makes the purchase. The third Broker bidding at 50 would not be entitled to "match," because his bid is not as large as the amount offered.

14

The losing Broker's customer might be notified that the Broker had "matched and lost." This is to answer any question the customer might have should he notice a print on the tape at his price and wonder why his order was not executed. The winning Broker in such cases does not report that he has "matched and won," since the customer, of course, is notified that his order has been executed.

Most "match" situations occur as a result of a basic auction market rule which provides that every sale "clears the Floor" and starts a new auction. For example, let's say that a Broker enters a "crowd" with the market 49⅞-50¼ and bids 50 for 100 shares. A few minutes later another Member enters the "crowd" and bids 50 for 100 shares. Still another Broker comes in five minutes later and makes an indentical bid. Any willing seller at 50 would sell to the Broker making the first bid at 50. However, let's assume that another Member enters the "crowd," bids 50⅛ for 100 shares and buys stock at that price from a seller who has been standing in the "crowd." This transaction at 50⅛ clears the Floor and places the three Brokers bidding at 50 on parity so that they will have to "match" against one another in the event that 100 shares of stock come into the market to sell at 50.

In representing the orders entrusted to him, the Specialist often competes against other Brokers in the market, so that it is frequently necessary for him to "match" against them.

In order to illustrate the problems of a broker, we present an imaginary "book" for Broker A as is shown in Exhibit I; we are also showing a "book" for Broker B as is shown in Exhibit II. The assumption has been made that XYZ Corporation has two specialists on the New York Stock Exchange.

The sample appearing in the booklet of the New York Stock Exchange is over-simplified. It has only eleven (11) entries, some of which have been cancelled. To make the imaginary books presented in Exhibit I and Exhibit II more realistic for a company the size of XYZ Corporation, more and larger entries have been made. (For corporations much larger than XYZ Corporation, these "Books" would undoubtedly be too small.) A reader will discover that Exhibits I and II conform to the Books used by specialists on the New York Stock Exchange.

EXHIBIT I — XYZ Corporation
Order Book — Broker A, One of Two Specialists

BUY		SELL		
Price	Shares	Price	Shares	
10		10		
⅛		⅛		
¼		¼		
⅜		⅜		
½		½		
⅝		⅝		
¾		¾		
⅞		⅞		
11	1,100	11	200	
⅛	800	⅛	400	
¼	1,500	¼	1,000	(market closed)
⅜	3,800	⅜	700	
½	500	½	600	
⅝	200	⅝	200	
¾		¾	500	
⅞		⅞	100	
12		12		
Total	7,900		3,700	

Figures as 3,800 shares at *one* price on *one* specialist's book may come from a dozen sources. (Brokers not specialists in XYZ Corporation stock will have turned their orders over to this specialist (or another) for execution.) Of course, the exact origin of each buy or sell order will need to be recorded, but will only complicate this explanation, which aims at simplicity here.

Broker A, when he examines his book, will immediately realize that he can "match" orders to buy or sell as follows:

$$200 \text{ shares at } 11$$
$$400 \text{ shares at } 11\frac{1}{8}$$
$$1,000 \text{ shares at } 11\frac{1}{4}$$
$$700 \text{ shares at } 11\frac{3}{8}$$
$$500 \text{ shares at } 11\frac{1}{2}$$
$$200 \text{ shares at } 11\frac{5}{8}$$

TOTAL 3,000 shares

It is "matching" buy and sell orders which "makes the market." Matching buy and sell orders is the quintessence of the function of brokers.

The problem, however, arises that there will be six (6) different prices—all the way from 11 to $11\frac{5}{8}$, a range of five-eighths. The customers will hardly be satisfied. (It may be remembered from information on page 209 that the high on August 11 was $11\frac{3}{8}$, and the low was 11; a range of three-eighths.

The problem of price uniformity will be considered later.

Broker B, when he examines his Book, will realize that he can "match" orders to buy and sell as follows:

$$400 \text{ shares at } 11$$
$$1,000 \text{ shares at } 11\frac{1}{8}$$
$$1,400 \text{ shares at } 11\frac{1}{4}$$
$$400 \text{ shares at } 11\frac{3}{8}$$
$$200 \text{ shares at } 11\frac{1}{2}$$
$$100 \text{ shares at } 11\frac{5}{8}$$

and of course the customer willing to buy as high as $11\frac{7}{8}$ can pick up 200 shares of the 600 offered at $11\frac{3}{4}$. The total will be 3,700 shares "matchable" by Broker B.

There are seven different prices, however, and that will be a problem in this case, too. More on this later.

There will, however, be some "matching" possible from the left-overs of Broker A and Broker B, shown in Exhibit III, which please see.

EXHIBIT II

XYZ Corporation
Order Book
Broker B, One of Two Specialists

BUY			SELL	
Price	Shares		Price	Shares
10			10	
⅛			⅛	
¼			¼	
⅜			⅜	
½	2,000		½	
⅝			⅝	
¾	800		¾	
⅞	900		⅞	
11	1,200		11	400
⅛	1,000		⅛	1,300
¼	1,400		¼	1,600
⅜	400		⅜	900
½	200		½	2,000
⅝	100		⅝	700
¾			¾	600
⅞	200		⅞	
12			12	
Total	8,200			7,500

EXHIBIT III

Further Potential Sales by Matching Residual
Orders on Books of Broker A and Broker B

Price	Broker A's Residual Orders		Broker B's Residual Orders		Obvious Further Sales That Can Be Made
10 ½			buy	2,000	
10 ⅝					
10 ¾			buy	800	
10 ⅞			buy	900	
11	buy	900	buy	800	
11 ⅛	buy	400	sell	300	B can sell 300
11 ¼	buy	500	sell	200	B can sell 200
11 ⅜	buy	3100	sell	500	B can sell 500
11 ½	sell	100	sell	1800	
11 ⅝			sell	600	
11 ¾			sell	400	
11 ⅞					
				Total	1,000 shares

EXHIBIT IV
Summary of All Shares Matched of Brokers A and B
(in shares)

Price	Broker A	Broker B	A and B To Each Other	TOTAL
10 ½				
10 ⅝				
10 ¾				
10 ⅞				
11	200	400		600
11 ⅛	400	1,000	300	1,700
11 ¼	1,000	1,400	200	2,600
11 ⅜	700	400	500	1,600
11 ½	500	200		700
11 ⅝	200	100		300
11 ¾		200		200
11 ⅞				
TOTAL	3,000	3,700	1,000	7,700

So much for *simple* matching. But there are different and many "permutations and combinations" possible. To avoid confusion not even examples of such "permutations and combinations" will be given. Every such "permutations and combinations" will yield variable prices, that is, at a given time on the market there will not be perfect equity on the price; the "market" will be *unjust*.

The question ends up in this form: Will *any* system of "permutations or combinations" yield a uniform price and permit a maximum number of deals at that one price? That is exactly what this Computator will do.

One final word, at this point, on what *one* broker specialist *can* do; or two or more brokers. The answer is: *practically nothing*. Transactions on the New York Stock Exchange are fast, the data change momentarily. No human mind exists which has the capability to make the "matchings" fast enough. More on this later, too. The very fact that there is more than *one* specialist results in the ideal answer not being discoverable. For a *perfect* market *all* the data must be collated at only *one* location, such as in the Computator.

II ∙ The New Method of Price Determination By the Computator

The crucial question is: Can some agency other than Broker A, and/or Broker B, arrive at one ideal price for *all* the orders they have on each Book respectively? The answer is: There is such an agency. But no broker can humanly do this; a Computator is necessary. See Exhibits IV, V and VI.

In the case of Broker A, the opportunities on his Book are:
> Shares he can move (100 shares each) 2,400
> Single price at which he moves them $11\frac{3}{8}$

In the case of Broker B, the opportunities on his Book are:
> Shares he can move (100 shares each) 2,300
> Single price at which he moves them $11\frac{1}{4}$

But when the orders of Brokers A and B are combined, the following is possible:
> Shares that can be moved (100 shares each) 5,400
> Single price at which they can be moved $11\frac{3}{8}$

The requisite steps are simple:

1. All orders must be fed into the Computator as buy or sell orders.

2. The machine must be capable of sorting the orders out according to price.

3. The machine must sort out *buyers according to their capability,* the highest priced buyers coming first.

4. The machine must sort out the *sellers according
   to their capability,* the lowest priced sellers coming first.

5. The "marginal" buyers and sellers must be determined.

   In the case of Broker A the marginal pair is
   the 23rd and the price is 11⅜.

   In the case of Broker B the marginal pair is
   the 23rd and the price is 11¼.

   When the orders of the two are combined, the
   marginal pair is the 54th.

6. The 54th buyer will pay 11⅜; the 54th seller will
   accept 11⅜. But although the 55th seller is ready
   to sell at 11⅜ also, there are no more buyers who
   will pay 11⅜, because the 55th buyer will pay
   only 11¼; this deal cannot be made.

7. At that time in the market for XYZ Corporation
   stock, every would-be buyer and every would-be
   seller who can agree on the price will be determined. If *all* orders for the stock to buy or to
   sell were fed into this one Computator, there
   would be *perfect competition,* and then the price
   would be 11⅜. Of course, on a different day or a
   different hour of the day, the market might be
   different.

All the foregoing is shown as simply as possible in
Exhibit V for Broker A, in Exhibit VI for Broker B,
and in Exhibit VII for the whole market.

EXHIBIT V

The Feeding of Data and the Principles of Sorting Which Determine the "Matching" of Orders on the Book of Broker A

BUYERS Willing to Pay	Shares	SELLERS Willing to Sell for	Shares	BUYERS Willing to Pay	Shares	SELLERS Willing to Sell for	Shares
11 ⅝	100	11	100		100		
	100		100		100		
11 ½	100	11 ⅛	100		100		
	100		100		100		
	100		100		100		
	100		100		100		
	100	11 ¼	100	11 ¼	100		
11 ⅜	100		100		100		
	100		100		100		
	100		100		100		
	100		100		100		
	100		100		100		
	100		100		100		
	100		100		100		
	100		100		100		
	100		100		100		
	100	11 ⅜	100		100		
	100		100		100		
	100		100		100		
	100		100		100		
	100		100		100		
	100		100	11 ⅛	100		
	100*		100*		100		
					100		
	100	11 ½	100		100		
	100		100		100		
	100		100		100		
	100		100		100		
	100		100		100		
	100		100	11	100		
	100	11 ⅝	100		100		
	100		100		100		
	100	11 ¾	100		100		
	100		100		100		
	100		100		100		
	100		100		100		
	100		100		100		
	100	11 ⅞	100		100		
	100				100		
	100				100		

*The marginal pair; the last buy and sell orders that can be matched. Regarding "marginal pairs," see pages 203 and 120.

EXHIBIT VI

The Feeding of Data and the Principles of Sorting Which Determine the "Matching" of Orders on the Book of Broker B

BUYERS		SELLERS		BUYERS		SELLERS	
Willing to Pay	Shares	Willing to Sell for	Shares	Willing to Pay	Shares	Willing to Sell for	Shares
11⅞	100	11	100		100		100
	100		100		100	11½	100
11⅝	100		100		100		100
11½	100		100		100		100
	100	11⅛	100	10⅞	100		100
11⅜	100		100		100		100
	100		100		100		100
	100		100		100		100
	100		100		100		100
11¼	100		100		100		100
	100		100		100		100
	100		100	10¾	100		100
	100		100		100		100
	100		100		100		100
	100		100		100		100
	100	11¼	100		100		100
	100		100		100		100
	100		100		100		100
	100		100	10½	100	11⅝	100
	100		100		100		100
	100		100		100		100
	100*		100*		100		100
11⅛	100		100		100		100
	100		100		100	11¾	100
	100		100		100		100
	100		100		100		100
	100		100		100		100
	100		100		100		100
	100		100		100		100
	100		100		100		100
	100		100		100		
	100		100				
11	100	11⅜	100				
	100		100				
	100		100				
	100		100				
	100		100				
	100		100				
	100		100				
	100		100				

*The marginal pair; the last buy and sell orders that can be matched. Regarding "marginal pairs," see pages 203 and 120.

EXHIBIT VII

The Feeding of Data and the Principles of Sorting Which Determine the "Matching" of Orders in the Total Market

BUYERS Willing to Pay	BUYERS Shares	SELLERS Willing to Sell for	SELLERS Shares	BUYERS Willing to Pay	BUYERS Shares	SELLERS Willing to Sell for	SELLERS Shares
11⅞	100	11	100		100		100
	100		100		100		100
11⅝	100		100		100		100
	100		100		100	11½	100
	100		100		100		100
11½	100		100		100		100
	100	11⅛	100		100		100
	100		100		100		100
	100		100		100		100
	100		100		100		100
	100		100		100		100
	100		100		100		100
11⅜	100		100		100		100
	100		100		100		100
	100		100		100		100
	100		100		100		100
	100		100		100		100
	100		100		100		100
	100		100		100		100
	100		100		100		100
	100		100		100		100
	100		100	11⅛	100		100
	100		100		100		100
	100	11¼	100		100		100
	100		100		100		100
	100		100		100		100
	100		100		100		100
	100		100		100		100
	100		100		100		100
	100		100		100	11⅝	100
	100		100		100		100
	100		100		100		100
	100		100		100		100
	100		100		100		100
	100		100		100		100
	100		100		100		100
	100		100		100		100
	100		100		100		100
	100		100		100	11¾	100
	100		100	11	100		100
	100		100		100		100
	100		100		100		100
	100		100		100		100
	100		100		100		100
	100		100		100		100
	100		100		100		100
	100		100		100		100
	100		100		100		100
	100		100		100	11⅞	100
	100	11⅜	100		100		
	100		100		100		
	100		100		100		
	100		100		100		
	100*		100*		100		
					100		
11¼	100		100		100		
	100		100		100		
	100		100		100		
	100		100		100		
	100		100		100		
	100		100		100		
	100		100		100		
	100		100		100		

*The marginal pair; the last buy and sell orders that can be matched. Regarding "marginal pairs," see pages 203 and 120.

III · Significance of the Principles Underlying the Computator

Careful analysis of data in Sections I and II will bring a reader to conclusions such as the following:

1. No one will realize how difficult the "problem" of "making a market" is unless he spends several hours trying to discover what sales can be made—what "matching" of a particular buyer with a particular seller—and at what price. The analyst will become frustrated, and unable to justify any of several methods that he may test, except he hit upon the principle which controls the design of this Computator. It is that, or else confusion, and chaos, and arbitrary manipulation, and injustice to disfavored buyers or sellers.

2. The existence of a "market" such as the New York Stock Exchange is evidence that there has been a clear awareness that the greater the number of buyers and sellers that can be brought together at *one* location, the better the market for those buyers and sellers. But a further legitimate and reliable generalization consists in the realization that there must be a "brain" in *one* big market capable of sorting more data than any human brain can accept, appraise, classify and "rank" item by item. Granted that brokers and specialists on the New York Stock Exchange can develop great skills and speeds, none can do the job in the case of a company of large size. (Therefore, there are two or more specialists in such cases.) But these specialists cannot coordinate *systematically;* they never do more than approximate the right market price, and can only guess who should be able to buy and to sell. Unless the sorting is done so perfectly as in this Computator—unless the sorting is done *in this way* only—no perfect results are possible. Therefore the New York Stock Exchange needs

dozens of these Computators. Maybe for transactions in General Motors' stock the Exchange should have a particular Computator which would accumulate data for fifteen-minute intervals, then clear and yield its results, and begin over. For smaller companies one Computator might alternate between Corporation K and Corporation L. Maybe in other cases involving still smaller companies one Computator might alternate between three or more companies. When the New York Stock Exchange thinks in terms of new and more modern quarters, it should visualize a building filled with Computators and not frenzied and shouting men.

3. There is, of course, a monumental job to be done co-ordinating the supplementary (existing) *informational equipment* with the needed *trading* equipment itself. Present equipment is ancillary to the *trading* function—the "matching" of buy and sell orders. No equipment presently exists which has behind it the boldness of the idea of doing the real job of trading itself. In the latest dozen years, the writer has asked brokers to whom it was fit to address the question, *How do you match buy and sell orders?* In no instance was a responsive answer ever given. (The brokers consider their activity to be an *art* and a gift or a skill, by which they mean that they cannot explain it, which in turn means (but it is not admitted) that they do not really understand their *art*. Brokers really hold that what this Computator proposes to do cannot be based on a "science.")

The same people who supply the information-transmitting equipment naturally ought to undertake to manufacture (in a figure of speech) the real engine in the vehicle—the piece of equipment that does what no broker or group of brokers—no matter how capable—*can* undertake to do.

4. The Securities and Exchange Commission has the responsibility of regulating markets as the New York Stock Exchange. The SEC undoubtedly does its work excellently, considering the circumstances; but the SEC

relies on the cliché of "supply and demand." Probably, too, nobody has undertaken in the history of the XYZ Corporation to determine HOW supply and demand should determine the price of XYZ Corporation stock before it was done (as an example) in Exhibits V, VI and VII. There, *supply* and *demand* were each measured in detail and exactly. Every buyer (with *his* ideas on price) who was CAPABLE of buying, and every seller (with *his* ideas on price) who was CAPABLE of selling were matched together. Every buyer whose idea of price was such that a matching seller could not be found was excluded. Those who could buy or sell influenced the price; those who could not buy or sell did not influence the price. These considerations warrant the following comments:

(a) SEC should, after it undertakes to understand this new and revolutionary Computator, welcome it. The task of SEC can be much simplified by this Computator.

(b) SEC will probably wish to influence supplementary matters in the design of the equipment—to facilitate discovery of irregularities in regard to what is put into the machine.

(c) SEC can solve or reduce many problems by promoting one specific, centralized market for a particular stock.

5. The "theory of free markets" versus the "theory of regulation," and the "theory of manipulation via Specialists" (called supporting the market or some other euphemistic term) are really conflicting. A manipulated market is not really "free." The theory that Specialists make and support markets gets down to this, that the initiated (who have a supposed esoteric knowledge), whose activities are not understood by the uninitiated, will do or will have done the right thing. This is an ages-old but useless myth. There is only one way to get the facts, namely, to earmark the purchases and sales of the Specialist and see how that affected the outcome as in Exhibits V, VI and VII.

6. The reader is referred back again to Pages 12, 13 and 14 photostated from the New York Stock Exchange booklet, *Now, About the SPECIALIST*. There is a description there of what happens when buy and sell orders appear out of balance, because of sudden and new developments. If the rapidly changing data were put into a Computator, it would show at fantastic speed how many shares could be matched and at what price. Then instead of the Specialist and a Governor of the Exchange coming in and trying to match orders clumsily, the input into the Computator, based on what *all* brokers decided to do rather than these two or few only, would work its way out of the imbalance faster, better, and with steadier markets.

7. The problem of big blocks of stock coming on the market from insurance companies, bank trust departments, mutual funds, etc., which now can hardly be put through regular channels of the New York Stock Exchange, would be more easily managed, by there being developed a big input of wider-ranging prices. Such transactions would become routine.

8. The New York Stock Exchange was founded on May 17, 1792, or one hundred eighty years ago. In that one hundred eighty years no broker on the New York Stock Exchange has left any record of having utilized the principle underlying this Computator. The circumstantial evidence for this is conclusive. On the following page, page 4 of the booklet, *Now, About the SPECIALIST*, is reproduced a second time. An inventive mind among the members of the Exchange might have discovered that the "Buy" column should be inverted; the left hand column should have had the 50 on the line of $50\frac{7}{8}$, and the $50\frac{7}{8}$ should have been on the top line. If that were done, then there would have been evidence that one part of the method of the Computator had been understood in principle. Contrast the "difference" between Exhibits I, II and III with the standard Book used by brokers. The "Book" of the Computator has new principles, making obvious its uniqueness, namely:

[Continued on page 233]

BUY			SELL
50	1 *Loper* 2 *Gaw* 1 *Green*	50	
1/8		1/8	
1/4	2 *Evans* 1 ~~*Brown*~~ C	1/4	
3/8		3/8	
1/2	~~*+Kind CDE*~~ ~~*1 Sail*~~ FGH	1/2	
5/8		5/8	1 *Ball* 1 *Lean*
3/4		3/4	1 *moon* 1 *Pike*
7/8		7/8	

(The orders to buy at 50½ have been executed and notations made indicating the selling Brokers. The order to buy 100 at 50¼ has been cancelled.)

maintaining a market

The Specialist maintains markets by purchasing stock at a higher price than anyone else is willing to pay or by selling stock at a lower price than anyone else is willing to take. For example, let's assume that a stock has just sold at 55. The highest price at which anyone is willing to purchase more of the stock is 54¼ (the best bid), and the lowest price at which anyone is willing to sell is 55¼ (the best offer). The Specialist, acting as a dealer for his own account, may now decide to bid 54¾ for 100 shares, making the quotation 54¾-55¼, which narrows the spread between the bid and offer prices to ½ point.

1. That the buy orders must be ascending, and the sell orders descending, and
2. That every hundred shares must be individually "ranked" in amount and in time.

In short, the Computator outlines a program unknown, or at least unused, on the greatest auction market in the world in its own one hundred eighty years of existence, and the five-thousand years of recorded human history.

9. Industries in which there is a virgin use of the Computator include government bond trading, all other kinds of bond trading, foreign moneys (called foreign exchange), and commodity markets as the Chicago Board of Trade. And of course such markets are international in the broadest sense.

10. Economics is one of the youngest sciences. At first it dealt in general ideas based on *a priori* reasoning. Then the science veered to data-accumulating and data-averaging, and other empirical methods attempted by econometricians. The principle underlying the Computator breaks with these, with both *abstract* theory, and with the idea that an *average* of any kind (based on supply and demand) will yield a determinative price. Instead, the Computator method is "scientific," by which can be understood that every buyer and every seller counts as he should. Generalities and *approximate* calculations are abandoned and replaced by *specific* data and a *sound* method.

11. This new method is simple. It is simple in the same way that Newton added to an established idea, that things at rest will remain in rest, the corollary idea that things in motion will continue in motion in a straight line unless there is a counter force. That simple *addition* permitted deductions in regard to gravity and other fertile ideas.

Frederick Nymeyer

August 18, 1972

Böhm-Bawerk in History of Economic Thought

Böhm-Bawerk considered his position in the history of economics to have been determined by the role which the whole so-called Austrian Neo-Classical school of economics, of which he was a confident proponent, had played in the development of economic thought. He refers repeatedly and respectfully to his great predecessor, Carl Menger; and to his colleague, Friedrich von Wieser (who was his brother-in-law) ; and to many others. He sincerely believed that the Austrian Neo-Classical school had made noteworthy advances over all earlier thinkers and researchers in the science of economics. He claimed a great deal for the School, but was modest about a place for himself. (As the leading publisher of English translations of books by Böhm-Bawerk, we naturally think that he was actually one of the most significant of the Austrian Neo-Classical economists.)

Socrates and many of the greatest thinkers in the intellectual history of men have considered ethics to be the queen of all the sciences. There are cogent reasons for holding such an opinion. Ethics concerns itself with the *relationship of men to men;* all human cooperation depends on that relationship. We do not know how Böhm-Bawerk ranked ethics and economics. Maybe he would have conceded to Socrates that ethics is indeed the queen of the sciences, or higher than economics. But Böhm-Bawerk declared economics in at least one respect to take a prior and higher significance than ethics. His idea was that ethical problems stemmed largely from men's relationships to things—that men's relationships to things were antecedent in time at least—and secondly, and very importantly, that the relationships of men to things were exceedingly complex and required intensive study and the making of more meticulous distinctions than predecessor economists or ethical thinkers had ever undertaken. Böhm-Bawerk wrote (*Shorter Classics of Böhm-Bawerk*, pages 19 and 20) :

What, now, is the short meaning of this long story? What is the significance to the science as a whole of the advent of a set of men who teach this and that in regard to goods, value, cost, capital, and a dozen other subjects? Has it any significance at all? In answering this question I feel the embarrassment of belonging to the group of men whose activity is under discussion. I must, therefore, confine myself to the statement of what the Austrian economists as a body are trying to effect; others may judge whether or not they are successful.

What they (the Austrian economists) are striving for is a sort of *renaissance* of economic theory. The old classical theory, admirable as it was for its time, had the character of a collection of fragmentary acquisitions which had been brought into orderly relations neither with one another nor with the fundamental principles of human science. Our knowledge is only patchwork at best, and must always remain so. But of the classical theory this characterization was particularly and emphatically true. With the insight of genius it (classical economics) had discovered a mass of regularities in the whirlpool of economic phenomena, and with no less genius, though hindered by the difficulties that beset beginnings, it commenced the interpretation of these regularities. It usually succeeded, also, in following the thread of explanation to greater or less distance from the surface toward the depths. But beyond a certain depth it always, without exception, lost the clue.

To be sure, the classical economists well knew to what point all their explanations must be traced—to the care of mankind for its own well-being, which, undisturbed by the incursion of altruistic motives, is the ultimate motive-force of all economic action.

But owing to a certain circumstance the middle term of the explanation, by means of which the actual conduct of men, in the establishment of prices of goods, of wages, rent, etc., ought to have been joined to the fundamental motive of regard for utility—this middle term was always wrong. That circumstance was the following: A Crusoe has to do only with goods; in modern economic life we have to do with goods and with human beings from whom we obtain the goods we use—by means of exchange, cooperation, and the like. The economy of a Crusoe is explained when we succeed in showing what relation exists between our well-being and material commodities, and what attitude the care for our well-being requires us to take toward such material commodities.

To explain the modern economic order there is, apparently, need of two processes: (1) just as in Crusoe's economy, we must understand the relation of our interests to external goods; (2) we must seek to understand the laws, according to which we pursue our interests when they are entangled with the interests of others.

Böhm-Bawerk elaborates new ideas, such as: (1) that the relationships of men to things (i.e., economics) is indeed antecedent to ethics, because men in isolation, whether Adam or Robinson Crusoe, do have relationships to things even though they are perfectly alone and isolated; (2) that the complexity of the relationships of men to things was either not adequately appreciated by earlier economists, or was at least not worked out, and because it was not adequately worked out some of the greatest errors had been committed by economists and remained in the system, so that in fact the *foundations* of economics must necessarily be *re-laid;* and (3) that Austrian Neo-Classical economics had made magnificent progress in accomplishing just that. Böhm-Bawerk alleged that the old *definitions* in economics were loose and unsuited to clarify economic thinking.

Illustrative of the subjects that Böhm-Bawerk discussed in detail, see the following titles of the five essays, together with their Tables of Contents, in *Shorter Classics of Böhm-Bawerk,* Volume I:

I The Austrian Economists

Economics

Classical? Collectivist? Neo-Classical?

In economics, the three master categories are (1) Classical, (2) Collectivist (socialist, communist, interventionist) and (3) Neo-Classical.

Valid critique by collectivist economists unsettled enough of the ideas of the classicists (Adam Smith, David Ricardo, etc.) so that classical economics must be admitted to be inadequate now.

Socialism aims to eliminate *all* unearned income—interest, rents, profits. With *that* as his strategic objective, Marx made a flanking attack on capitalism, namely, he challenged all private *ownership* of capital, *because that gave claim to and control over income.*

Austrian *Neo-Classical* economics soundly analyzes the working of economic law under freedom of choice and right of private owner-ship of goods. Three of the greatest Neo-Classical economists are Carl Menger (1840-1921), Eugen von Böhm-Bawerk (1851-1914) and Ludwig von Mises (1881-   ).

Böhm-Bawerk is the pioneer economist who met Marx's attack head-on. In defense of capitalism, Böhm-Bawerk substituted new arguments for the defective arguments of classical economists. Böhm-Bawerk concluded that an employee is entitled to *all* that he produces with no deduction for the employer; but nevertheless that that employer will surely get a return. If justice is to prevail under socialism, the equivalent of what is called originary interest must exist even in a socialist economic order.

In his famous treatise, *CAPITAL AND INTEREST*, Böhm-Bawerk expounds a theory of distribution and of social cooperation which has exerted a profound influence on the thought of other economists.

First complete English translation in 1959
of the third and final edition, never before available

Capital and Interest

by His Excellency

EUGEN VON BÖHM-BAWERK

(In Three Volumes)

I History and Critique of Interest Theories

Analyzes fallacious interest theories. **512 pages**
(See pages 167-176 for Table of Contents.)

II Positive Theory of Capital

Contains the most comprehensive analysis that
has been made of capital and interest. **480 pages**
(See pages 177-180 for Table of Contents.)

III Further Essays on Capital and Interest

Supplements Volume II. **256 pages**
(See pages 181-184 for Table of Contents.)

**Deluxe, Boxed
Three-Volume Set**

**Economy Edition
Three Volumes in One
Unabridged, 1248 pages**

Schumpeter, in his biography of Böhm-Bawerk, published in
his *Ten Great Economists,* wrote the following, about Volume I:
...the greatest critical work in economics ... a monument of creative
analysis. With a minimum of effort, following the straightest possible

line, and with the most graceful elegance, he dispatches one [interest] theory after another; and—after having carefully exposed the cause of the disaster—he continues on his way without losing another word, or indeed without saying one word too many.

In regard to Volume II Schumpeter wrote:

It is in any case quite certain that this [*Positive Theory of Capital*] was an effort to scale the greatest heights that economics permits, and that the achievement actually reached a level where only a few lofty peaks are to be found.

Schumpeter also wrote:

To say that Böhm-Bawerk's work is immortal is to express a triviality. For a long time to come, the memory of the great fighter will be colored by the contending parties' hates and favors. But among the great achievements of which our science can be proud, his was one of the greatest. Whatever the future will do to it or make of it, the traces of his work will never perish.

Libertarian Press
South Holland, Illinois 60473, U.S.A.

[*This Book Review begins on outside back cover.*]

edition of the treatise which consisted only of two volumes. The new translation gives the full text of the revised and considerably enlarged third edition which Böhm-Bawerk completed a few weeks before his premature death in 1914.

A book of the size and the profundity of *Capital and Interest* is not easy reading. But the effort bestowed upon it pays very well. It will stimulate the reader to look upon political problems not from the point of view of the superficial slogans resorted to in electoral campaigns but with full awareness of their meaning and their consequences for the survival of our civilization.

Although Böhm-Bawerk's great opus is "mere theory" and abstains from any practical application, it is the most powerful intellectual weapon in the great struggle of the Western way of life against the destructionism of Soviet barbarism.

Ludwig von Mises

Reprinted from *THE FREEMAN*, August 1959
Published by Foundation For Economic Education, Inc.
Irvington-on-Hudson, New York 10533

Ludwig von Mises

casts his ballot without having to the best of his abilities studied as much economics as he can fails in his civic duties. He neglects using in the appropriate way the power that his citizenship has conferred upon him in giving him the right to vote.

Now there is no better method to introduce a man to economic problems than that provided by the books of the great economists. And certainly Böhm-Bawerk is one of the greatest of them. His voluminous treatise is the royal road to an understanding of the fundamental political issues of our age.

The general reader should start with the second volume in which Böhm analyzes the essence of saving and capital accumulation and the role capital goods play in the process of production. Especially important is the third book of this second volume; it deals with the determination of value and prices. Only then should the reader turn to the first volume that gives a critical history of all the doctrines advanced on the source of interest and profit by earlier authors. *In this historical review the most important part is the chapter that analyzes the so-called exploitation doctrines, first of all the doctrine that Karl Marx developed in his* Das Kapital, *the Koran of all Marxians. The refutation of Marx's labor theory of value is perhaps the most interesting, at any rate the politically most momentous chapter of Böhm's contribution.*

The third volume consists of fourteen brilliant essays in which Böhm-Bawerk deals with various objections raised against the validity of his theory.

The new translation was made by Professor Hans Sennholz, the chairman of the department of economics at Grove City College, and by Mr. George D. Huncke. Mr. Frederick Nymeyer is to be credited with the initiative to make the whole work of Böhm-Bawerk accessible to the English-reading public. The hitherto only available translation is obsolete as it was made from the first

(Continued on preceding page)

peoples of Western civilization into feuding parties were religious. Protestantism stood against Catholicism, and within the Protestant camp various interpretations of the Gospels begot discord. In the eighteenth century and in a great part of the nineteenth century constitutional conflicts prevailed in politics. The principles of royal absolutism and oligarchic government were resisted by liberalism (in the classical European meaning of the term) that advocated representative government. In those days a man who wanted to take an active part in the great issues of his age had to study seriously the matter of these controversies. The sermons and the books of the theologians of the age of the Reformation were not reserved to esoteric circles of specialists. They were eagerly absorbed by the whole public. Later the writings of the foremost advocates of freedom were read by all those who were not fully engrossed in the petty affairs of their daily routine. Only boors neglected to inform themselves about the great problems that agitated the minds of their contemporaries.

In our age the conflict between economic freedom as represented in the market economy and totalitarian government omnipotence as realized by socialism is the paramount matter. All political controversies refer to these economic problems. Only the study of economics can tell a man what all these conflicts mean. Nothing can be known about such matters as inflation, economic crises, unemployment, unionism, protectionism, taxation, economic controls, and all similar issues, that does not involve and presuppose economic analysis. All the arguments advanced in favor of or against the market economy and its opposites, interventionism or socialism (communism), are of an economic character. A man who talks about these problems without having acquainted himself with the fundamental ideas of economic theory is simply a babbler who parrot-like repeats what he has picked up incidentally from other fellows who are not better informed than he himself. A citizen who

 (Continued on preceding page)